Getting New Clients

Getting New Clients

RICHARD A. CONNOR, JR.
Dick Connor, Inc.
Springfield, Virginia

JEFFREY P. DAVIDSON
Certified Management Consultant
Falls Church, Virginia

JOHN WILEY & SONS

New York • Chichester • Brisbane • Toronto • Singapore

Copyright © 1987 by Richard A. Connor, Jr. and Jeffrey P. Davidson
Published by John Wiley & Sons, Inc.

All rights reserved. Published simultaneously in Canada.

Reproduction or translation of any part of this work
beyond that permitted by Section 107 or 108 of the
1976 United States Copyright Act without the permission
of the copyright owner is unlawful. Requests for
permission or further information should be addressed to
the Permissions Department, John Wiley & Sons, Inc.

This publication is designed to provide accurate and
authoritative information in regard to the subject
matter covered. It is sold with the understanding that
the publisher is not engaged in rendering legal, accounting,
or other professional service. If legal advice or other
expert assistance is required, the services of a competent
professional person should be sought. *From a Declaration of
Principles jointly adopted by a Committee of the American
Bar Association and a Committee of Publishers.*

Library of Congress Cataloging in Publication Data

Connor, Richard A.
  Getting new clients.

  Bibliography: p.
  Includes index.
  1. Professions—Marketing. I. Davidson, Jeffrey P.
II. Title.
HD8038.A1C665 1987   658.8   87-21657
ISBN 0-471-62778-X

Printed in the United States of America
10 9 8 7 6 5 4

To Susan,
who lovingly provided the space and support
for this book to be completed.

Preface

Getting profitable new clients in targeted niches is the key to both survival and profitable growth in the turbulent times facing professional-service providers.

The competition for virtually every type of professional service is increasing due to a number of factors including: 1) lifting of the restrictions on all forms of commercialism in the professions; 2) the corporate squeezing out of baby boomers and midlevel managers resulting in an unprecedented influx of new consultants; 3) the increased propensity of clients to change the professional-service providers with whom they work; 4) the effects of technology, particularly the personal computer, on the ability of clients to handle more tasks in-house; and 5) a lukewarm economy.

This book has been written by busy professionals for an equally busy readership of service professionals. In marketing and selling your services to qualified, high potential, prospective clients, we recognize that you seldom have the luxury of investing large blocks of time. Thus, we have written the book in a manner that will support "quick hits," allowing you to focus on just a few pages at a time if necessary.

Hereafter, the narrative will be written in the first person, reflecting the voice of the senior author. I will talk directly to you, just as if you and I were face to face, focusing our time and attention on improving your ability to attract and acquire new clients.

Throughout the text, I will stress that a "client-centered," industry-specific, new client acquisition program is the only appropriate marketing strategy for professional-service providers. In 1969, when I became the first full-time professional services marketing consultant, I developed and introduced the Client-centered Marketing™ approach to marketing and selling professional services. Today, the term is well accepted and in use throughout the world. The client-centered marketing approach positions the client and qualified prospective clients as the targets and beneficiaries of your time, talents, and focused expertise.

I will also refer to the principles of leveraging and concentration. As a busy professional, you must leverage the available, often discretionary, time by concentrating on the smallest number of actions to produce the largest result.

The techniques and tips presented in Getting New Clients have been field tested with thousands of clients worldwide in virtually every type of service firm. Companies providing business services also report excellent results in serving their customers and clients. I use the techniques presented herein on a daily basis in my own practice and am confident that you, too, will prosper through their application.

I am confident that you will receive a disproportionate return on your investment, a hallmark of value-added services. I also recognize, however, that it is difficult to put your present performance under the microscope and analyze it for improvement opportunities. It takes a special kind of resilience to put the status quo on trial and to scrutinize your patterns of behavior, which, after all, have been based on your assumptions, experience, and conventional wisdom.

To assist you in your efforts to generate profitable new clients, I have presented the material in this book in an action sequence. You will know what to do, when to do it, and why you should do it. You will also be shown how to execute the recommendations successfully; there are copious examples and ideas presented, supported by the psychological explanation of why they work.

RICHARD A. CONNOR, JR.
JEFFREY P. DAVIDSON

Springfield, Virginia
Falls Church, Virginia
September 1987

Acknowledgments

There are many individuals the authors wish to acknowledge in preparation of the book. Jeanne A. Wolfe's editing and proofreading were instrumental and crucial to the successful completion of the manuscript. Louis P. Baron and Erin G. Austin assisted in the copyediting stage. David Alan Yoho's expertise on telephone techniques and Ernie Kosty's valuable tips in proposal writing greatly bolstered Chapters 10 and 15 respectively. John Hartshorne's interest and support in our work continue to inspire us.

We would also like to thank our editor, John B. Mahaney, for his enthusiasm and vision. Thanks also to Steven Kippur, Ph.D., Richard McCullough, Peter Clifton, and Kathy Astor.

A special thanks goes to agent Dave Cutler, who used all the leverage he could to get us a fair deal and who got some new clients in the bargain. Finally our highest tribute goes to Judy Dubler, whose unparalleled word-processing capabilities converted the impossible into the possible.

R.A.C.
J.P.D.

Introduction

This book answers the key question facing today's professional-service providers. Consultants, accountants, attorneys, communication specialists, EDP and systems consultants, as well as a wide variety of other professional service providers in the fields of finance, real estate, investments, training, engineering, and advertising, ask this question daily.

The megaquestion is, "How can I obtain profitable, high potential, new clients that will enable me to meet my practice-development objectives without having to be a professional salesperson or use distasteful, unprofessional methods such as advertising and discounting?" The answer to this question is presented here. This book provides the insider's guide to using a client-centered approach as the basis for developing a new-client acquisition program.

The client-centered approach to getting new clients has been acid tested in the field by intelligent, practical, and often skeptical professionals. The ideas presented in this book are the ones that will enable you to survive and prosper well into the 1990s.

I have had the opportunity to present these ideas and techniques in a 3-day workshop of the same title to thousands of professionals around the globe. In most instances, these professionals readily accepted the client-centered marketing approach and recognized the importance of focusing on a targeted industry-market niche.

The niche approach enables the busy professional to leverage his or her available time, existing relationships, and resources for the purpose of attracting and acquiring high-potential, new clients in the niche. The niche approach is based on experiences you'll gain in providing value-perceived services to existing high-potential clients in the niche. This allows the professional-service provider to work from a comfort zone, that area of professional behavior where one is productive, confident, and forthright.

A service professional is able to work from a comfort zone when he or she can propose effective solutions already developed for and used successfully by the best high-potential existing clients in the niche. Thus, the professional is able to use similar vocabulary, skills, and solution statements that yield success.

Rather than trying to sell a service, a situation in which most professionals find themselves when using traditional marketing approaches, the client-centered-niche approach offers a perspective from which the professional is able to suggest ways the prospect can improve his business. Thus, the professional is able to raise the level of exploratory discussion from one of selling services to one of offering solutions to the current needs of high-potential prospects in the targeted niche. This is a superior marketing approach. The client-centered-niche approach enables the busy service professional to leverage her* time, talents, and experience to sense, serve, and satisfy the needs of target prospects in a target industry or market segment.

In 1985, John Wiley & Sons published our best-selling book, *Marketing Your Consulting and Professional Services*. This book, which was in its fifth printing after less than two years, offers a

*We will alternate use of he and she to avoid sexism in the book.

by-the-numbers introduction to the broad scope of marketing professional services. *Getting new Clients* is the logical extension of the earlier book and focuses on the art and science of obtaining profitable new clients. Many of the terms used throughout this book have been defined and discussed in *Marketing Your Consulting and Professional Services* and are included here for your convenience in the glossary that follows the text.

Many years ago, as the material for this book began to take shape, a seasoned professional said to me, "If I can get an appointment with a prospect, my experience and basic problem-solving and communications skills will usually see me through. But getting an appointment with Mr. Right Guy is my Achilles' heel. I don't have a consistent way to open up a contact's door and mind to me. If my referral sources ever dry up, I am dead!"

Opening the door to qualified prospects in targeted organizations is what this book is all about. It is also about the art and science of planning and conducting effective new-business discussions with the right contact(s) after you have succeeded in obtaining an appointment.

The goal of the successful professional-service marketer is to promote and produce a value-perceived service solution to an important need faced by prospective clients in a targeted niche. To do this, you need to know what drives the niche: What are the success factors? What are the profit factors? Successful use of the client-centered niche approach involves a transformation from providing services to answering the question, "How many different ways can I help the client to be profitable as it applies to my resources?"

Today, prospective clients are increasingly reluctant to meet with sellers of services who want them to open their corporate kimono and reveal needs during what are often regarded as stressful sessions. This book recognizes that the most difficult part of new-client development is finding a prospective client who will meet with the professional. Determining needs is relatively easy for the professional; developing solutions is the stock-in-trade of professional-service providers.

This book will show you how to identify the unmet or poorly met needs of prospective clients in the targeted niches. It will show you how to prepare and mail an initial contact package to selected, prospective clients that will be received favorably. It will also discuss how to telephone decision-makers in the targeted organization to obtain an appointment to discuss the need identified in the contact package. The book will show you how to prepare for and conduct an effective new-business interview and an effective follow up. You will be presented with the must know skills, knowledge, and insights, as well as lessons learned, to make the client-centered marketing approach work for you.

To survive and thrive in today's economy the professional practitioner is required to develop a continuing, cost-effective, new-client acquisition program. Gone are the days when a client gained was a client retained. Client "churn" is a fact of life even in the best run practices. *Getting New Clients* is of particular interest in the following cases: (1) When you want to or have to change the nature and scope of your practice; (2) When your practice growth from cross-selling additional services to existing clients is not sufficient to provide the profit required for your practice (i.e., sometimes you mine all the gold in your own backyard and it is time to find a new vein); and (3) When you need to replace the revenue from clients known to be lost and clients suspected to be lost.

Not all readers will have the same orientation and level of experience. A popular way of describing the levels of experience in a professional-service firm is with the terms *finder, minder,* and *grinder.* This book will serve all three types of readers:

1. For the finder who is proficient in generating new business from existing clients and wants to develop the capability and confidence required to attract profitable new clients.

2. For the minder, often a partner-in-training, who recognizes that the ability to bring in profitable new clients is always recognized and rewarded.

3. For the grinder, who recognizes that transition from "business doer" to "business getter" is the make-or-break activity for most talented professionals, and who wants to accelerate his progress on the path to partnership.

This book contains everything you will need to be successful in obtaining profitable new clients. This includes exhibits, checklists, sample letters, and new-business discussion guides. There are detailed discussions showing you how to develop an insider's understanding and reputation within a targeted industry-market niche. And you will also be shown how to develop a data base and library for your niche that will provide you with a competitive edge and help to position you as an insider among those you want most eagerly to know of your services.

Contents

List of Charts, Worksheets, and Exhibits

Part I
Developing Your Client-centered and New Client Acquisition Program

Part I introduces the client-centered marketing approach, explains the client-centered marketing model, defines a number of key terms, and shows you how to develop a targeted client-acquisition program.

1
The Client-centered Marketing Approach

Getting new clients is the continuing goal and sore spot of most professional-service providers. Yet, it need not be a painful, identity-rattling venture. In this chapter, we'll begin laying the foundation of a client-centered approach to attract profitable new clients. The goals of this chapter are to introduce the client-centered marketing approach; to explain the content, flow and use of the 4-element client-centered marketing model; to explain the use of leveraging; to introduce the notion of comfort zones; and to explain the AIDA model.

As defined in our book *Marketing Your Consulting and Professional Services*, client-centered marketing refers to:

> Organized and coordinated activities designed to develop and enhance relationships and manage the firm's image with clients, prospective clients, and other influential people. These clients and others are, or can be, interested in using, retaining, and referring your firm and its services if you are able to sense, serve, and satisfy their needs and expectations.

The term *client-centered marketing* will be used throughout the book. The concept behind it is crucial to the process of attracting and retaining profitable, high-quality new clients.

Because marketing is an evolving discipline, words such as markets, niches, and so on are used interchangeably by many practitioners. This can be troublesome because it assumes understanding when misunderstanding is more likely.

The term *industry* will mean a specific 4-digit classification as defined by the U.S. Department of Commerce; therefore, *industry* will refer to all clients, prospects, and suspects (defined in Chapter 4) in your practice area that have the same Standard Industrial Classification (SIC).

Market, as used in this book, is synonymous with the postal zip codes that comprise your practice area for a specific SIC. Thus, your market is a defined geographic area in which clients, prospective clients, suspects, and nonclient influentials are located.

The term *niche* will be used as an abbreviation for industry-market niche. *Niche* will refer to clients, prospects, and suspects with the same SIC that are located in your market of zips.

THE CLIENT-CENTERED MARKETING MODEL

To describe how the client-centered marketing approach can work for your firm, let's examine the four elements that comprise the client-centered marketing model shown in Figure 1.1 and describe each in detail. The four elements of the model include the following:

Existing practice factors

Existing referral relationships

Targets of opportunity and targets of influence

New business development factors

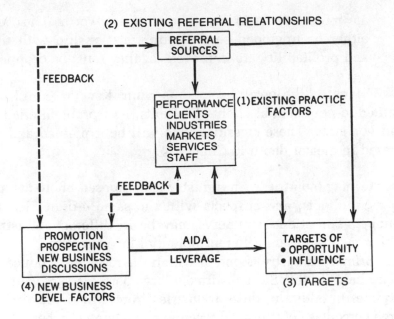

FIGURE 1.1. Client-centered Marketing Model

Existing Practice Factors

Existing practice factors include existing clients, industries, markets, services, and your staff.

Your Existing Clients. Your various clients represent different potentials and can be classified as follows:

1. High-potential opportunity clients who need and want additional client-centered services.

2. Limited-to-no-potential clients you want to retain, but because they seldom use additional services you continue to serve them in the traditional manner.

3. Problem clients who give you headaches and cause grief, particularly regarding fees and collections. These clients

are more trouble to you than they are worth. They must either be upgraded so that your relationship with them and profitability are improved, or they must be dropped.

We'll call high-potential clients your Key, or A, clients, limited-to-no-potential clients B clients, and problem clients C and D clients. These classifications will be explained and discussed in greater depth in Chapter 4.

Your Existing Industries. An industry is composed of clients, prospective clients, and suspects with the same 4-digit SIC code number. The clients you serve may be in different industries, which may represent different potential for your firm.

A *primary* industry is one in which the revenues produced by your clients in this SIC constitute a large percentage of your total revenue. In addition, those industries from which you derive a large percentage of your total revenue and a large number of high-potential clients are deemed high-potential primary industries.

Secondary industries represent those from which the revenue viewed from all of your clients in the SIC constitutes a small percentage of your total income. High-potential, secondary industries are the same as above except that you have several high-potential clients or several high-potential prospective clients who may well pan out.

Your Existing Markets. Your markets are the geographic arenas in which you promote and conduct your practice. Your goal is to identify high-potential industry-market niches for special attention.

Your Existing Services. There are several ways to look at the services you currently provide. One category contains those services needed by your clients even though they are not happy paying for them. Often viewed as necessary evils, these include accounting, auditing, actuarial, tax compliance, and benefit-plan reporting. Your goal is to add enhancements to the basic services and to develop value-added solutions. This in turn will increase the perceived value of your service to the client.

A second category of services is those both needed and wanted by your clients. These services could include anything clients perceive as assisting them in improving their business, such as cash-flow planning, marketing strategy, or business reorganization.

A third service area is what I call fad or "in" services. Since these tend to have a very short shelf life, you can use them to skim the market and earn high margins before competitors enter the marketplace or interest among clients wanes. Service leadership in this area tends to be brief and transitory, especially in today's turbulent environment. Examples include video wills and balloon mortgage financing.

The knowledge, skills, and attitudes you have acquired by serving your existing clients constitute a large portion of your current *comfort zone* (more on this later). In subsequent chapters, we will focus on how you can work from your comfort zone and leverage your existing strengths to get new clients.

Your Staff. One of the most critical issues facing professional-service firms, and one that has remained largely unaddressed, is role clarification. "Finders," "minders," and "grinders" comprise the three classes of professionals found in all firms.

Finders, traditionally representing less than 5 percent of senior partners, are marketing oriented. Their focus, and indeed, loyalty, is often the next contract or new client to be gained. Finders associate with one another and may enjoy celebrity status within the firm. They can relate to the activities and contributions of minders, but often have difficulty understanding or interacting with grinders.

Minders are task or engagement driven as well as people driven. Minders provide the glue that cements the relationship between a firm and its clients. They are personality people and enjoying working with others. They spend anywhere from 60 to 80 percent of their time on-site with clients. Minders support marketing efforts through cultivating referrals and opportunities for additional services. They communicate with both finders and grinders, and understand their respective contributions and needs.

Grinders are technology driven and often are the founders of the firm who carried it during its early days. The majority of professionals are grinders. Grinders are happiest when working at their desks, solving the firm's or its clients' problems through study and analysis. They love to work on projects, and deep down they wish there were no need to market to or interact with clients and prospective clients.

Existing Referral Relationships

The second element in the client-centered marketing model is your existing referral relationships. These consist primarily of existing clients and others who influence people to use your services.

Your existing clients, satisfied with the nature and quality of the services you provide, will frequently give you referrals. One client of mine, an accountant, makes it a point to deliver additional services during his initial engagement with high-potential clients. His motto is, "You never have a second chance to make a favorable first impression." Thus he often gains referrals upon conclusion of the first engagement. His current conversion rate is about 25 percent, an exceptionally good percentage.

There are also numerous nonclients who may never become your clients but may serve as referral sources for your firm. These nonclient influentials may include attorneys, bankers, editors, executive directors of industry associations, and accountants. These professionals are familiar with your firm and will frequently provide you with leads and introductions to prospective clients and other nonclient influentials.

Of the four major elements in the client-centered marketing model, the two discussed thus far, existing practice factors and existing referral relationships, represent the bedrock of your current practice. They are within your current marketing comfort zone, that area in which you comfortably and confidently initiate and respond to client and prospective-client needs.

The data to be collected and analyzed to gain a firm grasp of these two elements generally can be readily assembled. This information then can be used to identify targets of opportunity and targets of influence.

Targets of Opportunity and Targets of Influence

Targets of opportunity include existing high-potential clients with additional needs and a sizable budget. They also are prospective clients who may not have agreed to your proposed solutions but who may be interested in having you serve them. A third group of targets of opportunity consists of potential clients or suspects whom you have not yet contacted to discuss their needs. However, they have passed your initial screening and eventually may become new clients.

The focus of this book is on targets of opportunity in primary industry-market niches that you intend to penetrate and eventually dominate. Your ability to acquire profitable new clients hinges largely upon your ability to sense, serve, and satisfy the needs of targets of opportunity in a targeted market niche.

Targets of influence are additional nonclient influentials that you wish to develop into referral sources. Often, targets of influence include other professionals who serve your clients in noncompetitive ways. They may also consist of regulatory, political, or community officials and leaders who affect your clients.

Your ability to identify and track targets of opportunity and targets of influence directly affects the strength of your practice and your future profitability. *Favorably influencing your targets serves many purposes, including the following:*

Replacing lost clients

Converting prospective clients into new clients

Developing an insider's understanding and reputation in a targeted niche

Developing relationships with new nonclient influentials who are members of the infrastructure of your targeted niche.

The future of your practice is based upon successful interactions with these selected targets. Your activities in this area must be based on a well developed strategy and must be executed and monitored carefully.

New-business Development Factors

The fourth element of the client-centered marketing model, new-business development factors, consists of three activities: promotion, prospecting, and new-business discussions.

Promotion refers to the personal and nonpersonal activities involved in managing your image and reputation with targets of influence, and informing and reminding your key clients and prospective clients that you are willing and able to solve their needs and problems.

One of my target niches is the management-consulting profession. I have given the keynote speech at the annual conference of the Institute of Management Consultants several times. This speech is always well researched and well delivered and, among other things, serves as a valuable promotional vehicle. The contacts I make and the resulting favorable publicity have attracted inquiries from a number of conference participants.

An effective, ongoing promotion program can provide many benefits, including the following:

Creating name awareness within the targeted niche

Creating and maintaining a favorable awareness of your firm and its professional staff

Informing and reminding clients and prospects about your

willingness and ability to sense, serve, and satisfy their
needs

Building interest among clients and prospects to discuss their
needs and learn about your services

Building and maintaining a desired image

Attracting additional targets

Paving the way for new-business development activities

There are two forms of promotion: horizontal and vertical. A
horizontal promotion is one that cuts across numerous industries in your market. A vertical promotion is industry specific
and focuses on the needs of the various players in the industry
infrastructure. In addition to an ongoing promotional program,
many firms also undertake a prospecting-specific promotion,
discussed later in this chapter.

A second essential activity of new-business development is
prospecting. Prospecting is the process of finding and contacting high-potential suspects to secure appointments with
decision-makers willing to discuss their situation and ways in
which you can assist them. A suspect who agrees to meet with
you becomes a prospective client.

Effective prospecting enables you to find those who ultimately
may become your Key, or A clients. It also enables you to replen-
ish lost clients. If you have made the strategic decision to alter
your existing client and industry mix, effective prospecting is a
handy tool for implementing the desired change. Prospecting
represents the execution of a strategic decision. It enables you to
shape and formulate the nature and scope of tomorrow's practice.

Industry-specific prospecting is the process of (1) identifying
suspects in your targeted niche, (2) obtaining appointments with
one or more members of an organization's decision-making unit,
and (3) discussing a need mentioned in an initial contact mailing. Effective planning and managing of an industry-specific
prospecting program enables you to work within your comfort

zone, maximize your marketing efforts, and minimize the time and effort required to keep your potential new-business pipeline flowing.

The third activity area of new-business development is *new-business discussions*. These are discussions conducted for the purpose of defining a prospective client's need situation and suggesting a solution that involves your services. A successful new-business discussion is characterized by obtaining a commitment from a prospective client to take a mutually beneficial step, such as becoming a new client, or accepting a proposal.

When properly undertaken, new-business discussions enable you to focus and to leverage your time, resources, and relationships as you work with your targets of opportunity. I am a solo consultant who must perform the engagements I sell. Even though my time for new-business development is limited, by focusing my new-business activities on high-potential targets of opportunity, my promotion and prospecting efforts regularly generate a fair number of new clients.

THE CLIENT-CENTERED MARKETING MODEL IN PERSPECTIVE

Having now discussed the four elements of the client-centered marketing model, let's briefly review how they are interrelated. Please follow closely; the explanation is a little tricky. Elements 1 and 2 (existing practice factors and existing referral relationships, respectively) represent the existing practice. Both elements 1 and 2, along with element 4 (new-business development factors), can be used in the generation of *additional* targets of opportunity and targets of influence (element 3). Existing practice factors 1 and 2 may lead directly to element 3, or may first lead to element 2 or element 4, either of which then leads to element 3. Existing referral relationships primarily lead directly to element 3. The relationships between element 1 and element 4, and between element 2 and element 4, are essentially one directional—new-business development factors often provide feedback that strengthens existing business practice factors or existing referral relationships. (See Figure 1.1.)

THE CONCEPT OF LEVERAGING

Leveraging refers to the process of using the smallest number of targeted actions, resources, and relationships to produce the greatest results. The client-centered marketing approach to getting new clients firmly embraces the concept of leveraging. Good results can be obtained by targeting prospective Key and A clients, those organizations to whom you can offer high-margin services for potentially high fees. With these high-potential clients, your goal is to earn not just your daily rate, but also value-added hours. For example, a tax professional researches a client problem and bills the client $1500 for the solution. She then sells 25 tailored sets of solutions to other clients for $750 each. In this instance, she was able to extract value from the hours she spent researching a problem for the initial client by leveraging her efforts and making additional sales to others.

Value-added hours differ from cost-added hours in that you are able to bill for more than just your daily rate (your per diem) or the time that was actually logged in. You will have the greatest opportunities to use leverage with your Key and A clients. These clients traditionally represent no more than 20 percent of your total client base.

Leverage is a multiplier type of activity that produces a cascade effect. You apply leverage when you obtain the names of attorneys who serve your types of clients from a friendly bank lending officer. Leverage also refers to the use of information tools to amplify your single effort.

Often, the service practitioner who markets his services is also the one actually providing the service. This results in the inevitable double bind of selling an engagement and then delivering the service. Mastering the art of leveraging enables the solo practitioner to stretch his available time and resources to an optimum degree.

Closely tied to leveraging is the strategy of marketing the *end result* of a product or service, as opposed to the delivery. For example, one Las Vegas-based management consultant provided clients with short-term consulting sessions that mapped out a 12-month marketing strategy. While the consultant was offering a few hours of his time, the client was buying something completely different. What was the client buying? Security, peace of mind, the ability to focus on a prosperous market niche, and the ability to keep his present staff employed. If the consultant were to charge on a strict hourly basis, he would be limited to his hourly or per-diem rate. However, if he were to charge based on the end result, a result that was appropriately conveyed to the client in advance, the fee for such a service would be considerably higher.

Two other areas in which leverage can be used include use of time and use of technology.

TIME

Personal chargeable hours—investing your time with Key clients, not D clients.

Others you manage—multiplying yourself through the empowerment of those you manage.

Nonchargeable hours—investing in high-payoff promotions such as speaking to target groups.

TECHNOLOGY

Computers and EDP equipment—using them to provide recurring service solutions.

Audio recorders—using them to capture your ideas, impressions, and so on, and having a low-salaried employee transcribe them.

Video recorders—to showcase your capabilities and your key personnel.

Car phones—taking and making calls while stuck in traffic.

WORKING FROM YOUR COMFORT ZONE

I used this phrase earlier and now will explain this concept in detail. When undertaking new-business development activities, such as identifying targets of opportunity, most people find they get the best results when they call on clones of their existing Key and A clients. Working from your comfort zone means calling on those types of prospects with whom you have some affinity. You feel comfortable calling on them and you can speak their business language. Your anxiety level remains manageable.

The unspoken goal of professional service marketers is to clone their best existing client! This is achieved by identifying more prospective clients who have the characteristics of your best client. Working from the comfort zone enables you to initiate effective marketing behavior.

Your comfort zone can be expanded on new-business calls by winning early and often, developing insider smarts, and maintaining a balanced perspective and approach. For example, those effective in product sales know that every "no" brings them closer to a "yes." Others have been able to use the process of visualization to achieve desired behavior in otherwise unfamiliar territory. One target niche I serve is the accounting profession in the English-speaking countries of the world. My comfort zone depends on the degree to which I stay abreast of the pending legislation that will affect the professions, the economic factors, and impact of the competitors in each country. I use this information as insider small talk that leads to new-business discussions.

Many professionals are very comfortable talking with referrals, but not in initiating phone calls. Your comfort zone will not be uniform throughout the marketing and selling process. You must become familiar with the boundaries of your comfort zone and remain within close proximity of its boundaries as you systematically work to expand it.

Frequently, when speaking before groups, I share with them the fact that I am a scuba diver. My current comfort zone in diving is about 50 to 60 feet. I could dive to 90 and 100 feet, and on occasion have done it, but I have not been comfortable. I get no joy out of it, and I can't wait to get out of the water. So it is with your comfort zone when seeking new clients. If you move outside it too quickly, the discomfort may be so great that you withdraw entirely. To increase the size of your comfort zone effectively, you must do so slowly.

THE AIDA MINIMODEL

The AIDA model has been used traditionally in product marketing to describe the phases involved in the capture of a new customer (attention, interest, desire, action). However, the model lends itself well to adaptation for services marketing. The model's four phases must be planned and executed for your new-business development activities to be effective.

The first *A* represents the goal of obtaining the *attention* and favorable awareness of targets of opportunity and targets of influence. The *I* represents *information* you send to targets, information designed to interest them so they agree to meet with you after you have successfully completed a telephone contact.

The *D* represents *directed* new-business *discussions* with members of the decision-making unit in the targeted organization. These new-business discussions are designed to define the gap between what *is* and what is *desired* or *required* by the prospective client. Your ability to convince the prospective client how your proposed solution will decrease the deviation between what currently is and what is desired is at the heart of the new-business discussion.

The final *A* represents the agreed-upon *actions* you and the prospective client will take to meet a mutually defined need. Actions may include the preparation and presentation of a proposal or the execution of a scoping survey whereby the client allows you to interview additional key people.

In examining the individual components of new-business development, one sees that promotion involves obtaining attention and generating interest (AI). Prospecting involves generating interest and obtaining appointments for new-business discussions (ID). New-business discussions involve managing the discussions and moving toward agreed-upon actions (DA).

The client-centered marketing approach should not be directed to every client, prospect, and niche. Rather, it should be used selectively with those Key and A clients, prospects, and niches where you will receive the greatest return for your efforts. This approach to new business is an extension of the problem-solving approach you use daily in handling your own affairs; consequently, it should be well within your professional-marketing comfort zone.

This chapter has presented the client-centered marketing approach and the client-centered marketing model. We are now ready to proceed to Chapter 2 where the client-centered approach to attract and acquire high-potential new clients is discussed.

2
Getting New Clients by Targeting a Market Niche

The essence of client-centered marketing is satisfying the selected needs of high-potential targets of opportunity. It is also developing relationships with influentials who can serve as resources for achieving your marketing and new-business development goals. In this chapter, we will expand on the definition of client-centered marketing. Specifically, our definition will be in terms of a targeted-niche approach for obtaining profitable new clients.

Client-centered niche-marketing is the process of leveraging the time, technology, and resources available to you to sense, serve, and satisfy the selected needs of high-potential clients and prospective clients. It is important that your service offering be perceived as valuable by *all* involved. Perceptions about your service occur at all times during the client-centered marketing process, including the promotion, delivery, and application of the service.

To successfully penetrate a targeted niche you must offer "silver bullets." These are solutions to the "hot-buttons" needs, issues, or concerns that suspects have and for which they will readily meet with you to discuss how you can be of assistance.

A partner in a Big Eight accounting firm recently developed just such a silver bullet. He capitalized on the uncertainty surrounding the Gramm-Rudman-Hollings Act by providing workshops and individual counsel to anxious service providers to the U.S. government. Time magazine reported that this one partner was responsible for generating in excess of $800,000 in less than a year.

Client-centered niche-marketing is a results-driven, continuing process designed to focus and leverage the relationships and resources available to you. You then use these relationships and invest the resources in developing value-perceived solutions to the important needs of your existing high-potential clients and prospective clients in your targeted niche. The key question that effective client-centered marketers ask themselves is, "How many different ways can I assist my clients and targets to better their business?" (Or, "To better their personal situation?")

If you are an attorney preparing a will for a client, from your perspective you could say you are simply preparing a will. However, from the more important perspective of the receiver you could be seen as providing the following:

Peace of mind

Orderly transfer of assets

Education funding for offspring

Financial security for the widow, and so forth.

The effective client-centered marketer provides value-perceived solutions in ways that generate mutual benefits. Value-perceived means that the client perceives great value for his or her dollar. I discovered a way to avoid having a down market with my accounting clients during their busy season. I carefully developed, marketed, and conducted a 3-hour course, "Developing New Business During the 'Too-Busy-to-Market Season.'" Recognizing the firm's needs to keep staff accountants on engagements during the clients' normal business hours, I conducted the course from 9:00 A.M. until noon or 2:00 P.M. until 5:00 P.M. on Saturdays.

The service practitioner who generates large fees doesn't do so because she is providing a specific service per se. She generates large fees because of her ability to recognize a client's needs and to provide solutions in such a manner that the clients recognize the value of such solutions. To put it another way, you get no credit for developing an ingenious way of solving a problem unless you are able to convince a client that your ingenuity in meeting his or her needs will have an economic and/or personal payoff.

MARKETING IS EXPENSIVE

Let's face it—marketing is an expensive function that must be carefully planned and managed. Properly executed, a client-centered marketing program requires a substantial investment of time and out-of-pocket costs to properly develop and promote value-perceived services. Yet, as you proceed through this book, you will see that client-centered niche-marketing, on balance, is far less costly than traditional marketing approaches.

Client-centered marketing begins when you sense, serve, and satisfy important needs of your targeted, high-potential prospects in ways in which they perceive the value; it ends when you acquire new, prompt-paying clients.

This niche-marketing process enables you to work from your comfort zone in virtually all the marketing and selling activities involved in the client-centered marketing approach. Your targets in the niche, the prospective clients, could be clones of your best existing clients. It is a continuing process, because the approach is structured to enable you to engage in some targeted marketing and selling every day as you serve your high-potential clients; develop and strengthen relationships with key influentials in the infrastructure of the targeted niche; and promote, prospect, and sell to your targeted prospective clients in the niche.

Client-centered marketing is a self-initiated, proactive approach. I describe it as the marketing approach that pays homage to what I call the Platinum Rule[tm]: Serve others as they need and want you to. You must strive continuously to deliver value-perceived solutions by providing cutting-edge services, maintaining an image and reputation that you are different from and/or better than the competition, and develop the resources to stay in the forefront of your profession.

NOT WITH ALL CLIENTS

A client-centered marketing approach should be used only with approximately 20 percent of your existing clients and 20 percent of prospective clients. The reason for this is that only with your Key and A clients and prospective clients will there be a vibrant, dynamic atmosphere in which *continuing* and *additional* opportunities exist for you. It is with the upper 20 percent that the client-centered marketer continuously seeks ways to:

Assist targets better in *doing what they are in business to do*
Serve as a conduit to the resources available to deliver value-added solutions
Ensure quality control and delivery of agreed-upon services
Deliver value-perceived services

TARGETING A NICHE

The client-centered marketing approach works best when used to focus on targets of opportunity that are members of a specific industry (SIC) and are in the geographical location (zip codes) that comprise the practitioner's market area. Thus, the primary targets of opportunity become those high-potential prospective firms and individuals in the industry-market niche.

Secondary targets of opportunity represent those B-level potential clients (suspects) that are part of the industry and are located in the practice area. Contacting B-level suspects requires a lot of time because there are more of them. The best way to handle secondary targets is to use your insider's reputation (Chapter 7) to create sufficient interest for them to contact you.

Targets of influence are the additional nonclient influentials that are located or reside in the niche, and others throughout the region or nation who can interact with and influence members of the niche infrastructure with whom you have yet to develop a relationship. For example, I leverage my time by developing relationships with influential members of each niche's infrastructure. My targets of influence in the accounting profession are the editors of publications read by my best clients and targets of opportunity.

There are numerous steps involved in generating new clients by targeting a niche. I will summarize these steps, each of which will be explained in detail in Chapters 3 through 19.

ESTABLISHING OBJECTIVES FOR YOUR NEW-CLIENT PROGRAM

Your immediate goal as a professional is to ensure that your practice survives. Ultimately, your goal shifts to changing the nature and scope of the practice (1) to obtain larger, more profitable clients, (2) to enhance the image and reputation of the firm, and (3) to develop an industry specialization. A number of decisions need to be made. (See Chapter 3.)

Selecting Your Target Niche

Selecting your target niche is the first and most important step in the process of client-centered marketing. Most professionals find they must gather a substantial body of information to decide which niche to penetrate. Fortunately, much of this information already exists within the practice. During this stage, selection criteria must also be established. (See Chapter 4.)

Developing an Insider's Understanding of the Niche

Several key steps are involved in acquiring an insider's understanding. You must first identify industry success factors and the needs and wants of members of the industry. In addition, you identify targets of opportunity, targets of influence, and members of the industry infrastructure with whom you have a relationship. Finally, you must develop a data base that supports your efforts in marketing to the niche. (See Chapter 5.)

Tailoring Your Services-Delivery Program

While a client-centered marketing approach places the client's wants and needs at the forefront of your program, there are still many aspects of service delivery that you will want to standardize. In terms of clients, it is difficult to be everything to everyone. You must also consider in what form your deliverables will be packaged. (See Chapter 6.)

Developing an Insider's Reputation in the Niche

How does one create a favorable awareness within the niche and develop relationships with its key members? Some of the strategies involved include writing and speaking to your targets and leveraging memberships within key organizations. (See Chapter 7.)

THE FIRST APPOINTMENT

All of the foregoing lay the groundwork for face-to-face encounters with prospective clients. The next set of activities focuses specifically on getting and preparing for appointments with prospective clients.

Selecting the Needs and Prospect Organizations

This involves selecting a critical need known as a *hot button*, and finding supporting evidence to help you hook prospective clients. The needs you uncover should be ones you can and want to solve, at a good profit margin. Prospective clients with needs in this category become your current targets of opportunity. (See Chapter 8.)

Developing and Managing Your Mailing Program

Your major tasks here will be to develop and write initial contact letters, to prepare a telephone-interview guide, and to test and fine-tune the program. (See Chapter 9.)

Making the Appointment-Getting Telephone Call

What are the secrets of getting through to the appropriate contact person for prospective clients? Key activities in this area include handling resistance, stalls, and put-offs; turning the conversation your way; and securing an appointment. (See Chapter 10.)

Preparing for the Discussion

The importance of preparation cannot be overstated. Your tasks will include preparing a discussion guide and personal-contact kit. Your responsibilities will include arriving on time, alert and relaxed. (See Chapter 11.)

The next steps in getting new clients through a client-centered marketing approach involve the conduct of successful new-business discussions, which includes opening the discussion in a way that builds trust and rapport, defining existing-needs situations, defining the desired or required future situation of the prospective client, presenting your proposed solution, handling concerns and information needs, closing the discussion, and moving to action.

Opening the Discussion

Though you may not have considered it before, it is your responsibility to manage the introductions at the commencement of a new-business discussion. Your goals will be to reduce tension, build trust and rapport, and establish an atmosphere of openness and cooperation. At the same time you will be sizing up the contact and making mental notes for use later in the discussion. You then move on to the body of discussion. (See Chapter 12.)

Defining the Existing-Need Situation

This is a pivotal area and involves numerous steps, including: (1) verifying and determining the nature of the need, (2) defining the scope of the need, (3) determining its urgency, and (4) identifying the buying motive(s) of the contact person(s). It also involves determining costs to date, verifying your mutual understanding, and moving to the next phase. (See Chapter 13.)

Defining the Desired or Required Future Situation

What will the client get when you have completed what you have promised? Your task is to define the scope of the future situation and establish a realistic timetable. Other tasks include pinpointing your expectations and the client's, determining solution criteria, and specifying the products or services that will be produced or offered.

The second half of conducting winning new-business presentations involves presenting your proposed solution, handling concerns and information needs, closing the discussion, and taking action. (See Chapter 14.)

Presenting Your Proposed Solution. How do you effectively present the proposed strategy and goals that meet a client's needs? When is it appropriate to present a range of solutions? Your tasks include determining the best solution and making an effective verbal proposal that stresses the benefits of your method of handling the client's need. (See Chapter 15.)

Handling Concerns and Information Needs. Client objections are a predictable and normal occurrence during new-business discussions. The effective client-centered marketer must understand the anatomy of an objection and, subsequently, welcome objections and use them to her advantage. (See Chapter 16.)

Closing the Discussion and Moving to Action. Your task is to recognize when to close the discussion and debrief the contact person using client-centered scenarios. You must then deliver the closing statement and complete the administrative details. (See Chapter 17.)

Having laid the groundwork for the client-centered marketing approach, prepared for appointments with prospective clients, and conducted winning new-business discussions, you are almost home free. Next, we will discuss the importance of follow through, which includes preparing a winning proposal (if necessary in your practice) and reinforcing your client's buy decision.

Preparing a Winning Proposal

What does a winning proposal look like? What does it contain, and what does it offer? Your task is to prepare a proposal that meets the needs and expectations of the client while avoiding some of the common pitfalls of proposal writing. (See Chapter 18.)

Reinforcing Your Client's Choice

The effective client-centered marketer understands the importance of handling postpurchase concerns of the client. Touchdowns are not scored until the ball is over the goal line and the official's hands are raised. (See Chapter 19.)

3

Establishing Objectives for Your New-client Program

Establishing objectives for your new-client program involves first determining what you are trying to accomplish in acquiring new clients. Objectives, when fortified by action, lead to a measurable result. Another term for measurable results is *goal*. The nature, scope, and potential of your new-client program, indeed its very thrust, will depend on the objectives you establish. In addition, your long-term success will depend upon your ability to use leveraging to accomplish the chosen objectives.

REQUIRED AND DESIRED OBJECTIVES

Required objectives consist of those essential to your firm's survival. In other words, you have no choice in the matter, so the objectives confronting you tend to be of an immediate, urgent nature. An example of a required objective might be a new service launch, or changes in the way the firm operates. (See Fig. 3.1.)

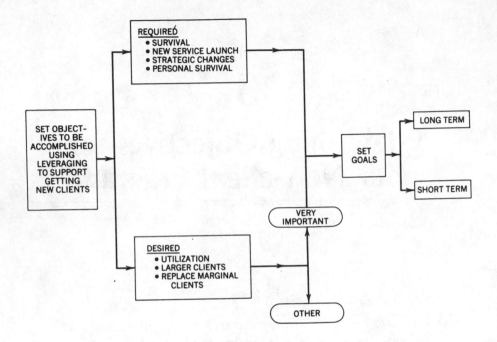

FIGURE 3.1. Setting Goals

Desired objectives differ from required objectives in that they may be something you strongly want, but are not necessary for survival. Examples of desired objectives include better utilization of existing resources, the ability to attract larger and higher paying clients, or the replacement of marginal clients. Only the most important desired objectives should be acted upon. Others should be put on hold and reviewed periodically.

Due to changes in the prevailing environment, in time these objectives may need to be reclassified as required, desired and very important; desired but not important; or not worth maintaining. I made a commitment to promote and teach the client-centered niche-marketing method to the providers of professional services in the English-speaking countries of the world. A highly desired objective is to be invited to present this method at international and national conferences attended by targets. Appearing at such gatherings lets me leverage my time and resources.

ESTABLISHING YOUR OBJECTIVES

To develop a prosperous practice, there are many types of objectives you could establish, including those in the areas of strategy, operations, financing, marketing, clients, personnel, and survival. *Strategic objectives* involve a change in the nature and scope of the practice, such as developing a different industry mix or creating conditions for service-industry specialization.

Operating objectives focus on improved internal procedures for achieving a more balanced work flow. *Financial objectives* focus on activities to improve profitability or loss of revenue, while *marketing objectives* are involved with transforming the present marketing mix or achieving greater penetration within a niche.

Acquiring larger-fee clients is one example of *client-related objectives*. *Personal objectives* may be as basic as surviving as a professional in public practice or generating more work.

Listed below are a number of objectives you may want your new-client program to accomplish:

GETTING NEW CLIENTS: OBJECTIVES

Strategic Objectives	Required	Desired
To change the nature and scope of the practice.	_____	_____
To develop and provide more high-fee services.	_____	_____
To develop a different industry mix.	_____	_____
To create conditions for service-industry specialization.	_____	_____

	Required	Desired
To enhance the image and reputation of the firm.	_____	_____
To _____	_____	_____

Operating Objectives

	Required	Desired
To use existing capabilities better.	_____	_____
To reduce peaks and valleys by developing an industry-market niche with a business cycle different from others.	_____	_____
To maintain and increase profitability by providing more high-priced services to better clients.	_____	_____
To expand present client base.	_____	_____
To _____	_____	_____

Financial Objectives

	Required	Desired
To improve net profit.	_____	_____
To ensure the survival/profitability of the office/firm.	_____	_____
To offset the loss of good clients through attrition.	_____	_____
To replace revenue lost resulting from pruning poor clients.	_____	_____
To provide more recurring sources of new business.	_____	_____
To replace revenue lost from recently terminated/lost clients.	_____	_____
To _____	_____	_____

Client-related Objectives

	Required	Desired
To acquire larger-fee clients.	_____	_____
To expand the base of high-potential clients.	_____	_____

	Required	Desired
To transform the client base from a volume to a cluster practice.	_____	_____
To establish a new industry-market niche to offset a slump with clients in an existing niche.	_____	_____
To obtain larger, more profitable clients.	_____	_____
To _____	_____	_____

Industry-related Objectives

	Required	Desired
To develop specialization opportunities.	_____	_____
To transform the market mix from diversified to concentrated.	_____	_____
To _____	_____	_____

Personal Objectives

	Required	Desired
To survive as a professional in a public practice.	_____	_____
To determine if I have the temperament to stay in public practice.	_____	_____
To obtain favorable visibility among partners as a condition for advancement and election to the partnership.	_____	_____
To begin building my confidence and capability so that I can be effective when I need to be.	_____	_____
To _____	_____	_____

Staff-related Objectives

	Required	Desired
To provide more interesting work for partners and high-potential non-partners.	_____	_____
To develop more specialists.	_____	_____

Any of the objectives listed above, as well as those you add, can be viewed as required or desired based on your particular situation.

Establishing objectives, upon first reading, appears deceptively simple. Yet, this is a task that cannot be taken lightly. The most successful firms choose no more than a handful of objectives at best. Because these objectives are virtually defining and shaping the future practice, they are given careful consideration.

Let's take a look at a mini case history of a professional in a consulting practice who established objectives for a new service in his office.

ESTABLISHING A NEW SERVICE OFFERING

Ira Snyder is a manager with Pannell Kerr Forster in their Los Angeles office. Ira's mission was to launch a new practice area for the firm in health-services management. He was given six months and a reasonable budget. He knew the benefits to be gained from niche-marketing and building relationships with the key players in the southern California health-care infrastructure.

Ira established the following objectives for the first year:

To develop name recognition in the niche area

To prepare and submit detailed qualifications packages to the niche

To identify and communicate with all niche contacts of his home office

To develop contacts and working relationships with other service producers to the niche (nonclient influentials)

To obtain memberships and become active in organizations serving the niche

To conduct a needs survey and publish alerts

To accumulate articles

To make 50 new contacts among the industry providers

To obtain 5 engagements.

You'll note that the last two items in the first-year list are really bottom-line goals.

The same is true of the last item in Ira's second-year list. He established second-year objectives, realizing that these could change depending upon what he accomplished during the first year. His second-year objectives include the following:

To promote and extend recognition in the niche

To upgrade the level of participation in high-potential local organizations

To expand contracts and maintain working relationships with other service providers in the niche

To publish at least one article in a local periodical

To obtain 12 engagements.

By establishing these objectives and bottom-line goals, Ira was able to focus on the job at hand. Whenever he could spend a few minutes, he used a bits-and-pieces marketing approach to reach the objective and meet the bottom-line goals. The objectives and goals provided Ira with a baseline for measuring his progress.

SETTING GOALS TO ACHIEVE YOUR OBJECTIVES

Setting goals, synonymous with achieving measurable results, is essential for accomplishing desired objectives. The goals you choose must be challenging yet reachable. It is of no use to you or your firm to set goals that only lead to frustration, misallocation of resources, or diminished spirits. Peter Drucker says you must ask yourself, "What are my goals? What should they be?" As with establishing objectives, goal setting appears simple. Let's lay the groundwork for setting realistic, achievable goals.

1. You must set goals that enable you to work from your comfort zone. Remember the illustration about scuba diving in the

last chapter? You don't want to dive into waters that are too deep or bite off more than you can chew because you may do damage to your psyche; then you'll become ineffective even within your comfort zone.

2. Set some goals that let you win early and often. A win is getting an appointment with a decision-maker or influential. Winning early bolsters your confidence while you are still learning and gathering information about the niche. It also serves as a springboard for your attempts to achieve more challenging goals.

3. Set goals that are achievable on a bits-and-pieces basis unless you have large blocks of time available. Look for ways to divide goals into manageable steps so you can make continuing progress.

A common financial goal among professional-service practitioners, and really anyone in business, is to obtain a certain dollar revenue from new clients by a specified date. To achieve that goal, other supporting goals must first be set. These usually involve some type of prospecting activity. How does the level of prospecting translate into the realization of financial goals?

INPUT, OUTPUT

Marketing, and particularly prospecting, has been described as a numbers game. Prospecting is an ongoing process and part of the niche-learning process. If you plan to be in business for a long time, you will have to embrace prospecting as the crucial activity in the success of your practice.

The level of prospecting efforts required can be established through a few simple equations. Suppose you have a financial goal of $60,000 in revenue from new clients for the next 12 months. If your average fee is $3,000 per client, then the number of additional clients required at this average fee is 20. If you are in a start-up situation, then the number of new clients required equals 20. Suppose you use mailings without telephone follow-up contacts (which are stressed in Chapter 10) to obtain inquiries. How many pieces mailed result in one inquiry? Let's say the number is 50. If you send 5000 pieces of mail, with a 50 to 1 ratio (2 percent return), you are likely to obtain 100 inquiries.

Now, in handling all of those inquiries, how many appointments can you generate? If you are able to get appointments with 25 percent of those making inquiries, then obviously you will have 25 new appointments. What number of appointments will be required to obtain one new client? Three? Five? Ten? Let's say for every five appointments kept, you obtain one new client. Following along in our example, you would then have five new clients. Based on the financial goal we established earlier, the number of new clients you require is 20. Thus, to obtain 20 new clients your level of effort (or efficiency) must be increased. You could increase your mailing to 20,000 pieces which, all other things being equal, would result in 20 new clients. Or, if the effectiveness of your mailing were improved (using the techniques in Chapter 10) the number of inquiries would surely increase beyond 2 percent (1 out of 50).

Improvements in your phone technique might increase your appointments from 25 percent to a somewhat higher figure. Finally, improvements in the way you handle appointments or simply having more appointments will bolster your efforts to achieve the number of clients you desire.

While it is difficult to determine the hit ratios (i.e., how many mailings to obtain an inquiry, how many appointments to obtain a client), if you have been in business for a while, hopefully you can calculate some type of historical average or make reasonable estimates. Realistically, whatever level of prospecting you think is necessary is almost always far below the level that is actually required to achieve your goals.

When determining the appropriate level of prospecting, you must also establish a time and money budget to achieve your goals. The typical service provider underestimates the time necessary to effectively prospect by as much as 70 percent and underestimates necessary expenditures by about 50 percent.

FIGURE 3.2. Prospecting Funnel

Prospecting can be likened to a funnel that requires numerous inputs through the large opening for a few outputs from the narrow end. (See Figure 3.2.) By following a client-centered, niche-marketing approach and employing leveraging, the output will be high-potential clones of your high-paying, existing Key and A clients.

ACTIVATING YOUR PROSPECTING PROGRAM

If prospecting represents a new activity for you, then learning how to prospect may well be one of your goals. (See Part II: Getting and Preparing for Appointments with Prospective Clients.) If prospecting is not new to you, you may nevertheless need to establish a goal of improving your prospecting capabilities.

To the degree that you can identify the divisible units of activity that support your prospecting efforts, you are ahead of the game. If your goal is to call on 100 new prospects in the coming 12 months, supporting goals that support your overall prospecting goal may include the following:

Preparing a realistic time and money budget by June 1.

Reviewing the file of previous no-sale prospects for leads by June 15.

The following chart contains a representative list of prospecting goals that successful practitioners have used to get new clients. Review this list carefully to determine which items are appropriate for your situation and will accelerate your ability to accomplish your overall objectives. You will probably need to modify some of the items to fit your needs.

Each of the goals you set must be accompanied by a time frame. How long will it take? By what date will you accomplish your objectives? A goal without a time frame is not a goal at all, but rather a vague notion of where you would like to be.

Prospecting Goals—a Representative List

- ☐ Establish goals of prospecting during coming period by   / /
- ☐ Inventory prospective clients in your business pipelines by   / /
- ☐ Review new-client acceptance criteria by   / /
- ☐ Define target individuals by   / /
- ☐ Define target groups by   / /
- ☐ Define target niche(s) by   / /
- ☐ Develop introductory letters for ( ) by   / /
- ☐ Obtain membership list(s) for ( ) by   / /
- ☐ Select key client referral sources to be contacted by   / /
- ☐ Select key nonclient referral sources to be contacted by   / /
- ☐ Review file of previous no-sale prospects for leads by   / /
- ☐ Inventory existing organizational memberships by   / /
- ☐ Identify hot-button and current problems in ( ) by   / /

☐ Establish a time-phased, contact-by-
   telephone plan by   / /

☐ Search for new and/or unusual sources/
   lists/directories by   / /

☐ Prepare a realistic time and money
   budget by   / /

☐ Integrate new leads into existing lists of
   prospects by   / /

☐ Determine the sources of assistance in
   prospecting by   / /

☐ Determine the name(s) of initial contacts
   to call by   / /

☐ Develop a profile to educate our referral
   sources by   / /

☐ Assemble resources for this period's
   prospecting program by   / /

In Chapter 4, we will discuss how to select your target niche and how the objectives and goals you have set translate into sensing, serving, and satisfying the needs of the niche.

4

How to Select Your Target Niche and Organize to Serve It

Unless your marketing comfort zone is large enough to handle the inevitable rejections that accompany wide-angle, horizontal prospecting, selecting an industry-market niche for analysis and action is a much easier way to conduct your prospecting activities. The key to fairly predictable, significant growth is to be "somebody special to a special group of bodies." You must be perceived as being different and better.

This chapter will help you select an industry-market niche for analysis and action, and introduce key ideas for organizing to serve the niche.

SOME KEY DEFINITIONS

So that we are talking the same game, here's a review of some working definitions.

Industry—All clients and prospects with the same 4-digit SIC-code number, offering the same basic type of product or service, and therefore competing with one another. Some of the industries you presently serve, or will be examining, are more appropriately termed professions. For example, I work with many firms in the accounting profession, although the phrase "accounting industry" probably conveys a similar meaning.

Market—The postal zip codes that comprise your practice area(s).

Niche—The clients, prospective clients, and nonclient influentials in the SIC-zip code area.

Prospects—Nonclients who agree to meet with you; or those with whom you have met whose needs you believe you can serve, but who are not yet clients.

Suspects—Nonclients who meet your minimum selection criteria, but who haven't been contacted by you or agreed to meet with you yet.

Nonclient-influentials—Individuals who have influence within the niche, such as editors and association executives. They may also be government officials with national status. Nonclient influentials may or may not be located within the niche; the determining factor is their degree of influence.

Infrastructure—The players in the niche: the clients, prospective clients, suspects, nonclient influentials, and organizations serving or affecting the niche.

A STRATEGIC DECISION

Choosing an industry-market niche for concentration is one of the most important strategic decisions you can make regarding the long-term viability of your practice. Niches change concurrently with and in reaction to changes in technology, competition, regulations, social trends, and so on. Change provides you with opportunities to develop and take advantage of the use of leverage. You can capitalize on leveraging opportunities best by developing an insider's understanding of and reputation with members of a high-potential niche.

You can't be all things to all people, and you certainly can't be all things to all clients. You must direct your attention to industry-market niche(s), where you can most readily serve and most prosperously penetrate. As I mentioned earlier, it is likely that your task of getting new clients must be accomplished with limited resources. Even if you had unlimited resources, you would want to allocate them wisely.

Previously, you may not have given much thought to the types of clients you should be acquiring. Wrong choices, however, can be costly. If you settle for C and D clients, you will not enjoy your work because you'll have fee and collection problems. While muddling through the problems of marginal clients, you will also miss the leveraging opportunities created by your interaction with Key and A clients.

THE SELECTION PROCESS

Choosing an industry-market niche on which to concentrate is an evolutionary process. It starts with examining appropriate industries (by 4-digit SIC code number) and ends with getting new clients from commitments supported by realistic time and dollar budgets and time-phased work schedules.

As a rule of thumb, you want to select a relatively stable niche(s) not dominated by one or more of your competitors. It is helpful if your technological capability is perceived as state-of-the-art at least (leading edge would be better). If you already have some clients in the niche you ultimately select, or if you have relationships with niche influentials, these are certainly plus factors. Likewise, if you or your staff is experienced and enjoys working in the niche, this is a big plus.

As we discuss the steps involved in selecting your niche, keep

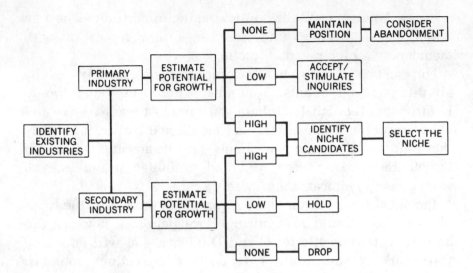

FIGURE 4.1. Selecting Your Industry-Market Niche

an eye out for leveraging opportunities. Can your services be specialized and delivered profitably? Can you reach prospective clients relatively easily? Is there an established infrastructure that you can identify and penetrate without too much time and cost? If so, you may be tapping into a gold mine. Figure 4.1 shows the steps involved in selecting a niche.

1. *Identify the Industries you Presently Serve.* This step is easy to complete if you have classified your clients by the 4-digit SIC mentioned earlier. If you have not yet entered the SIC data for your clients, you will want to do this now. The chart starting on page 47 contains a complete list of U.S. SIC numbers and industry titles. Compute the total revenue produced by all clients in each SIC for the most recent 12-month period.

2. *Determine Your Primary and Secondary Industries.* A primary industry is one from which you derive a relatively large percentage of your total revenue. A secondary industry is one

that currently generates a relatively small percentage of total revenue.

3. *Estimate the Potential for Growth in each Niche.* In assessing industries, ask yourself, "Are my primary industries the ones I should, or want to, be in?" If not, examine secondary industries that warrant further attention and that may be shifted to primary status.

In choosing your industry-market niche, it is more important to estimate the potential for future growth among primary and secondary industry candidates. Past trends are one thing. If the estimates for potential growth within a primary industry are poor, either abandon further action within that industry or maintain your current level of effort in serving it. Even if the potential for growth is low, you can elect to accept all inquiries regarding your services. You may even choose to follow through if you are in a survival mode. Your goal, however, is to focus upon primary industries that have a high potential for growth. Examining these industries in relationship to their geographic representation, including proximity and accessibility, aids in identifying niche candidates.

One source of information for estimating potential growth is *Predicasts*, by F&S Publications. It forecasts growth of all industries by SIC number and is a useful tool to accelerate your understanding of the growth and future direction of the niche. *Predicasts* is available in the business reference section of any major city, university, or federal government library. Industry and professional trade associations also make available a wealth of information regarding trends in their respective industries. (More on information sources in Chapter 5.)

4. *Determine the Size of the Niche.* You will need to obtain all the relevant information to make your final decision regarding which niche(s) to select. Among the basic information you need are the *raw numbers* of prospects within the niches being examined. There are several excellent national mailing list com-

panies that offer free catalogues with this type of information. Additionally, these companies can provide you with actual target lists, including the name, address, and phone number of companies by SIC number, zip code, and other selection criteria.

American Business Lists, Inc.
5707 South 86th Circle
P.O. Box 27347
Omaha, NE 68127
402-331-7169

R. L. Polk and Company
6400 Monroe Boulevard
Taylor, MI 48180
313-292-3200

Hugo Dunhill Mailing List, Inc.
630 3rd Avenue
New York, NY 10017
212-682-8030
800-223-6454, Outside NY State

Dun's National Business List
16 Progress Drive
Shelton, CT 06484
800-654-7834
800-435-3742, In Connecticut

The Educational Directory
16 Progress Drive
Shelton, CT 06484
(800) 243-5538

All of these companies can assist you in identifying nearly every suspect in any particular industry-market niche.

5. *Developing Your Preferred Prospective-Client Profile*. An effective way to select your niche is to develop a preferred

prospective-client profile. In other words, you put the cart before the horse. What would you like your new clients to look like? Act like? What makes them desirable? To develop the profile, define the characteristics of your desired new clients in the targeted niche.

First copy the following and fill in the chart on page 46. You will want to keep these profiles and refer to them for a visible record of your practice needs and preferences. Then you can monitor your needs and assumptions.

Next, think about the best clients you now have in the niche—the clients you really enjoy working with and serving. What are their characteristics? Are their size, management style, habit of prompt payments, stage in the growth cycle, and so on, attractive to you? List these characteristics on lines 1 through 9, using more space if necessary. Though you may not have realized it, the positive characteristics of Key and A clients help to define your comfort zone. Now, attempt to identify the two or three factors that really set these clients apart from all others, and put an asterisk after them.

Favorable characteristics of Key and A clients that might be listed include the following:

Pay on time

Have potential for growth

Are highly visible within their industry

Manage with integrity

Have a year-end in an off-peak season for you

Maintain a good accounting staff

Have streamlined management

Have experienced relatively rapid growth

Are a prestige client

Pay the full per-diem rate

Easily won—no costly proposals required

Date ___ / ___ / ___

PREFERRED PROSPECTIVE CLIENT PROFILE IN:

_____

(INDUSTRY SIC# AND NAME)

POSITIVE CHARACTERISTICS OF KEY AND A CLIENTS

1. _____
2. _____
3. _____
4. _____
5. _____
6. _____
7. _____
8. _____
9. _____

KNOCK-OUT FACTORS—C AND D CLIENTS

1. _____
2. _____
3. _____
4. _____
5. _____
6. _____
7. _____

Agriculture, Forestry, Fishing

SIC	SIC Description	Total Compiled Names
0721	Crop planting & protection services	4,062
0721A	Crop dusting services	3,871
0781	Landscape architects	5,683
0782	Landscape maintenance services	31,914
0782A	Landscape contractors	24,840
0782B	Landscaping & lawn maintenance	11,242
0783	Tree & shrub services	10,045

Mining

1381	Oil well drilling contractors	3,639
1382	Oil & gas exploration services	11,373
1389	Oil & gas field services, N.E.C.	20,313
1400	Nonmetallic mineral mining	4,471

Contract Construction

1521	Contractors—one-family units	80,643
1521A	Contractors—remodeling	45,133
1711B	Heating & ventilation	43,145
1711C	Air conditioning contractors	39,093
1731	Electrical work contractors	50,174

Manufacturing Firms

2711	Newspaper publishing & printing	13,440
2721	Periodical publishing & printing	7,300
2731	Books—publishing & printing	5,852
2791	Typesetters	10,365
3599	Machinery—nonelectric, N.E.C.	39,764
3599A	Machine shops—grinding	34,239
3662	Radio & TV communication equipment	2,329

Transportation, Communication and Public Utilities

4212	Trucking companies—local	27,172
4212A	Delivery services—local	7,505
4212B	Baggage transfer services	2,161
4212C	Trucking & carting—general	14,837
4213	Over-the-road trucking companies	32,116
4213C	Trucking—heavy hauling	25,851
4225	General warehouses	16,488

FIGURE 4.2. Selected SIC Numbers (continued on pages 48–51)

Transportation, Communication and Public Utilities (Cont.)

SIC	SIC Description	Total Compiled Names
4225C	Warehouses	15,188
4722	Passenger transportation services	35,607
4722A	Travel agencies	27,183
4722B	Airline ticket offices	10,257
4811	Telephone companies	5,508
4821	Radio broadcasting cos. & stations	9,089
4832	Telegraph services	1,977
4833	Television broadcasting	1,773
4899	Communication services, N.E.C.	9,104
4899A	Cable TV transmission & equip. cos.	8,064

Wholesale Trade

SIC	SIC Description	Total Compiled Names
5021	Furniture, whols.	23,371
5021A	Office equipment, whols.	13,289
5065C	Radio equipment, whols.	6,668
5065D	Sound systems, whols.	4,696
5065E	Telephone & intercoms, whols.	7,887
5081Q	Copying machines, whols.	7,498
5086	Professional equipment, whols.	36,417
5099F	Importers	9,031
5099G	Exporters	7,076

Retail Trade

SIC	SIC Description	Total Compiled Names
5734	Data processing equipment—retail	37,046
5734A	Computer stores & dealers	31,216
5734B	Computer supplies & parts dealers	7,044
5812	Restaurants—seated service	157,390
5812A	Restaurants—dinner, exc. 5814B	140,423
6020	Banks	55,442
6020A	Banks—commercial	23,799
6020B	Banks—savings	4,811
6020C	Banks—foreign	3,472
6052	Foreign exchange establishments	134
6059	Bank related services—misc.	2,744
6059A	Check cashing services	2,720

Finance, Insurance, Real Estate

SIC	SIC Description	Total Compiled Names
6120	Savings & loan associations	21,493
6141	Credit unions	27,767

FIGURE 4.2. Continued

48

Finance, Insurance, Real Estate (Cont.)

SIC	SIC Description	Total Compiled Names
6141A	Credit unions—federal	10,683
6141B	Credit unions—state	9,330
6162	Mortgage companies	20,242
6211	Security brokers	17,161
6211A	Investment security companies	10,348
6211B	Stock & bond brokers	9,184
6211C	Mutual fund brokers	2,929
6281	Investment advisory services	13,909
6300	Insurance companies—home office	1,467
6311	Life insurance companies	1,169
6321	Health & accident insurance cos.	988
6411A	Insurance adjusters	5,028
6411B	Insurance consultants	6,666
6411D	Pension plan consultants	911
6512A	Office building management	5,883
6512B	Shopping center management	5,697
6531	Real estate agencies & services	158,983
6531A	Real estate appraisers	10,673
6531B	Real estate management firms	10,616
6531C	Real estate agents	139,181
6541	Title abstract companies	8,895
6552	Subdivider & developers, exc. 6553	20,949

Business Systems

SIC	SIC Description	Total Compiled Names
7311	Advertising agencies	21,981
7312	Advertising services—outdoor	2,721
7313	Radio, TV & publishers advg. reps.	8,726
7313A	Newspaper advertising reps.	3,515
7313B	Magazine advertising reps.	2,687
7331	Direct mail advertising services	7,123
7331B	Mailing list brokers & compilers	1,606
7333	Commercial photography & art	39,284
7333B	Commercial artists	16,151
7333C	Commercial photographers	18,942
7361C	Resume services	3,213
7361D	Executive recruiters	3,539
7362	Temporary help supply services	9,549
7372	Computer software services	19,923
7372A	Computer systems consultants	10,671
7372B	Computer programming services	2,953

FIGURE 4.2. Continued

Business Systems (Cont.)

SIC	SIC Description	Total Compiled Names
7372C	Computer software & service	5,273
7372D	Computer graphics	522
7374	Data processing services	21,141
7379	Computer-related services, N.E.C.	5,370
7379B	Computer service and repair	3,867
7392	Management consulting & p r srvcs.	63,146
7392D	Business management consultants	19,717
7392E	Market research services	3,729
7392F	Personnel consultants	3,218
7392G	Public relations & publicity	4,731
7392L	Marketing consultants	3,534
7392M	Financial consultants	2,538
7392N	Educational consultants	2,822

Professional Services

SIC	SIC Description	Total Compiled Names
8011	Physicians & surgeons	203,483
8021	Dentists	115,187
8031	Osteopathic physicians	8,396
8041	Chiropractors	23,680
8042	Optometrists	22,750
8049	Health practitioners, N.E.C.	34,064
8049A	Podiatrists	10,119
8049B	Psychologists	16,795
8059	Nursing & personal care facilities, N.E.C.	21,687
8071	Medical & x-ray laboratories	6,579
8071A	Medical laboratories	4,580
8111	Attorneys	171,836
8231	Libraries	36,078
8231A	Public libraries	14,736
8231B	Special libraries	5,118
8231C	College & university libraries	2,688
8911A	Architectural services	21,146
8911B	Structural eng. services	2,164
8911C	Engineers—designers—industrial	2,481
8911D	Consulting engineering services	12,761
8911E	Civil engineers	4,182
8911F	Surveying services	10,345
8931	Accounting, auditing & bookkeeping serv.	69,350
8931A	Accounting services	53,248
8931B	Calculating & statistical services	11,834
8931C	Bookkeeping services	5,034

FIGURE 4.2. Continued

Government Offices

SIC	SIC Description	Total Compiled Names
9111	Executive offices	22,362
9111A	City halls	19,052
9111B	County government seats	3,181
9112	Government offices	90,888

FIGURE 4.2. Continued

In addition, any client with whom you enjoy working, who offers challenging work, or who you simply wouldn't want to be without, we'll term a "key" client. Your key and A clients represent the backbone of your firm.

Now, think about the worst clients you have served in the niche. These are the ones you would like to eliminate from, or avoid bringing into, your practice. What are the characteristics of these C and D firms? What among their attitudes, management styles, or operating procedures turns you off? List these knock-out factors on lines 1 through 7 on the chart on page 46, using more space if necessary.

Some knock-out factors could include:

Not following your advice

Lagging behind their industry

Haggling over your fee

Unchallenging work

Clients so large you are seen as an extension of their work force

Seek unreasonable or unethical services

You will want to limit the number of absolute knock-out factors that can cause a no-go decision. If a prospect has any one of these factors, say to yourself, "This one does not come aboard." Remember, you are shaping your future practice right now with every client you accept. Reexamine these lists to be sure you included all of the positive characteristics and the knock-out factors.

You have now prepared a very valuable profile. You have a current picture of the type of client you want to attract. In a sense you will be seeking clones of your best clients. You will be able to use this profile as a cookie cutter, to educate your referral sources, brief your staff, focus your prospecting time and efforts on preferred targets, and develop new-client acceptance guidelines.

If you have done a good job of analyzing your practice or maintaining up-to-date client engagement summaries, the task of producing a preferred prospective-client profile need not be difficult. If you have never undertaken any kind of analysis of this sort, then you must gather some basic information before you can proceed.

Frequently, professionals seek referrals and leads for new clients by telling their clients and influentials, "If you have any leads, send them my way." This is not a sound practice. Too often you'll end up with C and D clients. Specify the type of new clients you are seeking. When you have this knowledge, generating new leads by referral becomes much easier. You can then say to your A clients, "I would like to 'clone' you. I am looking for additional clients just like you that have the same management style and orientation." This is the highest compliment you can pay to a client; consequently, it opens many new doors.

6. *Establish Selection Criteria.* Ideally you serve at least two industry-market niches that have counterbalancing business-activity cycles, which enables you to level your workload and offset any unexpected variances. There are many criteria that could be used for selecting your niche. Over the years, I have found that the following are among the most important:

The number of existing Key and A clients in the niche

The nature of your competition

Existing and expected growth patterns

The interests of you and your key staff

The ability to transfer your technology developed from serving clients in a closely related industry

The number and strengths of your nonclient influentials

The estimated costs of identifying and contacting the target

The costs of developing sufficient insider's understanding

The costs of developing appropriate technologies required to provide support services

The support and cooperation of partners with relative experience in the niche

The existing and expected growth patterns in targeted industries should be examined further. For example, is the industry growing at a rapid pace or is it relatively stable?

7. *Identify the Resources On Hand and Experience in Serving the Niche.* Were you to select this particular niche, what specific experience do you have in serving it? What resources would you use, including existing relationships, industry data, or other inside information or competitive advantages? What is your current image and reputation within the niche? What promotion techniques could you use to stimulate interest? Are the organizations and memberships you currently maintain sufficient for meeting prospects and nonclient influentials? Or would you have to join other organizations?

8. *Make the Go/No-Go Decision.* Now comes the moment of truth, the time in which a go/no-go decision must be made regarding the industry-market niche you have been analyzing. It would be nice to use a simple formula to make the most appropriate choice. Unfortunately, there isn't one; at least, I haven't encountered it. Niche decisions are of a qualitative, subjective nature.

Your decision to go with a particular niche must feel right. By now, you have done your analysis and determined the areas in which you want to specialize. Hopefully, you have identified something different and better about your services so that you can attract those "special bodies." The niche that you choose must be one in which you are willing to commit and invest your time, technology, and resources, so that you can stand out from the herd.

Making the niche decision involves taking calculated risks. The analysis you have undertaken provides you with more informed decision-making capabilities. You must have confidence in your capabilities to enter and successfully penetrate the niche that you define. This will involve dropping what does not fit, unless it is needed for short-term survival. If you have any doubts about selecting a particular niche, don't select it.

A "gut check" is in order: Is it dominated by a few companies? Are the needs of typical prospective clients in this industry such that any work you do for them will be challenging to your staff and transferable to other clients?

Check it out and analyze it further. A bad choice can be very costly. Remember, your decision sets strategic practice decisions. It's similar to steering a huge ocean liner. If you choose in haste—spin the navigation wheel around too quickly—you will capsize or take a long time to right the ship and resume smooth sailing.

As with any decision, there are always costs involved. Perhaps the hardest decision to make is to abandon a niche that you had previously penetrated. After all, you have already invested time and resources. Abandoning the niche would force you to acknowledge time and money lost and engender feelings of guilt and second guessing.

Organizing to Serve the Niche

There are several organizational tasks that you must complete to serve the niche. These include preparing your niche data base, organizing your library, assembling and codifying your experience in serving the niche, and developing your service delivery system for the niche. For the balance of this chapter, we will focus primarily on preparing your niche data base and library. Subsequent chapters will discuss the other tasks.

Developing your data base and organizing your library involve asking the fundamental question, "What information do I need to sense, serve, and satisfy the needs of this niche?" This information must be *organized* and maintained on a regular basis so that it supports you in your continuing client-centered marketing efforts. Barbara Hemphill, an organizing consultant, points out that organization helps to reduce costs. "Research shows that the average white-collar professional is responsible for eight file drawers of paper—18,000 documents," Hemphill emphasizes. "The average professional spends 20 percent of his time looking for misplaced information."

It is absolutely critical that you handle the nuts-and-bolts side of getting new clients. You must keep your data base and library in superb condition. They are as much a part of your overall marketing efforts as the clothes you wear and your in-person presentations. In fact, as we will see in subsequent chapters, you must also keep your presentation materials, traveling files, appointment books, expense records, client correspondence, and briefcase in the same superb condition in which you keep your office prospect files.

Preparing Your Data Base

To manage and maintain the data you will be collecting, and to capitalize on the information contained in the library you will be assembling, you will need to choose an appropriate data base software package. This software must have the capability to do word processing and mail merges. When contacting the niche, your ability to immediately turn out custom-tailored computer-assisted hard copy such as a promotion letter, an engagement letter, and a proposal will help you win more clients quickly and keep your marketing costs at a minimum.

There are seven steps involved in preparing your data base, four of which are discussed in this chapter; others are covered in later chapters.

1. Determine the files you need
2. Determine the nature and number of fields to be used in each record

3. Build the form for producing each record

4. Enter information already on hand

5. Identify additional data needed and the best source(s)

6. Acquire and enter the data

7. Maintain and update the data base

1. *Determine the Files You Need.* A file is a collection of information that is related to a single subject or topic. There are three files that must be created:

Existing clients

Prospective/potential clients

Nonclient influentials

2. *Determine the Nature and Number of Fields to be Used in Each Record.* A field refers to a single-entry item of data, such as "name," "classification," SIC, and so forth. A record is composed of related fields. Experts who design data bases caution against using too many fields. More is not always better. Your goal is to enter only the information you need to accomplish your objective.

For your existing clients, the *minimum* fields should be:

Name

Address

Zip code

Telephone number(s)

Name(s) of contact person(s)

Firm's internal identification number (if used)

Class of client—Key/A/B/C/D

Past three years' revenue

Services provided past 12 months

Major needs, problems, and opportunities

Proposals outstanding

Essential background information

For your prospective/potential clients in the niche, the following fields should be sufficient:

Name

Address

Zip code

Telephone number(s)

Name(s) of contact person(s)

Probable potential class of client—Key/A/B/C/D

Major needs, problems, and opportunities

Services to suggest

Proposals outstanding

Essential background information

Preparing records for the nonclient influentials (NCIs) file requires a bit of thought.

There are three broad classes of NCIs:

Multipliers—individuals who, because of their responsibilities, have the potential to provide you with multiple promotion and prospecting opportunities. Included in this group would be:

Executive directors of industry/trade/professional associations in the niche

Editors of key publications read by your clients and prospective clients

Academics who interact with members of the niche

Sponsors of conferences and other educational events

Reciprocals—others who serve your type of clients and prospective clients. These people expect you to provide them with leads in return for leads they give you. Included in this group would be:

Advertising agencies

Attorneys

Bankers

Others who are or can be influential to you.

Because this is such an individual matter, I've summarized a number of possible NCIs in the next chart, "Possible Nonclient Influentials."

POSSIBLE NONCLIENT INFLUENTIALS

Alumni of your firm who speak well of it
Alumni of your college
Association executives in niches you serve or are targeting
Attorneys
Bankers
Civic officials
Clubs frequented by your clients
Convention and tourism bureaus
Economic development department personnel
Editors of publications read by your clients and targets of opportunity
Former executives of clients who have moved to nonclient/ suspect organizations in your niche
Government officials
Insurance agents/CLUs
Management companies
Neighbors
Other professionals serving your client and targets
Politicians
Real estate salespersons
Stockbrokers
Trust companies
Universities

---

3. *Build the Forms for Producing the Records.* To manage and maintain the data you will be collecting, you will need to

design carefully the form used to enter the information for each record. The charts that follow are examples of forms used to prepare records for various files. They should provide you with some ideas.

FORM USED IN ENTERING PUBLICATION DATA

Publication:
Publisher:
Editor:
  Last: First:
  Gender:
Address:
Suite:
City: State: Zip:
Area Code: Number:
Subscription $:
Type:
Circulation:
Frequency:

FIGURE 4.3.(a) Form Used In Entering Publication Data

FORM USED IN ENTERING DATA ABOUT STATE SOCIETIES AND PROFESSIONAL ASSOCIATIONS

Last Name: First Name:
Title:
State Society:

Address:
Suite:
City: State: Zip:
Area Code: Number:
Publications:
          a:
          b:
Conferences:
          1:
          2:
Number of Members: Membership Directory?:

FIGURE 4.3.(b) Form Used For Entering Data About State Societies and Professional Associations

An important aspect of building your form is determining the fields you will use in sorting the information entered in the records making up each file. If you are building a data base from scratch, consult a data base expert in your community. You may be able to find one at the computer store where you purchased the software package. If not, hook into the user groups for your type of computer. You often can get the names of such groups from the computer stores or "hackers" in your community. I have successfully used a high school computer whiz as my consultant both in designing my forms and handling the data-entry task.

4. *Enter the Information On Hand.* Your goal is to get an early win by entering the data on hand. This gives you a feeling of satisfaction and provides the basis for subsequent steps. It will also help you determine what is needed.

A quick and easy way to gain and enter information on non-client influentials is to trade business card files with noncompeting professionals who also serve your niche. It is becoming increasingly possible to trade data disks containing such names with others. One consultant in New York City is a master of exchanging names. His goal is to develop name awareness and relationships with everyone who is and can be influential to him in reaching his marketing objectives.

Organizing Your Library

Much of the data-gathering you will undertake to develop your computerized data base will also support the development of your library. Here are some of the basic items to gather.

1. *The "Bibles" Used in the Niche.* Every industry or profession has certain key manuals or handbooks that are used by the members in their daily operations. These insider books contain vital information about the industry. The next time you are at a client's office, find out what the key reference handbooks are.

2. *Major Publications Read by Clients and Prospects.* Virtually all publications are cited in one or more of the following directories, located in your public library:

Writer's Market

Working Press of the Nation

Bacon's Publicity Checker

Oxbridge Directory of Newsletters

Hudson's Newsletter Directory

Gebbie's All-in-One Directory

Magazine Industry Marketplace

3. *Engagement-related Materials.* Assemble materials you will use and refer to frequently. There are four major categories:

Proposals—to be analyzed and entered into the word processor for rapid turnaround.

Engagement letters—to be used with proposals.

Final reports—to be used in new-business discussions as evidence of accomplishment.

Work programs, budgets, and so on—to be used in estimating the fees involved in proposed solutions to needs.

4. *Competitor Information.* This includes brochures, Statements of Capability, copies of their proposals, news clippings, and so on.

5. *Niche Data.* These include legislation, trends, and economic studies.

6. *Other Materials.* These include materials about your prospective clients and influentials. As you get more deeply into an understanding of the niche (Chapter 5), undoubtedly you will uncover other key directories, reference materials, and insider's reference materials.

Organizing to serve the target niche will pay off in spades when developing your niche service-delivery system. You will be able to tailor and/or routinize your systems as the situation demands (Chapter 6). Being organized will also accelerate the rate at which you can develop an insider's reputation in the niche (Chapter 7) and specifically:

Help you generate greater name awareness of your firm among targets

Facilitate your handling of inquiries and enable you to develop them further

Bolster your programs for prospecting and promotion.

In Chapter 5, we will examine those factors that assist you in developing an insider's understanding of the niche. Then you can appropriately tailor your service-delivery system and develop an insider's reputation, a coveted position among service providers.

5

Developing an Insider's Understanding of the Niche

"The aim of marketing is to make selling superfluous," says Peter F. Drucker in his landmark book, *Management: Tasks, Responsibilities, Practices* (New York: Harper and Row, 1973). "The aim of marketing is to know and understand the customer so well that the product or service fits him and sells itself. Ideally marketing should result in a customer who is ready to buy. Drucker says, All that should be needed then is to make the product or service available, i.e., logistics rather than salesmanship and a statistical distribution rather than promotion."

No matter how effective your client-centered marketing program, it is not likely that you will be able to make selling superfluous—at least not for a while. However, it is certainly a worthwhile goal and the foundation upon which this chapter rests. The ability to develop and convey services that are perceived as both different and better than your competitors can only come about through developing an insider's understanding of the niche. When you have an insider's knowledge, all of the remaining steps for obtaining new clients become easier.

This will be rather a long and analytical chapter. Up to this point, we have taken a broad, or "macro" look at the niche in which you will be competing. In this chapter, we will be taking a detailed, "micro" look at the niche. We will also be completing the preparation of your data base and library. Figure 5.1 is a graphic depiction of the tasks involved in developing an insider's understanding.

An industry analysis involves the identification of critical success factors, key ratios, the industry cost structure, typical gross-profit margins, net profitability; the factors improving the industry-technology changes; economic, social, and governmental factors, and so on.

The market-analysis side of understanding your niche involves determining the infrastructure and the factors affecting the market. Often, the term infrastructure is tossed about but not really understood. The infrastructure on a zip-code basis consists of the clients, prospects, suspects, nonclient influentials (local), competitors, and all others who serve or affect the niche. This also includes the trade and professional associations and organizations to which these players belong. Factors affecting the market include current economic conditions, and the population density of clients and prospects within the targeted industry by zip code.

The combination of industry analysis and market analysis adds up to a niche analysis. Let's examine each of these elements in detail.

DETERMINING THE CRITICAL SUCCESS FACTORS OF THE INDUSTRY

John F. Rockart, writing in the *Harvard Business Review*, observes that "Critical success factors for any business are the limited number of areas in which results, if they are satisfactory, will ensure successful competitive performance for the organization." Stated differently, they are the few key areas in which things must go right for a business to prosper. Rockart contends that the critical success factors are areas of activity that should

FIGURE 5.1. Understanding Selected Niche(s)

65

receive "constant and careful attention from management." Your ability to identify these factors and their prime measurements will put you at the head of the class of potential service providers on whom your clients and prospective clients will rely.

Critical success factors (CSF) consist of the three to eight factors or performance areas where things must go correctly for a business to flourish, given its location, stage of growth, mission, and growth strategies. There are two major classes of CSF. The first consists of all-encompassing, industry-based factors. In the automotive industry, for example, this would include styling, a high-quality dealer system, cost control, and meeting industry-based energy standards. In the supermarket industry, this would include the product mix, inventory turnover, and sales promotion.

The second class of CSF contains organizational-based factors. In the home entertainment industry, for example, Motorola has chosen not to engage in research and development. Thus, a CSF for Motorola would be the rapid replication of new developments made by others in the industry.

To identify the CSF in the industry you have targeted, first speak with your better clients in the niche and ask them what factors are important. Then read company annual reports and any other information that profiles the industry. "Must" reading includes the prospectus issued by organizations in the industry that wish to go public. Pay particular attention to risk factors spelled out in the analysis section. Review the U.S. *Industrial Outlook*, published annually by the Bureau of Economic Analysis of the Department of Commerce. This publication predicts the growth and profiles the development of over 200 domestic industries, arranged by SIC number for the next five years. Finally, you should talk with stockbrokers who specialize in the industry. It is their business to know the CSF of their respective industries and which companies are adept at meeting them head on.

The same process used in examining an entire industry can be used to examine individual clients. The following chart shows the industry-based CSF for trade associations.

IDENTIFYING INDUSTRY-BASED CRITICAL SUCCESS FACTORS

SIC # <u>8611</u>   Description of Industry <u>TRADE ASSOCIATIONS</u>
List the five to eight most important industry-based CSFs below:

1. <u>Legislation</u>

2. <u>Member communication</u>

3. <u>Membership</u>

4. <u>Economic indicators</u>

5. <u>Financial resources</u>

6. <u>Competitive environment</u>

7. <u>Lobbying efforts</u>

8. _____

IDENTIFYING INDUSTRY-BASED CRITICAL SUCCESS FACTORS

SIC # _____   Description of Industry _____
List the five to eight most important industry-based CSFs below:

1. _____

2. _____

3. _____

4. _____

5. _____

6. _____

7. _____

8. _____

IDENTIFYING PRIME MEASURES FOR A CLIENT'S CSFs

Name of Key Client _____

SIC # __8611__ Description of Industry __TRADE ASSOCIATIONS__

Critical Success Factors	Prime Measures
1. LEGISLATION	Pending Bills Voting Records of Politicians
2. MEMBER COMMUNICATION	Participation Level at Conventions Time Lag Between "News" and Communication to Members Amount of Feedback from Members Communication Costs vs. Other Associations
3. MEMBERSHIP	Ratio Members to Non-members in Industry Dues Structure Advertising & P/R $$ to Total Members & Revenues versus Other Associations
4. ECONOMIC INDICATORS	Insurance Rates GNP Unemployment Rate Interest Rates Balance of Trade
5. FINANCIAL RESOURCES	Member Dues Government Aid to Members
6. COMPETITIVE ENVIRONMENT	# Of Competing Associations & Membership # Of Non-members in the Industry Services Provided by Non-association Providers (For example, Consultants or Educators)
7. LOBBYING EFFORT	Bills Enacted vs. Association Position $$ Spent vs. Other Assoc. # of Lobbyists

FIGURE 5.2. Identifying Prime Measures For a Client's CSFs

Next, for each of the CSFs within an industry, there is a measurement that can be used to track the performance of individual companies. Figure 5.2 indicates the corresponding measurement, *prime measures*, which are used to determine the health and vitality of trade associations. Following this, Figure 5.3 provides an example of critical success factors and prime measures for a construction firm. A blank form follows (Figure 5.4) for your use in determining the prime measures for your industry.

CRITICAL SUCCESS FACTORS AND PRIME MEASURES

Industry: Construction firm

Critical Success Factors	Prime Measures
1. Image in financial markets	Price/earning ratio
2. Technological reputation with customers	Number of contracts won versus number of bids made Customer "perception" interview results
3. Market success	Changes in market share Growth rates of company
4. Risk recognition in major bids and contracts	Length of experience company's with similar products "New" or "old" customer Prior customer relationship
5. Profit margin on jobs	Bid profit margin as ratio of profit on similar jobs
6. Company morale	Turnover, absenteeism, etc. Informal feedback (Management discussions with employees)
7. Performance to budget on major jobs	Job cost budgeted/actual

FIGURE 5.3. Critical Success Factors and Prime Measures

IDENTIFYING PRIME MEASURES FOR A CLIENT'S CSFs

Name of Key Client _____

SIC # _____ Description of Industry _____

CRITICAL SUCCESS FACTORS	PRIME MEASURES
1.	
2.	
3.	
4.	
5.	
6.	
7.	
8.	

FIGURE 5.4. Identifying Prime Measures for a Client's CSFs

IDENTIFYING THE KEY RATIOS USED IN MANAGING THE INDUSTRY

There are numerous sources of ratios that can be consulted to form a composite profile of a firm:

Dun & Bradstreet annually publishes *Key Business Ratios,* in which 14 ratios for 125 lines of business are presented.

Robert Morris Associates publishes an annual financial statement study.

More and more, trade associations publish financial ratios for their members.

Talk with commercial bankers serving targets, and read the annual reports and prospectuses in the niche. Ratio analysis does nothing to correct a weakness in business operations, but diagnosis is a critical first step.

DETERMINING THE COST STRUCTURE OF THE INDUSTRY

I use the term costs to mean the financial resources that are used in the development and/or acquisition of other resources used in the performance of a business function or operating process.

A business function could be marketing, advertising, sales, and so forth. A business process would be manufacturing, administration, and the like. Mack Hanan, author of *Key Account Selling,* says that ". . .you must know the location of significant cost centers that are susceptible to reduction." Implied in this statement is the tag: through the use of resources available in you.

Every business function and business process is a cost center. Your goal is to identify the cost points in each business function that you can affect positively. If you're an accountant, the job is easier because you have ready access to the key financial data. If you do not have such access, you need to discuss costs with your clients in the niche, talk with others who serve the niche, and become a student of the cost structure for the niche.

TRACKING THE DYNAMICS OF THE NICHE

Tracking the changes, trends, legislation and other factors affecting the niche is a continuing responsibility. The easiest way to do this is to identify the major publications serving the niche and monitor the dynamics. As mentioned in Chapter 4, these industry-specific publications can be used in a variety of ways.

I shall complete our discussion of publications in this section.

IDENTIFYING THE PUBLICATIONS

Identifying the publications read by niche members is relatively easy. The directories presented in Chapter 4 collectively list over 10,000 publications in every topic area. You will be able literally to identify 90 percent or more of all publications serving your target niche.

Now let's examine the wealth of information available from these publications that can be used to support your client-centered marketing efforts.

1. *Readership Demographics.* All publications maintain information on their readership, including average age income, sex, job title, and other valuable data. Exhibit 5.1 on the following pages uses the readership demographics of *Forbes* magazine to offer a brief glimpse of the kinds of information available from the publications.

FORBES Mission: "To report on the world of business and finance clearly and concisely, but thoroughly, and with an eye for the revealing detail."
— Editor Jim Michaels

Circulation: Worldwide   733,255
           United States   710,679   (ABC: Dec. 1986)
           Rate Base   720,000

Page Rates/
Efficiencies:

Black and White	$24,930	CPM	$34.63
Four Color	$37,890	CPM	$52.63

FORBES SUBSCRIBERS RUN AMERICAN BUSINESS AND INDUSTRY

	Percentage	Number
Business, Industry and Professions	83.8%	603,360
Manufacturing	23.5	169,200
Finance (Banking, Insurance, Real Estate Investment Services)	20.1	144,720
Top Management	48.4	348,480
Chairman, Director, President	14.7	105,840
Chief Executive Officer/Chief Operating Officer/Chief Financial Officer	24.2*	146,013
General Management Function	45.6*	275,132
Board of Directors		
Own Company	32.4*	195,489

EXHIBIT 5.1.

73

	Percentage	Number
Own or Other Company	41.2%*	248,584

Involved in Company Purchasing Decisions

$10,000 or more	71.5*	431,402

Household Income

Over $25,000	95.7	689,040
Over $35,000	90.8	653,760
Over $50,000	74.9	539,280
Average $138,935		
Median $81,595		

Net Worth

Over $1,000,000	28.4	204,480
Average $1,146,363		
Median $512,620		

FORBES SUBSCRIBERS OWN AMERICAN BUSINESS AND INDUSTRY

Investment Portfolio (Stocks, Bonds, Mutual Funds, Etc.)

$50,000 or more	76.8	552,960
Median Value $217,655		
Average Value $717,798		

Stockholdings in Own Company	47.1	339,120
Median Value $76,031		

Stockholdings in Other Companies	82.8	596,160
Median Value $56,307		

Stockholdings in Own or Other Companies	87.9	632,880

EXHIBIT 5.1. Continued

Security Transactions	Percentage	Number
More than five in Past Year	46.5%	334,800

FORBES SUBSCRIBERS ARE KEY MEMBERS OF THE INVESTMENT COMMUNITY

Involved in Investment Decisions	51.6	371,520
On Behalf of:		
Individuals	43.8	315,360
Corporations	15.1	108,720
Pension Funds	10.0	72,000
Trusts	9.5	68,400
Estates	7.8	56,160
Institutions	5.7	41,040
Other Kinds	4.6	33,120

FORBES SUBSCRIBERS ARE WELL EDUCATED

College Educated	90.8	653,760
Graduated from College	75.7	545,040
Post-Graduate Work	44.7	321,840

FORBES IS READ AT HOME

	88.5	637,200

*Percentage of those in business, industry and professions.

SOURCE: FORBES Subscriber Characteristics—Don Bowdren Assoc., 1985. Reprinted with permission.

EXHIBIT 5.1. Continued

The key to obtaining such information is to write to the advertising department and ask for a copy of the advertising rate card and readership demographics. The advertising rate card will explain the various costs and procedures for placing a single or continuous ad within the publication. You can also use *Standard Rate and Data*, which contains information on all major U.S. publications and a directory of advertising rate cards.

2. *Editorial Guidelines.* Those who regularly write for magazines know that most editors maintain a published set of editorial or author's guidelines. Available to anyone who asks, these guidelines define the nature and scope of the material the editor is seeking to serve the interests of the readers.

3. *Special Issues.* Many publications periodically offer a special issue that highlights developments and trends in the industry. For example, in November 1986, *Purchasing* produced a special issue entitled the "Top 100" that "told the purchasing story as it has never been told before." According to the publishers, the issue added a totally new dimension to the collective knowledge of the U.S. industrial marketplace. Other publications such as *Forbes, Fortune, Business Week, Inc.*, and *Venture* are noted for their special directory and industry-focused issues.

The editorial calendar will pinpoint when a special issue will be published.

The calendar from *Business Marketing* (see Figure 5.5) outlines the topics and issues for a 12-month period.

4. *Subscriber Mailing Lists.* Most publications have subscriber mailing lists for sale. Although some publications sell their entire list of subscribers (representing overkill to you if you only want subscribers in a particular locality), others offer a more targeted list. In addition, many publications sell their subscriber lists to the direct-mail catalogue houses (a partial list appears in Chapter 4), who often can offer them to you at a lower cost than the publisher because of high-volume sales.

INSIDE THE MAGAZINE ITSELF

In reviewing any particular publication read by your targeted niche, pay close attention to the following:

1. *The Masthead.* Who publishes, edits, advertises, and circulates the publication? How often is it distributed? Who owns the publication? Is it published in affiliation with some association or other organization? The masthead provides this information.

2. *Table of Contents.* In addition to the normal feature articles, considering your new strategic focus, look for the following:

Book reports

Washington watch

Trend watch

Columnist

Reader surveys

Letters to the editor

"My say" or opinion pieces

Names in the news

New products and services

Advertising index

3. *Classified Ads.* This section, particularly if there is a job mart, is often a giveaway as to the needs of the industry. Yet, I bet you rarely read these even in your own industry publications.

Other things you will find inside publications are fairly obvious. Who writes the articles and what kind of bylines are printed? Are articles accompanied by pictures, charts, or art work?

Business Marketing Calender

Issue	Ad Closing	Strategy Features	Tactics Features	Special Features	Advertising Services
JANUARY	DECEMBER 1, 1986	· International Marketing	· Communications Effectiveness · Agency Relations	· Annual Budget Survey · Copy Chasers' Best Ad of the Year · Direct Marketing Clinic	· International Bonus
FEBRUARY	JANUARY 2	· Corporate Communications	· Direct Response · Media Evaluation	· B/PAA ProComm Awards Insert · Copy Chasers · Direct Marketing Clinic	· Action Card Mailing
MARCH	FEBRUARY 2	· Marketing Research	· Computer Aided Marketing · Meeting Planning	· Ad Volume Review & Forecast · Copy Chasers · Direct Marketing Clinic	· Special Issues and Readership Studies in Business Publications
APRIL	MARCH 2	· Strategic Planning	· Video/AV · Premiums & Incentives	· Copy Chasers · Direct Marketing Clinic · International Marketing	· International Bonus · Bonus distribution at AMA/Business Marketing Seminar
MAY	APRIL 1	· Advanced-Technologies Marketing	· Trade Shows · Market Segmentation	· Best Exhibit of the Year · Copy Chasers · Direct Marketing Clinic	· Action Card Mailing
JUNE	MAY 1	· Sales/Distribution Channels	· 100 Leading Business Advertisers · Computer Aided Marketing	· Annual Trade Show Trends · Copy Chasers · Direct Marketing Clinic	· B/PAA bonus distribution at national conference · Special Issues and Readers' Studies in Business Publications
JULY	JUNE 1	· New Product Marketing	· Meeting Planning · Communications Effectiveness	· Copy Chasers · Direct Marketing Clinic · International Marketing	· International Bonus

Month	Closing Date				
AUGUST	JULY 1	· Resource Allocation	· Premiums & Incentives · Direct Response	· Copy Chasers · Direct Marketing Clinic · Advanced Technologies Marketing	· Action Card Mailing · Media Resource File
SEPTEMBER	AUGUST 3	· Communications Strategy	· Media Evaluation · Agency Relations	· Ad Volume Review & Forecast · Copy Chasers · Direct Marketing Clinic	· Special Issues and Readership Studies in Business Publications
OCTOBER	SEPTEMBER 1	· Market Segmentation	· Computer-Aided Marketing · Meeting Planning	· Leading Advertisers mid-Year Update; · Copy Chasers; · International Marketing; · Direct Marketing Clinic	· International Bonus
NOVEMBER	OCTOBER 1	· Strategic Planning	· Trade Shows · Video/AV	· Copy Chasers · Direct Marketing Clinic	· Special Issues and Readership Studies in Business Publications · Action Card Mailing
DECEMBER	NOVEMBER 2	· New Product Marketing	· Direct Response · Communication Effectiveness	· Copy Chasers · Direct Marketing Clinic · Advanced Technologies Marketing	

FIGURE 5.5. Schedule of issues, showing projected features, ad services, and ad closing dates. Reprinted by permission of *Business Marketing*.

The publications read by your targets are among the least expensive, the most effective way to gain inside information—and all while seated at your desk.

IDENTIFYING OTHER DATA SOURCES

In Chapter 4, we discussed ways to gain information from directories, industry associations and key publications. *Marketing to the Fortune 500* by Jeffrey P. Davidson (Dow Jones-Irwin 1987) contains a wealth of information and data sources on industrial markets. Here are a few that will hasten your ability to develop an insider's understanding:

National Technical Information Service
   4285 Port Royal Road
   Springfield, VA 22161

American Management Associations
   135 West 50th Street
   New York, NY 10020

Directory of Conventions *Successful Meetings*
   1518 Walnut Street
   Philadelphia, PA 19102

U.S. Statistical Abstract
   Superintendent of Documents
   Government Printing Office
   Washington, DC 20402

U.S. Industrial Outlook
   Bureau of Economic Analysis
   Department of Commerce
   Washington, DC 20230

Special Libraries Association
   1700 18th Street, NW
   Washington, DC 20009

There are also numerous data base vendors and services that will provide you with information via your PC or computer-system terminal. Some of the major vendors include:

Dialogue
    3460 Hillview Avenue
    Palo Alto, CA 94304

The Source
    1616 Anderson Road
    McLean, VA 22107

CompuServe
    500 Arlington Center Blvd.
    Columbus, OH 43220

Bibliographic Retrieval Services
    1200 Route 7
    Latham, NY 12110

Find/SVP
    500 Fifth Avenue
    New York, NY 10036

Other key directories, such as *Ward's Business Directory* (Figures 5.6 and 5.7), are available in most public libraries.

This concludes our analysis on the industry level. By now your confidence in your ability to call upon suspects should be building. Let's see what is involved in understanding the market side of your niche.

IDENTIFYING THE NICHE INFRASTRUCTURE IN THE MARKET

The infrastructure refers to the organizations and players associated with the niche. We now turn our attention to identifying members of the infrastructure and completing the preparation of the niche data base.

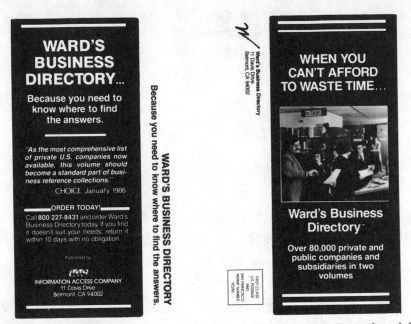

FIGURE 5.6. Advertisement for *Ward's Business Directory*. Reproduced by permission of Information Access Co., 11 Davis Dr., Belmont, CA 94002. For further information call 800/227-8431.

Identifying Clients, Prospects, and Suspects

Identifying existing clients in the niche is an easy task if you have entered their primary SIC number in your client file. If you have not yet done this, now is an excellent time to do so. Round up the names of all the clients you serve in the industry. Ideally, you have classified them in terms of their potential for growth, as recommended in Chapter 4.

Next, identify existing prospective clients. This is not difficult. Inventory prospective clients in your pipeline and assert the likelihood of converting them to new clients.

Third, identify the suspects in your niche. This is made considerably easier if you purchase the subscriber mailing lists for the key publication read by members of the industry. Suspects include both organizations and the names of specific contact

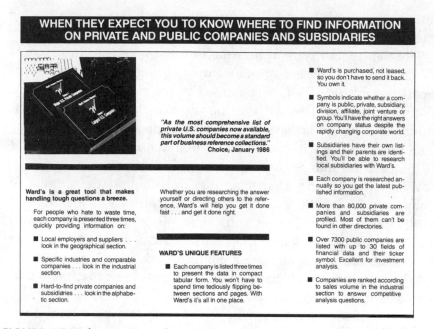

WHEN THEY EXPECT YOU TO KNOW WHERE TO FIND INFORMATION
ON PRIVATE AND PUBLIC COMPANIES AND SUBSIDIARIES

"As the most comprehensive list of private U.S. companies now available, this volume should become a standard part of business reference collections."
Choice, January 1986

Ward's is a great tool that makes handling tough questions a breeze.

For people who hate to waste time, each company is presented three times, quickly providing information on:

- Local employers and suppliers . . . look in the geographical section.

- Specific industries and comparable companies . . . look in the industrial section.

- Hard-to-find private companies and subsidiaries . . . look in the alphabetic section.

Whether you are researching the answer yourself or directing others to the reference, Ward's will help you get it done fast . . . and get it done right.

WARD'S UNIQUE FEATURES

- Each company is listed three times to present the data in compact tabular form. You won't have to spend time tediously flipping between sections and pages. With Ward's it's all in one place.

- Ward's is purchased, not leased, so you don't have to send it back. You own it.

- Symbols indicate whether a company is public, private, subsidiary, division, affiliate, joint venture or group. You'll have the right answers on company status despite the rapidly changing corporate world.

- Subsidiaries have their own listings and their parents are identified. You'll be able to research local subsidiaries with Ward's.

- Each company is researched annually so you get the latest published information.

- More than 80,000 private companies and subsidiaries are profiled. Most of them can't be found in other directories.

- Over 7300 public companies are listed with up to 30 fields of financial data and their ticker symbol. Excellent for investment analysis.

- Companies are ranked according to sales volume in the industrial section to answer competitive analysis questions.

FIGURE 5.7. Advertisement for *Ward's Business Directory*. Reproduced by permission of Information Access Co., 11 Davis Dr., Belmont, CA 94002. For further information call 800/227-8431.

persons in the organization—the very information included within subscriber mailing lists. Numerous data sources abound, including subscriber lists of key publications, association membership lists, Chamber of Commerce directories, and your existing A clients.

The business journal serving your local area usually offers theme and other special issues that list the leaders in particular industries and professional areas. In my own area the *Washington Business Journal* and the *Washington Post Business* frequently provide such lists as "the 100 largest employers in the Washington area," "the 25 largest advertising firms," and a "directory of area couriers." It is not necessary to subscribe to the publications. Often, the first or last issue of the year has an index of articles published in the preceding 12 months. If your local library cannot supply back issues, write or call the publication. They will be able to send you a back issue for a fee, or refer you to a library or repository with their back issues.

The nature and type of information you generate on suspects affects your data base design and upkeep considerations. When creating your data files, be generous in the amount of space you allow in each field while limiting the number of fields you include. It is better to have lots of blank space within your files than to be toiling with exotic codes that enable you to cram a lot of information into a small space.

When identifying suspects, the profile you developed in Chapter 4 of your Key and A clients becomes a valuable tool. This profile can be used as your "talk piece" in educating your referral sources. To gather information about suspects, the data sheet that you use need not be complicated. (See Figure 5.8.)

While gathering information on suspects, seek the name and title of the decision-maker(s) in charge of operations requiring your type of service. Also, who is the most receptive and positive influencer who can get you to the decision-maker? The title of the person with whom you wish to make contact might be determined by recalling the most recent discussions you had with new clients or prospects within the niche. Others within your firm, as well as nonclient influentials such as lawyers, bankers, and so forth, may be able to identify the appropriate title.

As you review the directories and information sources highlighted throughout this book, be on the alert for terms particular to the niche. For example, what is termed the personnel department in the insurance industry is called the human resources division within banking.

Another way to get the title of the proper person is to call the organization and ask the receptionist for the name of the person who makes decisions about engaging the type of services you offer. If you have already targeted the title of the person you will call, ask his or her secretary for a name. That way, you can honestly say when calling the officer, "I was told by your office you

DATE

NEW SUSPECT DATA SHEET

Name: _____ Industry: _____ SIC: _____

Address: _____

_____

Telephone: _____

Key Names:

_____

_____

_____

Founded: _____ No. employes: _____ Est. Sales/Yr: _____

Remarks:

_____

_____

_____

_____

_____

_____

How identified:
client referral	☐	nonclient referral	☐
association directory	☐	industry directory	☐
direct inquiry	☐	magazine article	☐
newspaper	☐	met personally	☐
civic, social org.	☐	trade show	☐
		other	☐

FIGURE 5.8. New Suspect Data Sheet

85

IDENTIFYING SUSPECTS

Name of SIC Code Existing Suspect	Nature of Services Needed	Next Steps

FIGURE 5.9. Identifying Suspects

were the right person to contact." (More on making telephone contact in Chapter 10.)

As you gain more information about suspects in the niche, begin to sort your information by your level of knowledge. The form in Figure 5.9 can be used for this purpose. The first column is obvious. The second column, "Nature of Services Needed," should be filled in to the best of your ability and updated as you gain more information about particular suspects. Ideally, you will have identified the hot buttons needs, issues, and concerns of suspects in your niche. Thus, the nature of services needed may begin to fall into a few categories, making your job that much easier. The third column, "Next Steps," requires that you identify what you do with each suspect on whom you are collecting information.

Suspects become prospects when they agree to meet with you. In most instances, the next step will be to call each suspect, either to get the correct name and title of the contact person, or to make an appointment with that person.

IDENTIFYING YOUR NONCLIENT INFLUENTIALS

Your nonclient influentials, those who serve and influence your targets, consist of two groups: those you know and those you need to know. Often your competitors and other nonclient influentials will lead you to them. There are many reasons and advantages for identifying and contacting nonclient influentials. Most importantly, any NCI that serves as a referral source for you enables you to have a higher hit rate when contacting the prospect because he or she has been pre-sold.

There are some disadvantages to using NCIs, including their expectation of a reciprocal lead and the possibility that the NCI misrepresented or oversold your capabilities to prospects. Also, an NCI referral may not be as meaningful as a client referral because he or she cannot personally vouch for your services.

The chart depicted in Figure 5.10 can be used to begin listing your NCIs and how you plan to use these relationships effectively. The middle column, "QOR," stands for *quality of relationship*. Those NCIs with whom you have a high-quality relationship, that is, a rating of 5, are the ones most likely to offer quality leads. Identifying your non-client influentials completes the infrastructure work.

NONCLIENT INFLUENTIALS

Names and Affiliations of Influential Contacts	QOR (1 to 5)	How Do I Plan to Use My Relationship With These People Effectively?

FIGURE 5.10. Nonclient Influentials

TRACKING THE MARKET-AFFECTING FACTORS

This step involves monitoring the economic conditions affecting your practice area. Included will be such factors as growth rate, unemployment, mergers and divestitures, strikes, and so on. Your goal is to stay current with the happenings in the market that could have an impact upon the receptivity and buying ability of prospective clients in your niche.

If the tasks you will need to perform, as laid out in this chapter, seem overly analytical or initially difficult, be comforted. They will minimize the level of sales proficiency you will need in face-to-face discussions. I find that the more technically oriented professional-service providers prefer this approach because it is a logical extension of their technical work-flow process.

Pursuing the steps that follow will place you in front of more prospects faster and easier and provide a simpler way to sense client and prospective client needs.

Distilling Your Knowledge

To distill your knowledge of the niche, prepare the worksheet shown in Figure 5.11, "An Insider's Analysis." In section 1a ask yourself, "What are the concerns of clients in this niche?" Then, list those concerns in the space provided. If your targeted niche were the construction industry, SIC-code number 1611, your answers might include "cost control," "timely reporting in control of multiple jobs," and "too much overhead."

For item 1b, answer the question, "What are the problems these clients face?" Even if you can't help the clients with these problems, you want to know because it gives you more empathy and opportunities for meaningful discussion. If your clients were in the retail office supply business, SIC-code number 5943, your answers might include "compliance with the new tax

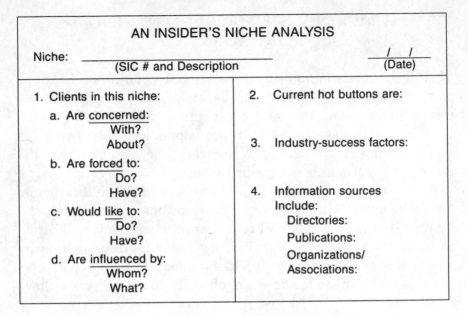

FIGURE 5.11. An Insider's Niche Analysis

laws," "employee pilferage," and "price instability among suppliers."

In 1c, ask, "What are clients in the niche vitally interested in that I can assist them in doing or obtaining?" If your client is an EDP-systems installer, the answer might be "to obtain cost-plus contracts versus fixed fee," "to maintain a smooth cash flow," and "more confident junior staff that can service client needs." Practically speaking, your ability to answer 1c-type questions is synonymous with your ability to identify new business opportunities for your firm.

In 1d, ask, "Who and what positively influences clients in this niche?" If your clients are realtors, for example, their answers might include "banks and savings and loan institutions," "corporate relocation officers," and "availability and condition of existing housing."

The top of the second column of the worksheet asks for the current "hot-buttons" in the niche. (This will be discussed in greater detail in Chapter 8.) Hot buttons consist of any topics, issues, or trends of a contemporary and keen interest to prospects within this niche. If your clients are members of the airline industry, for example, current hot buttons might include "shortages in air traffic controllers," "terrorism," "the effect of discount airfares," and "frequent flyer programs."

For number 3, determine as many of the industry-success factors as you can for this niche. If your clients are industrial launderers, SIC code number 7212, this list might include "efficient use of energy," "maintaining cost control over supplies," "eliminating waste," "passing EPA and OSHA inspections," "securing corporate accounts," and "maintaining schedules" and "customer deadlines."

For number 4, list the best directories for this niche, the ones that give you insider information. If your niche consists of one-to-five-person, public-accounting firms, SIC-code number 8931, you would certainly want to list the directory of the National Society of Public Accountants, with over 18,000 members. Next, list the publications read by your clients and prospects in the niche. If your target consists of design and product engineers, SIC code number 8911, publications of interest would include *Design News*, *Machine Design*, *Product Design and Development*, and *Product Engineering*. As I mentioned earlier, the subscriber lists to these publications can usually be purchased and used to identify targets of opportunity in your market area.

Next, identify the organizations and associations to which your clients and prospects belong. If your clients consist of machine shops, SIC-code number 3599, these organizations might include the National Association of Manufacturers, the National Federation of Independent Businesses and the Chamber of Commerce of the U.S. Figure 5.12 is an insider's analysis completed for the construction industry, SIC code number 1611.

AN INSIDER'S NICHE ANALYSIS

Niche: <u>#1611 Construction Industry</u>   <u> /   / </u>
          (SIC # and Description)   (Date)

1. Clients in this niche:

   a. Are <u>concerned</u> with/about:

      Cost controls

      Timely reporting & control of multiple jobs

      Too much overhead

   b. Are <u>forced</u> to:

      Too much executive involvement at lower levels

      Crisis management-reaction

      Customer deadlines and schedules

      Financial pressures of jobs and vendors

   c. Would <u>like</u> to:

      Delegate and still maintain control

      Lower overhead

      Cost plus contracts v. fixed fee

      Adequate financial resources

   d. Are <u>influenced</u> by:

      Banks and S&L's

      Real estate owners and operators

      Economic upturns and downturns

2. Current hot buttons are:

   Microcomputers

   Organizational review

   Personnel resource utilization

   Income tax planning

3. Success factors include:

   Obtaining a line of credit

   Availability of bonding

   The weather

   Front-loaded billing

4. Information sources include:

   Directories:

      List of contractors from state registrar of contractors

      Local homebuilder guides

      GCA Directory

      AB&C Directory

   Publications:

      Builder Contractor

      Construction

      Engineering News Record

      Construction Equipment

   Organizations/Associations:

      Registrar of Contractors

      Associated Builders & Contractors

      National Association of Home Builders

      General Contractors of America

FIGURE 5.12. An Insider's Niche Analysis

A MASTER MENU OF NEEDS

The research and analysis you have done of the targeted industry will enable you to develop and maintain a master menu of needs. This is analogous to the menus in a software program. The main menu lists the major topics or activity areas covered in the software program. Each major topic or activity area is further described or delineated as a submenu. Submenus have a number of tasks or options listed.

Figure 5.13 is the *Main Menu of Needs* that I created for the accounting profession. Figure 5.14 is the submenu of needs for existing clients, item 1 of the main menu. Figure 5.15 is the submenu of needs in industries, item 7 on the main menu.

The main menu and corresponding submenus of needs grow out of the development of an insider's understanding of the niche.

DICK CONNOR, INC.
MAIN MENU OF NEEDS
ACCOUNTING PROFESSION

1. Clients, existing
2. Prospects, existing
3. Suspects
4. Referral Sources
5. Industries
6. Markets
7. Industry-market niches
8. Services
9. Promotion
10. Prospecting
11. New-Business Discussion/Selling
12. Managing the Marketing Function

FIGURE 5.13. Dick Connor, Inc., Main Menu of Needs

SUBMENU

1. EXISTING CLIENTS

	HB	R	E
1. Determine the nature and potential of existing client base.		X	
2. Retention of Key & A clients		X	
3. Providing additional services		X	
4. Developing referrals		X	
5. Up-grading/replacing marginal clients			X
6. Serving high-potential Key & A clients in client-centered fashion	X		

HB = hot button
 R = recurring
 E = emerging

FIGURE 5.14. Dick Connor, Inc. Submenu

The term *need* refers to something in a suspect's situation that:

Is present but unwanted, a negative need situation such as excess costs, poor morale, subpar performance of a success factor, etc.

Is desired but is missing or in short supply, a positive situation such as marketing expertise, advanced technology, etc.

Needs to be done, a short-term task situation that requires the use of resources available to us, such as managing a project for the client, performing a diagnostic analysis, developing a program, and so on.

These needs are grouped in three categories including hot buttons, recurring needs, and emerging/potential needs.

Hot-button needs are those that are on the lips of your targets. They are current and deemed to be important by your targets.

SUBMENU
7. EXISTING INDUSTRIES

	HB	R	E
1. Identify existing industries (SICs)		X	
2. Classify in terms of existing revenues		X	
3. Estimate potential for growth	X		
4. Monitor the dynamics		X	
5. Develop an "insider's" understanding	X		
6.			
7.			

FIGURE 5.15. Dick Connor, Inc. Submenu

These needs will sometimes be one-time needs and thus require a modified or minipromotional system. Frequently, they will have enough staying power to become recurring needs; consequently, they merit a full promotional system.

While hot buttons will get you the appointment, handling recurring needs enables you to make a lasting contribution and earn the revenue that flows from satisfied clients.

PREPARING YOUR NICHE DATA BASE

As you complete the tasks involved in working with your market, you'll want to use the data-entry forms discussed in Chapter 4. Remember, more is not necessarily better! List only those names that have potential for your practice.

COMPLETING YOUR LIBRARY

Now is the time to index and file any additional directories, publications, annual reports, and so on that you've encountered in your library. Make readily available those books and materials you need for responding to new-business opportunities and to provide client-centered solutions to the important needs you serve.

In Chapter 6, "Preparing Your Service Promotion and Delivery Systems," we will discuss how to use the insider's understanding of the niche you have developed to showcase your professionalism and create solution packages for recurring services.

6

Preparing Your Service Promotion and Delivery Systems

Throughout this book, we have stressed using a client-centered approach. Client-centered marketing is not a substitute for high-quality service, nor is it a ploy to be used in selling a "plain vanilla" service in a "rocky road" package.

The approach was defined earlier as sensing, serving, and satisfying the selected needs of targets of opportunity in the niche. The information you have assembled now can be directed toward successfully promoting your services and profitably delivering your services within the niche.

PREPARING YOUR SERVICE-PROMOTION SYSTEMS

The purpose of preparing a service-promotion system is to maximize the efficiency and the effectiveness of your promotional program for the niche. The following goals will guide your activities:

1. To be perceived as a knowledgeable insider by all who receive the promotional materials.

2. To prepare need-specific, initial-contact packages designed to obtain appointments with targeted suspects.

3. To enable you to be cost-effective and highly responsive to opportunities to contact and converse with prospective clients.

4. To showcase your professionalism in the mind and emotions of the targets.

5. To position your services as different from and better than the competition.

6. To be able to respond to needs with what are perceived as value-added solutions by interested prospects.

Figure 6.1 shows the elements of a service-promotion system. With each element, for each client, a decision must be made whether to tailor (T) or treat routinely (R). Sometimes a combination of the two is necessary, R/T.

SERVICE-PROMOTION SYSTEM	T	R	R/T
1. Initial contact package			
a. Cover letter	X		
b. Need-specific enclosures	X		
c. Telephone contact guide			X
2. New-business discussion package			
a. Question sheet		X	
b. Testimonial letter		X	
c. Problem-approach-result write-ups (PARs)		X	
d. Approved client list		X	
e. Sample final reports and other "deliverables"			X
f. Other firm and promotional materials			X
3. Proposals	X		
4. Client-centered analysis	X		

     T = tailored for client
     R = recurring/standard
  R/T = minor tailoring of recurring standard factors

FIGURE 6.1. Service-Promotion System

1. *Initial Contact Package.* The preparation of the three elements in the service-promotion system is covered in detail in Chapters 9 and 10. Because the approach is need-driven, the cover letter and enclosure often must be tailored to each client. Your basic telephone contact guide should be slightly modified to include the contact's name and specific appointment information.

2. *New-Business Discussion Package.* The preparation of the five elements is discussed below.

   a. *The Question Sheet.* Used during the new-business discussion, this helps guide you through the prospect's potential new-business situation. The questions, of course, are different for each service being offered to the niche.

   Following is a sample of a Question Sheet I use with marketers of professional services who want to talk with me about establishing a marketing function in their firm.

QUESTION SHEET FOR DISCUSSING A FIRM'S READINESS TO
ESTABLISH A MARKETING FUNCTION

1. Do you have a recognized marketing "champion" in-house who is willing to and capable of heading the function?
2. Do you have a clearly developed and communicated mission statement or vision for the firm or office?
3. To what extent is marketing responsibility assigned, articulated, understood, and accepted?
4. To what extent is marketing built into your performance and reward systems?
5. What percentage of total gross fees has been invested in marketing over the past three years?
6. What is the current and desired nature and scope of the practice in each functional specialty?

7. How often do partners and others meet to discuss marketing?

8. To what extent is a keep-off-my-turf attitude and behavior alive and well in the firm?

---

b. *Testimonial Letters.* These are statements of praise and commendation from satisfied clients. The testimonial, since it is in the client's own words, is more believable and convincing than information you've prepared.

One client of mine periodically asks me to meet with a number of his clients for the purpose of acquiring testimonials. While we have a light lunch in a casual atmosphere, I chat with his client representatives to break the ice and make them comfortable. Then, I ask them to share what it is they like and dislike about the firm and the particular service for which I am developing the testimonial. To minimize notetaking and speed up the process, I get their permission to tape record their remarks.

When a particularly good testimonial statement is made, I replay it. We discuss the statement. Then, I ask for permission to quote the person. When this is given, I suggest that I write a letter on his stationery using the exact words as recorded.

During one 2-hour session, I was able to obtain four good statements and agreements. An important byproduct of such a meeting is the number of "I wish that. . ." statements made by the clients that provide insights into additional service opportunities.

c. *PAR Reports.* Each time you assist a client in the targeted niche, you are adding to your promotional system. You can document the problem, approach, and results (PAR) related to each client engagement and then use the capsule summaries to favorably influence prospect clients. Most of the well known consulting firms and Big Eight accounting firms, as well as other successful professionals, employ some version of PAR reports. Many firms use these in their marketing literature, including capability statements, brochures, pamphlets and proposals.

One large accounting firm described in a marketing brochure how it was able to help a hospital revive its financial management system.

A county-run hospital was facing great financial hardship; its advisory board had no faith in the accuracy of the hospital's financial statements. Worse, its chief financial officer had just been fired. The accounting firm was called in to provide financial management support for three months. This allowed the hospital staff to hire a permanent chief financial officer during the interim.

Within three weeks, patient registration, patient billing, and accounts receivables were analyzed. A 16-page work plan was developed to reduce the backlog in billing and accounts receivables. The accounting firm then began to study cost management and productivity improvement. With a strong foundation in place, the hospital now has a profitable future and strong management guidelines.

The above minicase was adapted from the marketing literature of an established, successful public accounting firm. Figures 6.2 and 6.3 present variations on how PAR reports can be prepared.

There are many advantages to using PAR reports. As mentioned, they can be used in proposals, brochures, and capability statements. They can also be used in newsletters and as exhibits and charts during new-business discussions, and in training new staff. PAR reports are excellent tools for educating your client-referral sources, including your existing clients and nonclient influentials.

If you have not used PAR reports before, go back through your files for the past two or three years and ask the managers on completed engagements to develop PARs for all situations that support your new targeted-niche focused-marketing efforts. Hereafter, develop a PAR report as each new-client en-

---

Problem–Approach–Results (PAR) Report

INDUSTRY: Local Government   OFFICE: Milwaukee

PROBLEM SITUATION:

A class-action suit had been filed against a city for releasing untreated sewage into public waters. The class action was for loss of business and punitive damages. Actual damages claimed were $1 billion from over 100 businesses. The client asked us to provide litigation support to substantiate damage losses.

ABC CO. SOLUTION

ABC would provide the professional and technical assistance needed to substantiate the business losses.

RESULTS EXPERIENCED BY CLIENT

The city provided a draft of the documentation request written by in-house legal counsel. This document was modified by ABC because of its expertise in the business environment. As a result of the documentation request, we were informed that all of the suits were dropped except one, and it was not being pursued at this time.

FIGURE 6.2. Problem–Approach–Results (PAR) Report

gagement is completed. Your PAR reports should be added to your niche data base.

d. *Approved Client List.* Be certain you have a current list of clients you have served in the niche who have given you approval to use their name. Experienced marketers do not banter this list around freely, but rather keep it in ready reserve and show it only if the hot prospect is skeptical of their experience level, and so forth.

e. *Sample Final Reports.* Use these and other sample deliverables to assemble a sample case of your final products involved in the solution program for the need under discussion.

A financial-planning firm in Virginia Beach prepared a montage of management-letter comments made in client re-

---

Problem–Approach–Results (PAR) Report

INDUSTRY: Local Government

OFFICE: San Francisco
Bay Area

PROBLEM SITUATION:

A city budget office had not received recognition from the California Society of Finance Officers regarding its financial reporting practices for 20 years.

ABC CO. SOLUTION

ABC assisted the city in (1) changing accounting principles to conform to GAAP, (2) designing a new financial reporting format, (3) typing the financial reports, and (4) resolving review comments regarding reporting deficiencies.

RESULTS EXPERIENCED BY CLIENT

The city received recognition in the form of an award presented to city officials at the Society's annual convention for outstanding financial reporting.

FIGURE 6.3. Problem–Approach–Results (PAR) Report

ports using graphics to illustrate ratios, trends, and so on. Actual pages from client letters were photocopied and the name and proprietary information blanked out. When the opportunity arises during a discussion with a prospective client, the financial planner says to the prospect, "You may be interested in the way we tailor our letters to reflect our client's needs and interests." He reports that the prospect is usually impressed with the client-centeredness of the document. Subliminally, he is also demonstrating that he can keep a confidence!

f. *Other Firm and Promotional Materials.* Other articles that deal with the need you are promoting should also be acquired.

3. *Proposals.* Accumulate several of your proposals that document your approach to delivering the solution program for the need under discussion. Some of your previous proposals may be

For: _____ Need: _____ Service: _____
    (Type of Client)

Client-centered Analysis (Blank Chart)

Improve or Enhance	Reduce, Relieve, or Eliminate
Protect	Restructure
Identify	Restore or Resolve

FIGURE 6.4. Client-Centered Analysis (Blank Chart)

reusable. Simply enter the client-specific information gathered during the new business discussion.

4. *Client-Centered Analysis.* This is another tool for enhancing your ability to promote your service-delivery systems. As explained in our 1985 book, *Marketing Your Consulting and*

Professional Services (John Wiley & Sons), prospective clients are not really seeking to purchase your services; rather, they are focusing on the end results that you will produce. Prospects purchase the possibility of enjoying a more favorable future and receiving expected benefits.

A benefit is something prospective clients perceive as valuable in their terms. It always relates to the purchaser's needs and expectations and how they will be met. By using the chart in Figure 6.4, "Client-centered Analysis," you will be able to identify benefits that are important to prospective clients and, more importantly, develop service descriptions to which the prospect can relate easily.

Your task is to identify a hot button or a recurring need for which you have a service solution. First, enter the name of the service you want to analyze at the top of the chart. Next, move to "Improve or Enhance" and ask yourself, "In what ways does this service enable the prospective client to improve or enhance the need area?" List your answers in the block. For example, sample answers might be competitive capability, internal operations, and so on. The remaining blocks are filled out in the same fashion. You might complete all blocks.

When finished, you will have developed a set of potential benefits in terms that can be used to promote your services to prospective clients. The service analysis can also be used in new business discussions, proposal writing, and in training your staff. An example of how a management consultant might complete the chart is presented in Figure 6.5.

Here are additional terms that can be used in completing the client-centered analysis:

Improve and Enhance

Market position
Cash flow
Product image
Service image

Client-centered Analysis	
For: Accountant **Need: Unfocused** **Service: Marketing** (Type of client) Marketing Strategy Efforts	
Improve or Enhance	**Reduce, Relieve, or Eliminate**
Client data base Profitability Telephone techniques Operations Internal control Revenues Capability statement	Misdirected efforts Paperwork Implementation bottlenecks Marketing errors Unnecessary expenditures
Protect	**Restructure**
Market share Credibility Reputation Profit Liquidity	Proposal development system Quality of reporting system Unprofitable operations
Develop or Install	**Restore or Resolve**
External reporting Marketing information system Cost systems Decision-making model	Prospecting system Resolve backlogs, uncertainty Inefficiencies, management anxiety

FIGURE 6.5. Client-centered Analysis

User needs
Competitive capabilities
Employee morale
Quality and reliability
Decision-making capability
Internal operations
External operations
Management information system

Reporting systems
Marketing information system
Profit potential

Protect

Assets
Self interest
Market position
Independence
Reputation
Proprietary information
Public image
Integrity
Industry position
Market share

Identify

Bottlenecks
Potentials
Needs
Decision factors
Strategies
Key problem areas
Option alternatives
Opportunities
Shortcomings
Action steps

Reduce, Relieve, or Eliminate

Inefficiencies
Congestions
Conflicts
Public pressure
Pilferage
Unnecessary costs

Peaking of demands
Service delays
Idle equipment
Excess capacity
Recurring problems
Local cost-benefit ratios
Deficits
Management headaches

Restructure

Internal operations
Compensation program
Planning process
Management structure
Business organization
Current operations
Incentive program
Training program
Financial systems
Plant layout
Technical approach

Restore or Resolve

Competitive edge
Profitability
Cash flow
Management skills
Plant and equipment
Quality-control procedures
Proposal-development system
Business outlook

As you can quickly gauge, some terms can be applied to more than one category. You may have several terms of your own to add. The headings for each category are not etched in stone;

almost any action-related verb will work. The exercise will help you to identify specific need situations of your clients and prospective clients; it will also help you relate and discuss in their terms relevant client benefits provided by your service.

PREPARING YOUR SERVICE-DELIVERY SYSTEM

When I worked for Booz, Allen, and Hamilton, an international consulting firm, at the end of each client engagement we would distill our experience to obtain the maximum mileage from what we had already done. Figure 6.6 shows the elements of the service-delivery system we used.

Client-specific Documents

1. The engagement confirmation letter can be prepared by entering the specifics of the engagement in a letter previously drafted and stored in your word-processing system. Remember to emphasize the solution goal, the importance of the engagement, and the benefits to be derived upon completion of the engagement.

2. Progress reports must be customized if you are to exhibit a unique approach for the client. You can develop boilerplate progress reports for the recurring aspects of the engagement, however.

3. The final written report or other deliverable(s) must be tailored. Prepare a final product of the engagement that justifies the budget allocated for it. The meeting during which the final product is delivered becomes the vehicle for discussing additional services.

4. The client satisfaction review, a check on the degree to which the client's needs and expectations were met, too often is bypassed by the busy professional. Referrals come from clients

SERVICE-DELIVERY SYSTEM

	T	R	R/T
1. Client-specific			
a. Engagement confirmation letter			X
b. Progress reports	X		
c. Final report/other deliverables(s)	X		
d. Client satisfaction review			X
2. Engagement Administration			
a. Work plan			X
b. Budget	X		
c. Activity schedules	X		
d. Quality-control procedures			X
e. Invoice preparation		X	
3. Engagement Wrap-up			
a. PAR produced		X	
b. Press release if significant engagement	X		
c. Recommendations for additional services	X		
d. Engagement distillation			
Inputs to standard practice			
manuals	X		
Purchase detail: trigger for			
the purchase, title(s) for			
best contact	X		
Standard patterns, fee ranges			
appropriate and expected			
jargon, buzz words	X		

FIGURE 6.6. Service-Delivery System

who are conscious of the fact that their needs *and* expectations were met, and that you took the time to bring your service to their attention so they could "vote" on the degree to which they think you met them.

Engagement Administration

1. Preparing a work plan in advance for this type of engagement enables you to estimate a fee quickly during the proposal phase of the new-business development process.

2. Because you have a range of costs associated with each task, you can quickly estimate the cost required to complete the current engagement. Your goal should be to develop and update a standard work plan and time and dollar budgets for completion of the deliverables for each task involved in the need-solution program you are promoting and delivering.

3. Activity schedules, the daily list of subtasks, must be tailored to meet the circumstances of the specific client situation. Having the work plan spelled out enables you to prepare the activity schedules to reflect the uniqueness of the situation.

4. Quality-control procedures can be standardized for most engagements. Your goal is to modify the standard process to reflect any circumstances in this engagement that need to be monitored to ensure quality.

5. Invoice preparation can be routinized. Some engagements require invoicing early and often, even though the actual hours invested lag the amount being invoiced. I do this for engagements with a lot of out-of-pocket expenses or where the final product is going to be delivered far down the pike.

Engagement Wrap-up

1. Finish each engagement with a PAR. The person managing the engagement should be held responsible for generating the report and reviewing it for accuracy and completeness with the engagement team and *the client*. This is a logical extension of the client-satisfaction review. The PAR can be a powerful relationship builder when reviewed with the client. Seize the opportunity of obtaining a testimonial letter at this time. The PAR can be used to prime the pump, to get the client in a responsive, helpful mood.

2. One of my more alert clients generates a press release along with the PAR if the engagement is deemed to be significant. A variation on the press release would be the development

of a joint article describing the engagement routine and the benefits the client obtained.

3. Prepare a discussion guide to suggest recommendations for additional services the client should consider at this time. Tailor it to meet the present buying conditions in this client's situation.

4. Engagement distillation is another task that frequently gets short shrift. My experience at Booz Allen taught me the importance of milking each client engagement for its maximum use in upgrading the niche-information base, increasing the experience, capabilities, and value of the staff, and generating new business. This was all done before the popular and widespread use of computers.

SUMMARY

Yes, there is advance preparation required before calling on new-business prospects. If you can weather the time needed for preparation, you'll experience the most productive marketing period of your firm's existence.

7

Developing an Insider's
Reputation in the Niche

Developing an insider's reputation in the niche provides at least two major benefits. First, it minimizes the amount of rejection you will experience when marketing to the niche. Second, it helps to stimulate new-business inquiries from those who know and trust you. When members of the niche regard you as one of them, it is a clear sign that you have built the trust and rapport necessary to be prosperous.

The strategy for gaining this reputation is to develop and employ a mix of promotional activities that fit your current, promotional comfort zone. This provides you with maximum leveraging opportunities. Such opportunities emerge by being involved in forums—organizations and groups comprised of your targets of opportunity and targets of influence; and, publications read by these same targets. As with many of the tasks outlined here in Part I, the bulk of the work to develop your reputation takes place before and during new-business discussions with targets. Thereafter, the reputation-building activities are executed on a continuing basis.

DEVELOPING OBJECTIVES

Successful firms have at least four basic objectives in developing an insider's reputation. These include the following:

1. Becoming an active, accepted, visible, working, and serving member of the infrastructure
2. Creating, maintaining, and enhancing a favorable awareness of you, your firm, and its services
3. Stimulating inquiries from high-potential suspects
4. Paving the way for gaining acceptance from targets of opportunity when you make need-specific mailings and telephone contacts. (See Chapters 9 and 10 for a discussion on this fourth objective.)

To pursue these objectives, your short-term goal is to create a favorable awareness on the part of those whom you "condition," the A and I in the AIDA process mentioned earlier. Your immediate goal is to obtain an appointment with the most appropriate decision-maker in suspect organizations, thus creating an initially qualified prospect, the D step in the AIDA process. (See Chapters 8, 9, and 10.) Your final goal is to convert the prospect into a new client and/or referral source, the last A step in the AIDA process.

Let's look at the first two objectives in detail.

OBJECTIVE #1. To become an active, accepted, visible, working, and serving member of the niche's infrastructure you will need to obtain a position of leadership in at least one, and hopefully several, targeted organizations. It is of no value to you or your firm to identify and join organizations comprised of targets of opportunity or targets of influence if they do not meet, get to know, and think favorably of you. Thus, your task is to identify and obtain memberships in viable organizations. You can do this by contacting existing high-potential clients to determine which organizations they belong to and recommend joining. At this point you should ask them to sponsor you for membership.

Next, contact the executive director of each target organization to gain further information. Interview him or her by phone to take an initial "gut check" about the organization. If this step is successful, ask for the name of the director or head of the new-member committee. These steps will help you decide whether to join.

If you previously looked askance at joining targeted organizations, this is an excellent time to reconsider. Involvement in targeted organizations is an important aspect of your professional and personal development as well as the development of new business for the firm. Moreover, you will be able to gain confidence in your ability to deal with influential people from different environments. Quality involvement with targets enhances the image and reputation of your firm and your profession in general.

Preparing for a position of leadership in a targeted organization requires spending several months as an active participant to gain visibility. When you become better known, and develop some relationships within the organization, you can use these contacts to spur your nomination to key positions and committees. Many organizations experience a shortage of high-caliber leadership; don't hesitate to throw your hat in the ring.

Heading up a committee will provide you with personal growth and leadership opportunities, perhaps beyond those you could achieve in your own firm. In addition to rubbing elbows with prospective clients and nonclient influentials, membership and involvement in targeted organizations strengthens relationships with your existing clients.

The role of activities chairperson is a high-leverage position because you're highly visible and have unlimited access to key people in the niche. For example, you could call the mayor's office to see if the mayor would be willing to speak to your group members. If the response is no, you could ask for an alternative official. When calling that person, you are able to say, "Mr. X, while speaking with the office of the mayor, it was mentioned that you are very knowledgeable regarding municipal zoning. Would you be willing to address our group?"

Serving on the new-member committee is also a valuable position, especially if the new members represent potential new clients or nonclient influentials who can lead you to new-business contacts. Other byproducts of earning a position of leadership include:

Organizing and managing volunteers who share your interest builds your communication and leadership skills.

Demonstrating the value of knowing your firm's personnel.

Gaining confidence in your ability to interact with community leaders.

Acquiring fundamental leadership and communication skills that further support your marketing efforts.

As you become a more active, accepted, and visible member of the niche, there are other, higher level activities that further the accomplishment of the objective. For example, you can entertain clients and nonclient influentials, host social functions, and donate the use of your office for a particular organization's events. You can attend conferences and seminars in the niche and conduct your own on-the-spot surveys.

A Provo, Utah law firm provides a small conference room for the biweekly use of a subcommittee from the United Fund. The partner in charge of practice development says, "This small gesture brings big names into our firm twice a month."

A Dayton, Ohio-based accounting firm conducts on-the-spot surveys during the annual business-accounting conference held in its city. Each day during the 3-day conference, several junior partners poll the attendees on a topic of the day. The results are posted by 8:00 A.M. the next day and copies on the firm's letterhead are distributed.

While so far I have focused primarily on membership in local groups, the same strategies and pay-offs apply on a national level. It never hurts to have a national reputation even though the scope of your marketing efforts is currently confined to your local market. Who are the high rollers of your industry? Who counts nationally and is known by everyone in the industry? Where and when are the national forums held? It is here that you will have the opportunity to meet the leaders of your industry.

In my own profession, management consulting, John F. Hartshorne, the executive director of the Institute of Management Consultants, and James Kennedy, publisher of *Consultant's News* and *Consultant's Bookstore*, are two of the most respected, visible, nationally-recognized leaders. Not coincidentally, I count these gentlemen, among others, as my friends and key business associates.

OBJECTIVE #2. There are numerous activities you can undertake that will create, maintain, and enhance a favorable awareness of you, your firm, and its services. Your goals in undertaking each of the activities are to generate greater name recognition for you and your firm; to educate your targets regarding what your firm is all about, the types of service solutions it offers, and some of its clients; and to have members of your firm and members of target firms become better acquainted.

SPEAKING TO TARGETED GROUPS

There exist many opportunities to speak to targeted groups, and you have the ability to create additional opportunities. Why is it important to speak to targeted groups, and what are some of the benefits? Probably the biggest barrier faced by many professional-service providers is the fear of speaking to groups. Consequently, you can turn this into an advantage. Speaking to targeted groups provides the following benefits. This activity:

Enhances your communication skills

Increases your self-esteem and perceived net worth to others

Enables you to be perceived as an expert in the field

Identifies you as an individual and firm to seek for professional assistance

Offers increased exposure, both internally and externally

Often generates immediate new contacts

If you refuse a speaking engagement, you have lost an opportunity. The seeds you plant today may take a while to bloom. If nothing is planted now, the results will be as expected.

A number of years ago, one of my objectives was to build a client base in Australia. To build name awareness, I accepted speaking assignments in the United States, Canada, and the Caribbean with accounting, consulting, and management groups that had affiliations in Australia. During my speeches, I indicated my interest in Australia and invited visiting "Aussies" to say hello upon conclusion of my talk. Within two years, I was booking four to six weeks of work "down under" per year.

Many leveraging opportunities develop for the service practitioner who speaks to targeted groups. For example, questions from attendees are invaluable. I have frequently held cracker-barrel sessions after the speeches in which attendees ask me questions on hot-button and recurring-need areas that were not addressed during my presentation. The issues raised during these sessions served as automatic guideposts for tailoring and enhancing my promotional and services-delivery systems (Chapter 6).

When speaking to a captive audience—and that is exactly what your listeners will be—you can poll them on various issues. In addition to bolstering your understanding of the niches, these minipolls can be developed as news releases. The information and feedback you gain from one presentation can immediately be used in subsequent presentations, rapidly increasing your reputation in the niche.

As you address the hot buttons and recurring needs of the niche, you further multiply your leveraging opportunities. *Marketing Your Consulting and Professional Services* contains an excellent description of how to identify target groups and secure a speaking engagement using excerpts from tape-recorded speeches. Many groups are in a state of perpetual need when it comes to finding speakers.

The amount of time and money you spend preparing and delivering a speech will depend on your goals and the type of organization you will be addressing. Your goals may be simply to practice your delivery, introduce your firm's new program to handle a need, be invited to speak at this group's national convention, or generate qualified leads for new business.

The time, the setting, and the format of the speech are usually set by the host organization. You will usually be requested to speak for 30 to 45 minutes, with 10 or 15 minutes for a question-and-answer session. The group's meeting planner or program host can fill you in on all the details regarding scheduling information. In any event, be sure to provide quality handouts reprinted on your firm's letterhead so that attendees may readily call you in the future. (See Figure 7.1.)

One technique I have used to good advantage is to ask the meeting planner for a copy of the membership directory and list of attendees. I also hold a business card raffle at the conclusion of my presentation. This has several benefits. First, it holds their attention and it enables me to establish personal contact. The prize I offer is an autographed copy of my first book. The prize you offer can be any book of quality, whether or not you wrote it. The recipient instantly becomes your friend and booster.

Many novice speakers make the mistake of "cutting and running" after their presentation. Stick around for at least 30 minutes and possibly longer. You should take full advantage of the leveraging opportunities that exist when you have a room full of prospective clients and nonclient influentials. There will always be time to rest later.

If you have arranged to have your presentation taped, then you

Jeffrey P. Davidson, CMC
3709 South George Mason Drive, #315E
Falls Church, Virginia 22041
(703) 931–1984

MARKETING PROFESSIONAL SERVICES:
JEFF DAVIDSON'S 11 PRINCIPLES OF SUCCESS

1. Write down what it will look like when you're there.
2. Use available help, but allow that you won't find another you.
3. Have many irons in the fire so that you are not depending on any one client.
4. Delegate often, concentrate on those tasks you must do personally.
5. Carefully research the range of available images, choose one, and then cultivate it.
6. Identify the 10 people who could accelerate your plans and then meet them.
7. Stay flexible, roll with the punches, and maintain perspective.
8. Make your work fun, or get out.
9. Ruthlessly discard what doesn't support your quest.
10. Think like your client.
11. Expect the journey to be hard and expect to make it.

FIGURE 7.1. Handout Example: Jeff Davidson's 11 Principles of Success can listen to it following the presentation and critique yourself. Also, by transcribing the tape, you may find that, with a few hours' work, you have a publishable article in the making. If the tape is a good one, get it duplicated. It will be a valuable tool when contacting other meeting planners and will increase the likelihood of your being invited to speak.

WRITING FOR TARGETED PUBLICATIONS

All of the publications you identified in establishing your niche data base and library are excellent places to send an article. Given all the information you have assembled about the niche, it would not be difficult to determine several interesting topics. Your article need not be more than 750 to 1000 words (three or four double-spaced typed pages). As long as you simply address one of the hot buttons or recurring needs of readers, the probability of your article being accepted and published will be high. (See Figure 7.2.)

The editor of an association-based publication is what I call a "megaleverage" nonclient influential (NCI)! Graham Goddard, editor of *The Practicing CPA*, is a case in point. He and I have worked out an agreement where I query him about an article topic I have. If he agrees that it's suitable, I send him a draft. He, in turn, edits, tightens, and, if necessary, restructures it to fit the needs of his readers. Graham's philosophy is, "I know best how to present your material for my readers, so give me your best presentation."

Each time you write an article make at least 20 copies of it. On the average, every 20 times you mail out a manuscript, you will ultimately achieve one acceptance. These days editors do not mind receiving simultaneous submissions—in other words, you are also mailing the same article to other editors. You can also mail two or three different articles to one editor at the same time. These mass-mail techniques increase your chances of getting into print.

WHEN SHOULD YOU CALL A CONSULTANT?

It's a plain matter of fact that there is a problem in the company. The quarterly figures show it, or the employees whisper about it. It may be that sales are eroding, or that employee morale is sinking, but you're not exactly sure why. Is it time to call in a consultant?

For any management consultant to do the job well, he first has to know precisely what the problem is that you want investigated. That may be the hardest part. Before hiring a consultant, a management team may want to sit down together and try to define and write out the problem, its effects on the company, its probable causes (as the management sees them), and possible solutions. In doing so, you may find you don't need a consultant.

Yet, certain problems inherently lend themselves to solution by someone from outside the organization, according to Jeffrey Davidson, a management consultant in Falls Church, VA and co-author of *Marketing Your Consulting and Professional Services* (John Wiley & Sons, New York, NY). Following are a few of his suggestions for determining when you need outside assistance:

- The time and talents are not available in house to solve the problem.
- The true state of affairs can be determined only by the objective examination of someone not involved in daily operations.
- Management has already tried, and failed, to solve the problem.
- Unfamiliarity among management with the specialized field.
- A desire for fresh ideas or new techniques.
- A conflict of views within the organization.

Davidson warns that calling a consultant should not be used as a status symbol, to back up an unpopular decision, or as a political weapon to discredit the views of a rival in the corporation.

For more information, write: *Jeffrey P. Davidson, 3709 S. Geo. Mason Dr. #315-E, Falls Church, VA 22041. (703) 931-1984.*

FIGURE 7.2. Short Article Example in *Industrial Distribution* (Vol. 75, No. 1, January 1986). *Reprinted with permission.*

If you have never had an article published before, take heart. Each year between 800,000 and 1,000,000 people in the United States alone have their first article published.

Take advantage of the pyramid process when trying to get published. It is far easier to get a small column published in a newsletter than in a major, nationwide magazine serving your targeted industry. Once you get published in a newsletter, make an attractive reprint, write the words "previous publication" in the corner and include that reprint when sending out other manuscripts to editors of larger publications.

Having been already published in any other publication influences editors favorably and multiplies your chances of getting published again. When you have been published several times, you begin to benefit from the "halo effect." As publishers and editors see that you are well published, they automatically read more closely the manuscripts you send them.

Successful firms, those with well developed systems for getting new clients, seem to have mastered techniques for getting into print. Review the most prominent magazines in the niche, and you undoubtedly will find published articles authored by partners and principals of well known firms. It is no coincidence that the firms are well known and their key people are in print. Articles written by your competition are must reading. Study them to see how you might use their articles to help you make *your* selling point to suspects in your niche.

Perhaps the greatest obstacle to getting published is the concern that what you have to say is not important or how you say it is unacceptable. Both of these fears are unfounded. If you have done your homework, you *will know* what topics are of concern to the niche. If you are not particularly adept at writing, have others in the firm edit your manuscript; talk the details into a tape recorder and have a junior associate flesh out the article; or hire a ghost writer.

I learned to use ghost writers years ago after I met a respected contributor to the *Harvard Business Review*. I asked him where he found time to research and write the articles. He looked at me incredulously and stated, "Dick, *no one* who is really keen about using their time well writes their own stuff. I use a freelance writer to interview me for a one-expert story. She quickly prepares an outline and draft that she walks me through. I do the final editing before it's submitted." Good writers are available in every location; ask around and you'll find them.

Be on the lookout constantly for ways to extract articles from reports and written materials you have already developed. Transcribe the tapes from your speaking engagements and half the job is already done. Too many professionals who spent years writing compositions and term papers in school have been traumatized by the harsh remarks and comments of their teachers and professors. The editors who receive your manuscripts are not nearly as critical. If they like your basic theme, often they will help edit your manuscript.

There are several fine software programs available that can be used to improve your writing techniques. These include "Right Writer," a Write Soft (tm) product by Decisionware, Inc., among others.

At all costs avoid sitting at your desk staring at a blank screen or a blank page and attempting to write an article from scratch. You probably won't do it. Start by listing everything that comes to mind regarding a problem you can solve, a trend in the niche, or an opportunity to be exploited. Since most professionals view article writing as an elective activity, you should set a personal goal of completing one article every three to six months, or whatever time frame you choose.

Once you have actually written your article and had it published, many more leveraging opportunities become available. As mentioned, the article reprint can be used to influence editors and accelerate the process of getting published in the future. Beyond that, the article reprint can be used as a promotional tool when contacting suspects and prospective clients.

PREPARING ARTICLES THAT PROMOTE YOUR FIRM

An advanced strategy in preparing articles to develop an insider's reputation within the niche is to include you, your firm, and its services as the subject of your article. Done skillfully, the article in print and its reprint are effective ways of establishing a reputation and gaining high visibility. (See the article from *Marketing News* reprinted on pages 125 and 126.)

December 19, 1986

PATH FROM FADS TO PRAGMATISM CIRCLES THE GLOBE

FAD ENTREPRENEUR Fred Reinstein has made a name for himself by developing and marketing such products as the "Wacky Wallwalker," "Sydney Slush Muggs," and E.T. posters.

Now, Reinstein has created a practical household product—and a $50 million-plus business—by attaching a one-piece pressure washer to a garden hose.

Called Turbo-Wash and distributed by Reinstein's Turbo-Tek Enterprises, Culver City, Calif., the product features a black tank that holds eight ounces of soap and a tube with a high-pressure nozzle.

Primarily marketed as a device for washing cars, Turbo-Wash can also be used for houses, boats, and other outdoor surfaces.

Reinstein developed the idea for his product with inventor Rudy Proctor in late 1984. By May 1985—with the help of $2.5 million in start-up funds—he was marketing the product throughout the U.S., Canada, Europe, and Japan.

IN JAPAN ALONE, he expects to sell nearly 1 million units in 1986.

"We've created a market for the product and made it so we can sell it anywhere in the world at the same price," he said.

Although advertising and word-of-mouth sales have helped make Turbo-Wash a worldwide success, Reinstein gives the most credit to his company's in-house distribution and marketing division, Distribution Systems International (DSI). All of his previous successes have been merchandised through DSI.

Reinstein said DSI is comprised of a network of people who have contacts in the business world, including manfacturing agents and merchandise brokers, who have the ability to go into any major market area and move a product.

Reinstein refers to them as "bullets," because their contacts at drugstores, discount houses, and supermarkets allow them to get orders—sometimes on a day's notice.

"DSI HAS MADE Turbo-Wash happen," he said. "They'll tell us what to do to a product to make it fit a particular marketplace. We then do what we have to do to make our product fit their distribution needs."

Reinstein said input from DSI allowed his company to change 15 attributes of the Turbo-Wash package to make the product more marketable in Japan. Another plus for sales was the fact that the Japanese are very clean about themselves, their homes, and cars. Reinstein said many found the Turbo-Wash was an efficient tool for accomplishing those tasks.

"Also in Japan, you have a situation where if a product works, fills a need, and is from the U.S., it becomes a fad," he added. "Everybody's got to have one."

Reinstein called Japan "the simplest and most profitable place in the world to do business. They pay up front, they take the product and market it the way they say they are going to, and it's all done on a handshake."

"**WITH OUR** Turbo-Wash product. we went into Japan and worked with several distributors on a nonexclusive basis until we found one capable of selling our product." Reinstein's company finally chose a distributor who moved 600,000 units of the American-made product, bringing in gross sales of $10 million.

Reinstein sees a continuing market for the Turbo-Wash—unlike "108-day" fad marketing. He is currently planning the introduction of four accessory Turbo-Wash products this year, including a foam wax, a steel cleaner, a mildew cleaner and retardant, and a whitewall tire cleaner.

"We have developed high-gross products which can easily be merchandised and cross-merchandised," Reinstein said. "The bottom line is giving the consumer value for money."

Despite his success with Turbo-Wash, Reinstein has not totally forsaken his career as a fad merchant. He is currently working on a new novelty product he plans to market sometime next year. The only information he would offer is that "it levitates, and kids are going to love it."

Reprinted from *Marketing News*, published by the American Marketing Association, December 19, 1986.

If treated as a major feature story, the article should be loaded with illustrative applications of how your clients are better off since being served by you. Often, this type of article refers to anonymous clients by location but includes enough information so that readers within the niche think that it was a real case with a real company.

A variation on this theme is to prepare the same type of article but much shorter, focusing on a particular problem or portion of the problem-solving process. The PAR report can be used to get the article underway. The short feature presented on pages 125 and 126 accomplishes this task.

There are seven steps in the development of the major feature story we have been discussing:

1. Hook the reader into the case history by quantifying the benefits you helped the client achieve. In other words, at the outset of the article summarize what was accomplished and foreshadow what is to follow.

2. Place the story in perspective by describing the client organization and the management objectives, which could in-

clude improving sales, improving the quality of its products or services, reducing costs, or accomplishing some other objectives. It is important to state the client's objectives early in the article so readers with the same objectives will immediately identify with the company and other readers can relate more easily to the story.

3. Describe the problem in sufficient detail, providing such information as the prevailing environment, recent client experiences, current sales figures, and other pertinent data. Tell whether the problem had been an acute or longstanding need.

4. Present the solution in a before-and-after context, such as, "Previously ABC company's problem was XYZ. They found that by applying DEF they are able to achieve GHI. . . ." Discuss the various alternative solutions that your firm produced and how you and the client arrived at the ultimate solution. Next—and this is vital—relate your service's features and capabilities as the solution. This conveys to the reader that what you have to offer is different from and/or better than anything else available. Frequently, firms develop a system that is named based on their acronym, such as LASER. In this manner, readers know that you have something, but there is just enough mystery to make them want to know more.

5. Relate the benefits resulting from your service solution to the results the client was able to achieve. Use quotes or testimonials from the satisfied client. Also cite any statistical measures that support the improvement, such as sales figures, quality-control data, reduction in costs, and so on.

6. Elaborate on how the service you provided continues to be used to master the problem. Bring the reader up to the present. Offer an extended explanation of what the client is presently experiencing and how your system or solution continues to provide benefits. This portion of your article must leave the reader with a good feeling about the case history and your firm in particular.

7. Wrap up your article with a summary of the case history that restates the key benefits. Make this paragraph short, sweet, and uplifting.

The immediate goal of preparing this type of article is to have the reader clip and save it. Look through your own files and examine the articles you have saved. What was it that attracted you to them? What nugget or information gem satisfied your need to know? Now, the $64,000 question—whom have you contacted as a result of something you have read? Chances are it was the firm that had developed a good understanding of the niche and had an ongoing program for developing an insider's reputation.

CAPITALIZING ON PUBLICITY OPPORTUNITIES

To enhance your firm's image further, you need to identify and capitalize on other available publicity opportunities, such as writing letters to the editor, opinion pieces, and educational flyers. Letters to the editor, particularly in response to controversial issues, generate more exposure than most people are aware of. The magazines, journals, and newsletters in the niche are read eagerly by its members. A reply to the editor or an editorial opinion that reflects your understanding of the niche has a significant impact.

Don't hesitate to be controversial if you have a strong opinion. Figure 7.3 is a copy of a letter that expressed my opinion about an ad in *Advertising Age* that I thought was inappropriate. Fortunately, editors frequently clamor for these contributions, so the probability of having your views published is much higher than having an article published. Be certain to review recently published letters to determine their form and tone.

An educational flyer or brochure is also a useful tool to generate publicity. Many organizations, such as professional and industrial-trade associations, produce such items. At the

February 5, 1987

Viewpoint:Letters Editor
ADVERTISING AGE
740 Rush Street
Chicago, IL 60611-2591

The nature and tone of the ad for the Trout & Ries War College Workshop (page 23 in the February 2, 1987 edition) troubles me:

> "The true nature of business is not serving the customer . . . [it's] outwitting, outflanking, outfighting the competition." proclaim the lead statements.

Terrific, guys!

This warfare mentality, and the related strategy and tactics flowing from it, leads to many of the abuses we decry in the profession.

It's the other way around!

Sensing, serving and satisfying the marketing related needs of the client is the *only true reason* for being in business. Forget this fact and the end is soon in sight.

If competition's your game, learn to compete against the outmoded notions of marketing, service, sensitivity and responsiveness that linger in the minds and emotions of your only competitive resource, your people.

I'd welcome the opportunity to debate these two fine fellows in the forum of informed opinion, *Advertising Age*.

Very truly yours,

Richard A. Connor, Jr.
The Client-centered (tm)
Marketing Mentor

DC:io
Enclo.

FIGURE 7.3. Sample Letter by Dick Connor

individual-firm level, successful firms have produced printed material with titles such as:

"Eight Things to Look for in Selecting an Attorney"

"Five Services Your Accountant Should be Providing"

"How a Management Consultant Can Help You"

Notice that these are not titles that highlight the specific benefits you can provide. Rather, they provide general education about the profession, with the implication being that since your firm is aware of such criteria, it also meets them. The educational flyer can be converted readily into an article with a minimum of effort.

Most professional-service providers with whom I have worked either don't recognize the value of these additional publicity opportunities or never allocate the time to take advantage of them. Please view these activities with a new perspective. Anything that places you and your firm in the eyes of the target niche, and creates a favorable association with lasting benefits, is worth pursuing. To generate publicity you have to get the wheels in motion. The opportunities always exist. Those who have made the commitment to develop an insider's reputation (which includes some of your competitors) look at generating publicity as an ongoing, long-term activity.

All of the things I have discussed so far in this book, including name/service recognition and exposure, creation of an image, and generation of referrals and contacts, can be achieved as a result of capitalizing on publicity opportunities.

CREATING THE PUBLICITY EVENT

The creation of a publicity event, such as a national forum, is another advanced publicity strategy for those practitioners who are ready to make a bold statement about their relationship to the target niche.

Hosting events such as national forums makes some powerful declarations to the niche:

"We own the niche."

"We preempted it."

"We are the educational force."

There are many examples of firms that have achieved this position in their respective niches. As part of your task in developing an insider's understanding of your niche, determine which competitors, if any, are hosting such forums. A careful analysis of the brochure will indicate what is involved in staging such a forum. You could consider hosting a forum on a joint-venture basis with a noncompetitor.

DEMONSTRATING YOUR "D&B"

Another extremely effective way to create, maintain, and enhance a favorable awareness of your firm is to look for ways to demonstrate for your targets your "D&B" manner, or how your services are *different* and/or *better*. Always keep clients apprised of your industry activities, including speeches given, meetings attended, articles written, and so forth. If your firm monitors legislation, pass such information along to your targets. If you are offering some new type of service, issue a news release to the press and your clients. Many firms regularly invite clients and prospective clients to social and sporting events. Some professionals send postcards to key-client executives when traveling for business or pleasure.

Firms that are particularly adept at maintaining favorable awareness contact clients during periods when they are not actively serving them. In addition, the winners make follow-up calls about completed engagements and, if the situation is appropriate, offer incentives to contract for additional business, such as discounts for immediate follow-on work. Many firms sponsor get-acquainted tours of their company facilities; others host theme or after-work parties with wine and cheese or hors d'oeuvres.

Occasionally, entice prospective clients with free advice over the phone. At social, civic, and professional functions introduce clients and nonclient influentials to one another, as well as to key professionals they might be interested in knowing. Those who refer business to you appreciate having business referred to them.

Another excellent strategy for demonstrating your D&B manner is to put together a list of those who serve your targeted industry. This list could be as simple as the names and phone numbers of key sources of information, or as involved as a bound directory.

STIMULATING INQUIRIES

To further develop an insider's reputation, stimulate inquiries from high-potential suspect individuals in organizations within the niche. There are several ways to accomplish this objective:

Plan and conduct niche-centered seminars

Further leverage the use of speeches and articles

Develop and place advertisements

Contact suspects for research purposes

Distribute need-driven newsletters based on your research

Distribute niche-specific brochures

Plan and Conduct Niche-centered Seminars

In any metropolitan area, you can plan and conduct seminars that will provide educational benefits to attendees, generate revenue, and stimulate inquiries for your services. Such a seminar can be advertised through your newspaper, by using direct-mail lists, or in affiliation with a university or association. If you have sufficient space in your own offices, it can be held there or in meeting rooms at local hotels and conference centers.

Most sessions last either a half or full day, and lunch is included in the seminar fees. Much has been written on the seminar business in previous years. Several excellent texts are available, including:

An Executive's Guide to Meetings, Conferences and Seminars by James Jeffrey and Jefferson D. Bates. New York: McGraw Hill and Company, 1982.

Speak Like a Pro! by Maggie Bedrosian. New York: John Wiley & Sons, 1987.

How to Conduct Training Seminars by Lawrence Munson, New York: McGraw Hill and Company, 1984.

How to Create and Market a Successful Seminar or Workshop by Howard L. Shenson. Woodland Hills, CA: Howard L. Shenson Publications, 1985.

Further Leverage Use of Speeches and Articles

As previously discussed, any time you give a speech or get an article published you have created a tool that can be leveraged. One organized practitioner gave 14 speeches in the course of a year, and the speeches were in chronological sequence according to a book outline he had developed. At the end of the year, by transcribing his 14 speeches, he was able to assemble a 265-page rough draft of his book manuscript.

In the next six months, working with one of his junior staff members, he was able to complete a 280-page manuscript, which was ultimately published as a hard-cover book. Had he sat down to write a 280-page manuscript from scratch, the book never would have materialized.

A management consultant in Yorkshire, England, was able to convert an article he had previously published into a position paper that got him invited to the most prestigious symposium in his field. As a result of his presentation at the symposium, he generated five inquiries for his services, three of which led to new clients. He also was invited by two editors to submit articles.

One way to leverage your existing resources is to review your files and determine if any previous articles, client reports, outlines, or memos can be spun off into other articles. Make your speeches, articles, and publicity vehicles count two, three, and four times—never just once. That is the way to keep the inquiry pipeline flowing.

Develop and Place Advertisements

Since the Supreme Court ruled that lawyers may advertise as long as their claims are accurate (the Bates decision, 1982), all professions have gained added flexibility in their ability to attract new clients through advertising. Having researched the niche thoroughly, the probability that you will be able to develop and place an advertisement that will stimulate inquiries is far greater than that of the average practitioner. Developing and placing advertisements is never easy, and usually costly.

Any successful advertising program must be of an ongoing nature. Just one or two ads do not generate the kind of impact necessary to keep the inquiry pipeline open. If you choose to place advertisements, first identify the key publication(s) read by the niche. Then, carefully examine several issues of the publication, noting who advertises, what they offer, and the image they convey.

Next, write to the advertising department of the publication and ask for the rate card (see Chapter 5), a breakdown of the various prices the publication charges to run an advertisement. Normally, you receive substantial discounts by running an ad several times. To determine whether to place an ad, check the cost per thousand—the cost of reaching 1000 members of your targeted niche. If you are advertising in a national publication to reach local targets, the cost per thousand may be quite high. Depending on the target group, you may not have a choice; the key publications of the industry could well be national or international in scope. Nevertheless, the cost per thousand is a useful measure of the strength of your advertising dollars.

Contact Suspects for Research Purposes

You can stimulate inquiries by contacting suspects in the niche for research purposes. Those firms that are able to dominate the niche do so in part because they are continuously publishing the results of surveys and inquiries regarding trends, hot buttons, and developments within the niche.

The research conducted can be gathered by mail or phone surveys. Mail surveys have a far lower rate of response than phone surveys, but enable you to reach many more targets with far less effort. Moreover, those who don't respond still have received the message that you are conducting research. Calls directly to targets require considerable effort on your part but are likely to yield far more information about the suspect and often result in inquiries. A consultant to the architect-engineering profession uses the research contacts to good advantage. First, he keeps his name in front of the key players in the niche. The calls keep his finger on the pulse of the niche and alert him to immediate and emerging needs. Sometimes he obtains work that he otherwise would not have been considered for. Today, out of mind equals out of pocket.

Distribute Niche Centered Newsletters

Three years ago, while preparing *Marketing Your Consulting and Professional Services*, we decided not to include newsletters because the task of developing them, on even a quarterly basis, was seen as prohibitive. With the advent of desktop publishing and other available supporting software, the strategy of offering a quarterly or even monthly newsletter becomes much more viable.

If done properly, a newsletter can be an effective tool for establishing an insider's reputation. If not done properly, you're better off not issuing a newsletter because it will detract from your image. The key to producing and distributing an effective newsletter that stimulates inquiries is to stay on target. The size of the newsletter is relatively unimportant; it can have one page or as many as eight to twelve. The information must reflect your insider's understanding of the niche, the recurring needs, the hot buttons, and in general the issues that are on the minds of your targets. The preparation of a well targeted newsletter is best illustrated by example. (See Figures 7.4 and 7.5.)

A frequent mistake in distributing a newsletter is reiterating or encapsulating information published by other sources. This can be marginally effective, but fails to demonstrate your insider's understanding of the niche and the different and better aspects of your service(s). It is far better to use your newsletter to convey the results of your own research. Showcasing your own findings effectively conveys your deep understanding and separates you from the competition.

Distribute Niche-Specific Brochures

Your understanding of the niche and the research you have been compiling will also enable you to prepare a brochure that can stimulate inquiries. Refer back to the exercises in Chapter 6 on critical success factors and the client-centered analysis for the terminology and tools to prepare a brochure that hits home the moment it gets into the hands of the target.

The items about your firm that must be contained in the brochure include how long you have been in business, your size and location, and the qualifications of your staff. It is helpful to include information on the quality of your service(s) and your firm's reputation. Most important to the target is information on

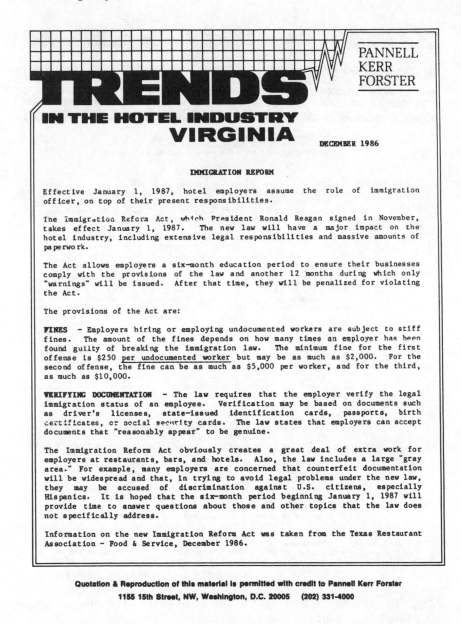

FIGURE 7.4. Newsletter from Pannell Kerr Forster. Reprinted with permission.

Management, Marketing & Design News Highlights
Compiled by David Voracek for clients and friends of
The Marketing Department • P.O. Box 3525 • Alexandria, VA 22302 • (703) 824-8787   Vol.4 No.4

NEW PRODUCTS ARE VITAL

"Fifty percent of a firm's profits could come from products less than five years old," believes one respected high-tech executive. By the year 2000, fast changing technology and new product developments will mean that company growth and profits will be heavily dependent upon the newest products in one's line. How's *your* new product development ?

HIGH TECH MARKETING IS DIFFERENT

Technological superiority alone no longer guarantees success. Bill Davidow, author of a new book titled *Marketing High Technology*, contends that "It's your marketing strategy that makes the difference. All your advertising is capable of doing is to create awareness. It doesn't sell product."

To be successful, Davidow advises firms to create "complete" products. That's the hardware itself, as well as its instructional materials and service procedures. In addition, you must work to convince prospects that your company will be around in the future. "Peace of mind" is one of the most important aspects you are selling.

Formerly VP of Sales & Marketing for Intel, Davidow's book includes numerous success and failure stories about other Silicon Valley firms.

SALARY VS. COMMISSION

Salary-only sales reps outsell their commission-only counterparts by nearly four-to-one. That's what a recent study of 738 firms by the Wyatt Company discovered.

In another study in the *Small Business Report*, it was noted that in many professional and technical companies, salespeople primarily act as consultants, and incentive pay simply doesn't apply.

Here are a few of the other findings to consider when structuring your firm's sales compensation program:

- Variable pay (commission) is prevalent at newer, smaller companies without big sales staffs.
- Of the companies studied, 6.4% paid only commissions to their sales force, while 19.6% paid on a salary-only basis. The balance offered various salary/commission incentive mixtures.
- Top salespeople paid a mix of salary and incentives earned an average of $65,000 at industrial firms.
- Straight salary compensation makes sense in some situations, though. When sales is merely a stepping stone to a management position, there is often no need to use commissions to "entice" people to stay. Or, when sales managers have set *realistic* goals, they can often motivate their people without using commissions.

THE BURDEN OF BEING FIRST

"The company with the most at stake is the one that launches an entirely new product. This company generally bares most of the costs, the tribulations, and certainly the risks of developing both the product and the market."
      Theodore Levitt, *The Marketing Imagination*

FIGURE 7.5. FOR YOUR INFORMATION—Management, Marketing & Design News Highlights. Reprinted with permission.

others who have used your services, and your firm's ability to sense, serve, and satisfy the needs of the niche. Quotes or endorsements from satisfied clients are always helpful. Figure 7.6 depicts a simple, three-panel brochure that typifies what I've been talking about.

A POSITIONING CASE HISTORY

Here is a look at how one accounting firm in Chicago positioned itself to gain an insider's reputation in its chosen niche. The firm decided to develop a series of niche "white papers" aimed specifically at the target market, which would immediately be recognized by the recipient as important information. To produce these papers, the firm hired a market researcher who would periodically gauge the current concerns of trade associations, periodicals, the firm's existing clients, some of its prospects, and other niche influentials. The researcher was specifically instructed to distinguish the very serious issues from the less serious so the papers could attract high-potential prospects with information specifically aimed at their needs.

Numerous steps were taken to carry out the strategy. It was determined that the white papers would be distributed on a monthly basis. Some of them provided how-to information, such as how to avoid problems. Other issues focused on new developments and trends and conveyed the message that the accounting firm understood these changes through its long tradition of being a leader in the field, its current research, and its ongoing surveys.

As the papers evolved, other features were added, such as checklists based on case histories. A perforated reply card for requesting more information was also added, as was a personal cover letter that introduced the philosophy and purpose of the paper. The letter emphasized that this communication was a public service on the part of the firm to maintain and upgrade the standards and sources of information available.

Reality versus theory

Business profit depends on a commitment to long term problem solving.

W. L. Nikel and Associates, Management Consultants

Executives attending seminars that we conduct at the American Management Association mention these critical problems in managing:

- Inflation, productivity and governmental pressures.

- Rapid changes in technology and competition; new competitors.

- Too little time to plan because of "alligators."

- Not easy to stay current with latest developments in management.

- Difficulty getting functional units to really work together.

- Too little time to evaluate competitive strengths and weaknesses in current and potential markets.

- Limited rewards for long term profit planning.

FIGURE 7.6. 3-panel Brochure (pages 140–145). Reprinted by permission of W. L. Nikel and Associates.

William L. Nikel
President

W. L. Nikel and Associates
Management Consultants
295 North Mountain Avenue
Upper Montclair, New Jersey 07043
201-744-1661

Professional experience:

Mr. Nikel has over 25 years of proven consulting and management experience in consumer and industrial products and markets, retailing and wholesaling. He leads executive seminars and courses with the American Management Association on a wide range of subjects and is a guest lecturer at Columbia University Graduate School.

His consumer marketing experience includes management and internal consulting at Exxon Enterprises and J.C. Penney Company. At Exxon Enterprises he managed dealer and electric utility sales, advertising and marketing programs. At Penney he developed and managed diversification programs and consulted on store and catalog operations, strategic plans, and consumer financial services.

Industrial marketing experience includes Lukens Steel Company and the Noland Company, a Southeastern wholesaler of plumbing, heating, electrical and industrial products. His principal assignments were strategic planning, diversification, marketing research and consulting for key customers.

FIGURE 7.6. Continued

Mr. Nikel received an M.B.A. in Marketing from the Wharton School of the University of Pennsylvania and a B.A. in Economics from Ursinus College. After graduating from the U. S. Naval Intelligence School he served as a Lieutenant (j.g.) during the Korean War.

He is a member of the Association of Management Consultants, Wharton Business School Club of New York, American Marketing Association, New York Organization Development Network and Appalachian Mountain Club. He is a former director of the Virginia Peninsula Homebuilders Association.

Mr. Nikel and his family have lived in Upper Montclair for many years and are active in church and civic affairs. He is an avid jogger, hiker and cross country skier.

Our approach as consultants is to:

Utilize experience from marketing, physical distribution, financial analysis, human resource development and other fields to provide a multi-discipline capability.

Improve cost-effectiveness of client assignments by:

- Clearly defining the opportunity or problem before moving out of the initial phase.
- Summarizing the situation in a written description, to sharpen the focus.
- Moving more quickly to solutions and into implementation.

Use a proven, systematic method to review long range market and competitive trends.

Provide a clear outline of work to be done, with a completion schedule and cost estimate.

Meet scheduled progress reports and completion dates.

We do not accept an assignment unless we believe that the value created by our services will be far greater than the cost to our client.

FIGURE 7.6. Continued

Key areas of management consulting experience:

Our experience and accomplishments include these representative areas:

Market Penetration. Developed a market measurement system that triggered a multimillion dollar expansion and acquisition program by a leading wholesaler.

Profit Improvement. Reduced expense by $600,000 annually through a comprehensive program to control catalog merchandise returns. Program included management information systems, transportation and warehousing, store/catalog operations, merchandise planning and customer service.

Diversification. Saved over $10 million by substantially reducing scope of diversification into building materials. Our evaluation pinpointed much higher distribution costs than projected by our client.

National Advertising and Merchandising. Developed a successful marketing planning and implementation system for 20 nationally advertised consumer product lines.

New Products. Saved an estimated $1.3 million through a conclusive market test that changed market development strategy because of consumer price resistance.

Client evaluations:

Clients' comments about our assignments include:

"Gave us more than we expected."

"Assignments demanded broad experience and skills."

"Excellent reasoning, analysis, planning, writing and oral presentations."

"Contribution was substantial, innovative and thoroughly professional."

"Excellent leadership in developing teams of executives."

References:

Client references can be readily provided.

FIGURE 7.6. Continued

Reasons for choosing
W. L. Nikel and Associates:

Our clients include retailers, banking and insurance, hospitals, manufacturers of home furnishings, sporting goods, heating and electrical equipment, contractors, professional organizations and investor-owned utilities.

We have found that our clients often choose us for one or more of these reasons:

Expertise in key businesses. This enables us to be useful to our clients immediately in specific problem areas.

Breadth and perspective. A broad perspective gained from many functional areas avoids overlooking less obvious but important aspects of client opportunities and problems.

Experience in both planning and implementation. This facilitates practical, cost-effective solutions and programs geared to capabilities of an organization and its people.

Track record in developing teams of executives. Our experience with many types and sizes of organizations permits us to develop and improve teamwork in key areas.

FIGURE 7.6. Continued

Management consulting services:

- Marketing and strategic planning
- Positioning
- Pricing
- Industry surveys and competitive analyses
- Marketing research
- Diversification
- Marketing audits
- Sales forecasting and financial analysis
- Marketing information and control systems
- Acquisition and divestiture studies
- Sales and merchandising management
- Distribution strategies
- Customer service
- Coordination of marketing and
    physical distribution
- Advertising and sales promotion
- Public relations
- Management development and training

ASSOCIATION OF
MANAGEMENT
CONSULTANCY

W. L. Nikel and Associates
Management Consultants
295 North Mountain Avenue
Upper Montclair, New Jersey 07043
201-744-1661

FIGURE 7.6. Continued

The implied message was that the accounting firm was very concerned with the standards and procedures of firms within the industry and wanted to help them stay up to date by providing current information. Contributory articles by industry leaders, which often focused on an explanation of their positions in dealing with previous problems, were included.

After several months, the paper evolved into a newsletter format. A professional writer/editor was hired to assist the marketing researcher in developing the end product. Each issue of the newsletter was numbered, but not dated, so that issues could be sent to prospects on an individual basis. The publication had a sturdy, substantial, elegant look.

Though the newsletter was only one page, front and back, the back was reserved for a brief description of corporate philosophy, more information, solutions to the problems discussed on the front side, and the firm's return address. Overall, the back page maintained a nonselling stance. The newsletter was positioned as an information service.

For nonclients who had already received three or four mailings, a decision was made to enclose a request card for the firm's other how-to lists, evaluation tools, and minimanuals. This strategy was undertaken in the realization that the targets wanted to receive this information, but were highly selective in reading advertising material.

As more issues were developed, requests from other firms in the niche, but not on the mailing list, started to come in. Using its computerized data base system, the accounting firm was able to keep track of which publication each recipient had received and bring them along in measured sequence. All envelopes were typed, rather than labeled, so that no one felt as if they were receiving a mass mailing. In addition, mail was stamped and sent first class rather than by postage meter or bulk mail.

The newsletters were distributed with the goal of creating the need for interaction—something that could not have been achieved if the recipients thought they were receiving an item from another direct-mail campaign by a company that wanted to sell them something. As a follow-up to this story, the firm is still employing these techniques and is generating a healthy percentage of inquiries as a result.

OTHER INSIDER STRATEGIES

A Lakeworth, Florida firm offering tax preparation assistance decided to reach key decision-makers in the niche by joining the most prominent trade association. By establishing a high degree of trust on an interpersonal basis, the firm was able to reduce sales and promotion costs.

Several members of the firm joined the association, and they examined the various committees of the association to see which firm members could participate as leaders. Having joined the appropriate committees, the firm's members immediately offered to do research for the committee or help prepare for upcoming events. During this time, they were able to become familiar with the terminology and language used by the target niche. They also were able to gain a fair understanding of the needs of the decision-makers in the niche. In this way they became sensitive to the changes taking place before most of their competitors.

Another firm that provided communications and public-relations services developed joint-venture programs with other types of noncompeting professionals. This enabled them to reduce research costs while maintaining an insider's understanding of their niche. On a periodic basis, staff members from the various firms who were responsible for maintaining the library and niche data base met and traded target lists, loaned key publications, and created reciprocal referral systems. In the course of 18 months, the initiating firm was able to substantially accelerate its understanding of, and reputation in, targeted niches.

A professional training specialist in Canberra, Australia, compiled a press kit consisting of her quarterly newsletter, some article reprints, her firm's brochures, and some endorsement let-

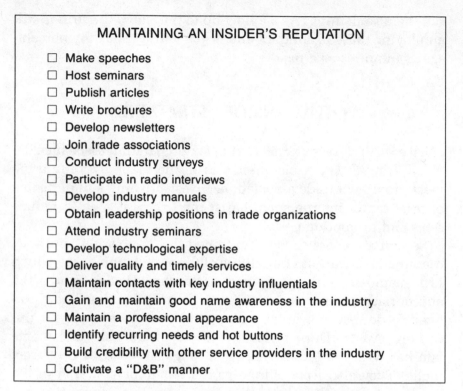

FIGURE 7.7. Maintaining An Insider's Reputation

ters from satisfied clients. She then identified five journalists who covered her beat. Every couple of months she sent them a cover letter explaining the latest trends in training and development and her specific experiences. After the first three mailings, a period of about nine months, no one had called. Undaunted, she mailed the next round and about a week later received a call from an international training magazine. This magazine was not on her list to receive her publicity kit. However, it turned out that one of the journalists to whom she had been sending her kit had attended a conference in Sydney with the editor of the training publication. The journalist was asked if he had ever encountered someone who had vast experience using a certain kind of training technique, and he offered her name to the editor. As a result, the trainer was featured in this prominent international industry publication and was able to leverage reprints of that article by favorably influencing a much greater percentage of her prospects and suspects.

MAINTAINING AN INSIDER'S REPUTATION

Figure 7.7 is a composite of what the most progressive, successful professionals do to maintain an insider's reputation in their targeted niche. Relax when reading this list; few firms are able to engage in all the activities listed.

So far, all of the suggestions and strategies outlined have required that you work in the trenches. You have had to do much analysis and planning and perhaps rethink some of your basic business objectives. The rest of the chapters in the book flow from what you have learned in Chapters 1 through 7.

Once you have assembled the information you need, getting new clients will become much easier. You will be able to talk their language and make your firm attractive to targets of opportunity and influence.

The chapters that follow are a bit shorter and represent easier reading and implementation. We begin with Part II: "Getting and Preparing for Appointments with Prospective Clients."

Part 2
Getting and Preparing for Appointments with Prospective Clients

The next four chapters focus on the steps involved in selecting the need(s) and the organizations to which you'll be presenting service solutions; developing and managing your initial contact program; making the appointment-getting phone call; and preparing for the new-business discussion.

8

Selecting a Need and the Right Suspects to Contact

You have spent considerable time researching the niche and increasing your insider's understanding. Now it's time to obtain appointments with high-potential prospective clients. This involves the following five steps:

1. *Selecting the Need to be Promoted.* Your goal is to select a current hot button or important recurring need that your targeted suspects have and want solved at this time.

2. *Developing a Preliminary Need Scenario.* Your goal is to visualize the probable need situation of the individuals in the suspect organizations to whom you will send your initial contact package. You want to get in sync quickly with the players in the organization.

3. *Selecting Suspect Organizations in your Niche for Contact.* Your goal is to target high-potential suspect organizations to contact during this specific promotional-prospecting campaign.

4. *Developing your Initial-Contact Mailing Package.* This package consists of a "grabber" cover letter and a need-specific

153

enclosure. Your goal is to find an enclosure that makes your selling point and grabs the contact's attention.

5. *Making Telephone Calls to Obtain an Appointment.* Your goal is to obtain an appointment with a member of the decision-making group in the targeted organization to discuss the specifics of their need situation and suggest how you can solve the need.

This chapter will discuss the first three steps. Chapter 9 will discuss step 4, and Chapter 10 will discuss step 5.

SELECTING THE NEED TO BE PROMOTED

As a general principle, the stronger the need, the easier it is to obtain appointments with the decision-maker in the targeted organization. Focusing on a need and the benefits you can provide, rather than pitching your product or the service you offer, is one of the best ways to use the Platinum Rule mentioned in Chapter 2.

Find a current need that is urgent and important enough to the contact in the suspect organization so that he or she will meet with you. It has been said that a problem well defined is half solved. This goes doubly for the notion of solving a need. Up to now, I've been using the term *need* generically to describe a situation faced by a targeted suspect. Let's take a few minutes to explore this topic.

1. *Negative Need Situations.* There are three need situations in which unwanted, negative conditions are present or probable. First, there may be a *deficiency* (yellow-red alerts; see next page) in some existing performance factor. Secondly, there is the *threat* of some unwanted condition occurring; and finally, there is a *decision* to be made that involves uncertainty on the part of the contact.

2. *Positive Need Situations.* There are two positive need situations. One occurs when some positive, desired/required condi-

tion is *lacking*. The other occurs when some positive condition (performance, people, system, etc.) exists but is in *short supply*.

3. *Short-term Task Situations*. These are situations that require your type of skills, knowledge, and technology. In today's economy, task-driven engagements are increasing as organizations seek to streamline their operations.

Remember, the purpose of all this analysis is to enable you to talk "suspect-talk" when you prepare your initial contact package (Chapter 9) and make your telephone contact (Chapter 10). If you can think like they do, use their vocabulary, and promise benefits, you quickly establish yourself as someone who is worth meeting. Each situation can be used in your practice.

A *deficiency* refers to subpar performance of an existing business function or process; that is, sales are off, scrap is up, morale is poor, or costs are above budget. Each of these unwanted conditions is an enemy of effective organizational management. Each condition requires analysis to determine the reason behind this subpar performance. You know how to do this; and, more importantly, you know how to correct the cause of this deficiency and bring the level of performance up to desired/required levels.

Hopefully a deficiency will occur in the performance of one of the critical success factors you identified while you were developing your insider's understanding of the niche. In addition, the subpar performance will be approaching the "red-alert" zone of what I call the "yellow-red alert" model.

Yellow-Red Alert

This is the first time I've written about this simple and powerful tool. I learned about it years ago when I was with Booz, Allen & Hamilton. Their best business developers had figured it out. Let's discuss the model to see how you can use it to obtain appointments with high-potential suspects.

Suppose that inventory turnover is an important success factor for suspect organizations in your niche and that your expertise enables you to prevent and solve such problems. Further, assume that nine turns a year for product X is the industry standard. You know this because you did your homework during the industry understanding phase.

You also know from discussing inventory with your key clients that a turnover of between nine and eight for product X is in their tolerance zone. Performance in this range is expected and does not alarm them. Promoting your need-solution program to suspects who are in this operating condition usually generates little interest on their part. However, if your initial contact package is well prepared, they may file it in their "consultants" file.

The next zone, eight to seven turns, is the yellow-alert zone. Management wants to prevent the now subpar performance from falling below seven into the red-alert zone, "where it hits the fan." Promoting your need-solution program to suspect organizations who are in the yellow-alert zone frequently generates a high degree of interest and acceptance on the part of the executive who is responsible for managing inventory.

Experience shows that when contact persons are operating in the red-alert zone, they may be more resistant to outside assistance at first, because they are being bombarded from within by superiors and others who have a stake in the operation.

Your goal for the deficiency-need situation is to design a solution program to bring the present performance up to the desired/required level of performance specified by the buyer.

A *threat* situation refers to one in which an unwanted occurrence is probable. Your solution goal is to prevent the unwanted condition from occurring, or should it occur, to minimize the adverse effects.

A *decision* situation is one in which the contact is faced with a choice and requires your expertise to make the right one. Alternative courses of action must first be identified and evaluated; then the optimal alternative must be selected and implemented. Your solution goal is to remove the uncertainty in the situation by assisting the contact in selecting and implementing a cost-effective course of action.

Positive Need Situations

A *lack* situation is one in which a desired/required positive performance factor, such as a niche data-base, compensation plan, and so on, is needed, and you can provide or develop the factor. Your solution goal is to develop and install a new performance factor that produces the desired/required results.

A *short supply* situation is one in which there is some level of positive performance that you can enhance. For example, some service firms are lucky to have a "rainmaker"—business developer—on board, but no one to back him up. I'm often brought in to leverage the existing rainmaker's contacts and begin developing the marketing capability of potential partners using my mentoring approach of doing, training, coaching, and appraising the performance.

Short-term Task Situations

In today's economy, many organizations are tightening their corporate belts and reducing the staff size by identifying and eliminating nonessential employees. This is creating a huge market for task-driven engagements that require your type of skills and knowledge. In effect, you are providing what many consultants call "rent-a-body" services.

RECOGNIZING NEEDS

Your solution program is to produce the results sought on a cost-effective basis for the contact and your firm. What are the *basic criteria* indicating that a need is present and worthy of your pursuit? First, the need must be recognized by the contact person in the suspect organization as being important enough to discuss at this time. If it is perceived as an issue for which resolution is mandatory or required, so much the better.

On your end, the need is something that you can fill in "D&B" fashion; you have the resources to handle it and you have evidence of past accomplishments, including PAR reports and testimonials. It is also important that you *want* to do this type of work on a repetitive basis if necessary.

Another important criterion is to make sure the competition is not excessive, and that they haven't devised the silver bullet that kills the vampire (need) once and for all. Finally, the need should be one in which you can make a reasonable profit.

There are several *benefits* in identifying hot button or recurring needs that you will use when making initial contact with suspects. You will be able to increase the probability of obtaining an appointment, thus minimizing the number of false starts. Nothing is more time consuming and mentally or emotionally draining than calling on nonreceptive, uninterested targets.

Another important benefit is that you maintain and build your self-esteem by minimizing the probability of rejections. Busy decision-makers are always interested in discussing a need situation, especially if they think they can pick up some free information that might enable them to do the job themselves. When you call upon them to discuss a hot button, you have already answered the foremost question in their minds, "What can I gain from talking to you?"

By focusing on a specific hot button or recurring need of qualified suspects, you can save your time and energy by narrowing the number of contacts you make; those that respond to the hot button you have addressed are much more likely to become your clients. Finally, you continue to build and enhance your insider's reputation with the targeted niche.

Hot-Button Identification 101

If you have already prepared one, refer to your main menu of needs in the backup folder for the niche. (Refer back to the passage on menu of needs in Chapter 5.)

Next, talk with existing clients in the niche. Your mission here is to convince them that you have genuine interest in their

well-being and improving the value of your services to them.
You can do this by simply asking them about their operations.
Using nondirective, open-ended questions, ask them about specific critical success factors, such as:

"What do you have to concentrate on to ensure survival and profitability?"

"What is the status of the XYZ problem?" (If you know about a problem or objective that is probably important throughout the niche.)

"Where are you focusing your attention during the next six to nine months?"

The answers to these questions will give you important insights into your potential clients' problems, as well as opportunities to improve their situation.

If you are serving large clients, try to do some walk-throughs. Visit the department heads and ask the same questions. Meanwhile, observe the operations, housekeeping, work flow, and so on. Be on the lookout for positive exceptions to industry standards. Also, look for opportunities to review client reports, which may provide clues to the needs of others in the niche.

To stay abreast of industry developments, you must also be able to identify hot buttons. By now, this should be old hat to you. Review key industry publications. Your goal in monitoring publications read by your best clients and your targeted suspects is to determine their current hot-button needs to obtain appointments. Hopefully, the publications you review include specific industry/professional journals, as well as general business and local business publications.

Reading general business publications, such as *Business Week*, *Forbes*, *Fortune*, and *Barron's*, for example, provides you with information about larger trends, such as green mail, restructuring, downsizing, legal actions, and so on. In the case of downsizing, look for ripple effects among suppliers to the major players in the industry. Help-wanted ads will point out high-growth organizations and those having trouble retaining good employees.

Some professional-service firms hire part-time graduate students to review recent literature on the industry to identify recurring problems, names in the news, people on the move, and key conferences. Monitoring the topics for yearly conferences can provide you with excellent insights on the needs of the niche. Because the topics and speakers must be selected well in advance of the conference, the topics will be of highest priority.

Another good source of industry needs are industry studies published by research organizations such as Frost & Sullivan and Standard & Poor's. While they may range from $300 to $1500, the information can be quite useful. Also, be sure to check the president's message in the annual reports of larger companies within the niche. This often provides useful insights into the trends and major problems of the niche players. When reading the annual report, look for accounting notes to significant financial changes; they could be clues to the gems that you will use in finding needs to penetrate the niche.

"Red herring" prospectuses for firms wanting to go public must discuss the risk areas, which translates into opportunity areas for the alert professional. After you have read a couple of prospectuses and seen the same risk areas identified, you know you have a hot one.

Tap the Industry Influentials

Those who serve, influence, and regulate members of the niche are well positioned to identify hot industry topics and those destined to become hot. Industry influentials can be identified by asking your A clients, reviewing publications, and purchasing directories and targeted mailing lists.

Another essential task, which cannot be neglected if you wish to dominate the niche, is to meet the industry influentials and establish relationships with them. This will allow you to find today's hot buttons, as well as tomorrow's. There are three basic ways to meet the industry influentials:

1. Call them directly and identify a topic of direct interest to them when you call. Later in the conversation, you can bridge to your interests. You don't get a second chance to make a favorable first impression. Consequently, your call has to have something in it for *them*. Remember the Platinum Rule: Do unto others as they would have you do unto them.

2. Attend meetings, conventions, trade shows, and civic, charitable and social functions at which industry influentials will be present. Before attending the event, you will need to identify a topic of direct interest to them.

3. Arrange to meet them at lunch using a mutual third party. This form of leveraging your existing relationships can easily double or even triple the number of industry influentials you personally contact.

In the months and years that follow take the necessary time to maintain your relationships with industry influentials by calling them, sending them notes ("I have been thinking of you"), and "alert information," anything that you come across that would interest them. This is a small favor that reaps large rewards. People genuinely appreciate receiving items or interesting clippings, which they may have otherwise missed.

Developing a Preliminary Need Scenario

By now you have identified at least one hot button or recurring need that you can use in your preparation for meeting with prospective clients. The purpose of preparing a need scenario (see Figure 8.1) is to get in sync with the target. You want to view the need situation from the contact's vantage point.

NEED SCENARIO

The need I will fill is _____

_____

The need is the *direct* responsibility of _____
                                                    Title

_____

Others who are involved in the need are:

        Who/title   Their stake in it

1. _____   _____

2. _____   _____

3. _____   _____

The *negative* consequences to the contact of not handling the

need include _____

_____

_____

The *positive* consequences of handling the need include

_____

_____

The *solution* goal for this need is _____
                                              Improve

_____

record, protect, build, regain, etc. _____

_____

Evidence I can cite includes _____

_____

_____

FIGURE 8.1.

162

Using an example from my practice let's look at each item on the Need Scenario worksheet.

The Need. State this as simply and powerfully as you can, using the suspect's vocabulary where appropriate. For example: "Improve the new client-getting capability of PITs (partners in training) in local CPA firms in the U.S."

Direct Responsibility. Who in the targeted suspect organization is directly responsible for the need you are able to fill? In my example, the managing partner of the local firm is typically responsible for the development of tomorrow's new partners. But not always. Some of the more aggressive local firms now have marketing people who are responsible for ensuring that the development occurs. This is where your insider understanding pays dividends.

Others Involved. Who else in the suspect organization is involved/concerned and in what ways? Who wants my need solution to succeed, fail? Why? Who will be affected by the solution and in what ways? Later in the chapter, I'll discuss the decision-making unit idea in more detail. In this section your goal is to identify the players in the organization. That way you won't overlook important, future relationships or communications that must be made once you get into the organization.

Negative Consequences. What costs and risks are associated with the unmet need? What additional costs and negative consequences are likely to be incurred if the need is not met at this time? What conclusions can you draw as to the nature of the negative consequences—not serious, acceptable risk, serious, critical, unacceptable risk, and so on?

In my example, the costs are both out-of-pocket and opportunity costs. Too often PITs are told to go out and get new clients without being shown how to go about it. The result is that too many PITs, if they do any new-client development at all, invest too much in entertaining and don't capitalize on their relationships with influentials in targeted niches. A serious, negative consequence of the lack of PIT training in new-client development techniques is the risk of turning them off completely regarding marketing.

Positive Consequences. What benefits are likely to accrue if the need solution is installed at this time? Will new revenue be generated? Will existing revenue be protected? What costs will be reduced or eliminated? What efficiencies will be introduced? Will performance be improved? Will morale be improved? If so, by how much?

In my example, the benefits are numerous and visible. PITs who have been trained in the how-to of client-centered marketing recognize that new-client development is largely the result of leveraging their relationships, problem-solving experience, and insider understanding. For the first time the PITs are enthusiastic and confident. They know what they must do to obtain new clients.

The Solution Goal. State the goal for this need situation here. If you have done a good job of defining the need, the goal will often be a restatement of the need statement. Frequently, the goal statement changes due to the in-depth analysis required to complete the scenario.

You have taken a giant step closer to being in sync with the targeted suspect organizations. The insights gained completing this document will be useful as you develop your initial-contact package, the subject of the next chapter.

SELECTING SUSPECT ORGANIZATIONS

Steps one and two have been completed. Now it is time to determine the targets for the upcoming contact program. If you delight in keeping your data base current, you need go no further. Simply search your mailing criteria. You may also come across new lists or have traded data bases with another professional. You may also draw names from new lists. Finally, there will always be newcomers to the niche no matter how on top of things you are.

Your goal is to select only those organizations and individuals that: (1) Are most likely to have the need you are promoting; (2) Want the need to be solved at this time; (3) Have the necessary funds.

For example, the buying cycle for my CPA suspects is *not* from January through April, because that's their busy season and most communications to them would be shelved. Since that is the case, my likely targets during that period are my other two primary niches—consultants and lawyers—who are not affected by the calendar as much.

Item 3, having the funds available, implies that these funds will be invested in your type of solution. I long ago quit trying to market to one niche on the more technical side of the professions. This group of firms is experiencing rapid consolidation and many business failures. But they are resistant to paying my daily rates, which are about 40 percent higher than theirs, so I no longer go after their work. I do accept new work from the better firms that contact me if they are willing to do what I recommend. We have covered the first part of who—the organizations to be contacted. Now let's look at who to contact in the organization.

The Decision-making Unit

Firms in your target niche characteristically operate in ways that can be identified and charted. By reviewing the history of your most recent engagements with key clients, you can begin to recognize patterns in how a new-purchase decision is made. Who is involved and what are their titles? How many steps are there in the go-ahead decision? Review your Preferred Prospective Client Profile again (Chapter 5) for the clues provided there.

A useful concept in understanding the way target firms are likely to respond to you is to isolate their decision-making unit (DMU). A DMU may contain the following roles:

1. *The Initiator.* This is a person who tends to look outside the firm for your type of services when a need situation arises. In addition to being a leading-edge thinker, this person is often the one who suggested seeking outside help. Quite often the initiator becomes the internal champion for your solution.

2. *The Influencer.* Influencers can be both positive and negative individuals; they are expected to give a yea or nay to the idea of retaining outside services. Since these individuals significantly affect the purchaser's decision, your message to each must be individually tailored and delivered.

3. *The Decision-maker.* This is the individual(s) who actually makes the decision whether to proceed and make a purchase.

4. *The Coordinator or Purchaser.* This individual may not make the decision or be a primary influencer, but will be involved in the purchase, use, and application processes. Often, this person is charged with liaison responsibility with the outside service organization.

5. *The User.* The individual(s) who will be directly or indirectly, intentionally or unintentionally affected by the results of the services you provide.

From previous research, the consultant will appropriately target her mailing to initiators. She recognizes that in smaller firms the initiator and the decison-maker are often one and the same.

What should be apparent now is that, if you have done your homework and have an insider's understanding of the niche, the process of preparing and securing appointments should no longer be the dreaded, feared task that it used to be. You are virtually paving the way for discussions with people who will want to meet with you, and you should be looking forward to them.

In the next chapter, we will integrate what we have learned so far to develop and manage an effective initial-contact program.

9

Developing and Managing Your Initial-contact Program

There are two major components to your initial-contact program: the package that you will be sending to suspect organizations, and the follow-up telephone call you will be making. In this chapter, we will discuss the elements of the initial mailing program. Preparing your telephone conversation guide and actually making the appointment calls will be discussed in detail in Chapter 10.

DEVELOPING THE INITIAL-CONTACT MAILING PACKAGE

Your ability to get clients is directly related to how well you execute your initial-contact mailing program. If you have chosen your targets appropriately, you will be triggering some of the basic buying motives of several recipients of your package.

Buying motives refers to the inner state of the contact person receiving your mailings. They are intellectual and emotional conditions that are present and either incite the person to contact you upon receipt of the package or be receptive to your subsequent telephone contact.

Managing and dealing with buying motives is an important task of the client-centered services seller. If the system you're using now works for you, don't let me mess you up. If you're open to a system that works, read on.

Think back to the three types of need situations I discussed earlier: negative, positive, and short-term task. Let's develop a practical approach to managing and dealing with these motives.

Negative need situations involve fear: fear of failure, and fear of the unknown. A deficiency in the performance of a desired/ required success factor causes fear of failure in most people. A threat situation or a decision that must be made causes fear of the unknown; consequently, fear is often a buying motive. Insurance pros tell me more insurance is bought out of fear than for any other reason.

Positive need situations involve meeting the requirements of the position, feeling good, and looking good to others. There is lots of self-interest. Approval, both of self and by others, is a need probably present.

Task situations primarily involve meeting the requirements of the position. The stakes are usually lower in these situations so the buying motive is probably efficiency and/or effectiveness.

The motive is triggered when a receiver in need reads your initial-contact cover letter and properly prepared enclosure. The appointment-getting telephone call will inflame him if you have properly prepared the scenario. We'll return to these motives a bit later. For now, let's look at what is involved in developing your initial contact package.

The package that you prepare and mail to the targeted suspect requires only two pieces—usually an article that makes your selling point and a cover letter that triggers the buying motive and interests the recipient in reading the enclosure.

Finding and Preparing the Enclosure

One of your key tasks in developing your insider understanding was to identify articles in niche publications that dealt with current changes, problems, and opportunities. Now is the time to turn to your file of niche articles to find one or more that relate to the need situation you are promoting.

Using reprints of articles that have appeared in the niche has at least two key benefits:

1. It demonstrates that you are an insider; you read what they read. This helps build rapport later when you contact the recipient.

2. You leverage on the authority and credibility of a niche influential. The article appeared because the editor was convinced it had reader interest and utility.

There are several criteria for selecting an article for use as an enclosure:

The article should be easy to scan with sidebars, insets, and graphics.

The article must address or relate to the need you are promoting in the cover letter.

It should be solutions oriented, unless you are selling think-tank types of services.

Once you have chosen an article and it has cleared all the hurdles, then contact the publisher. You will need to purchase professional, attractive reprints. Never photocopy the article or article abridgement. In addition to being an infringement of the copyright laws, it conveys a cheap image, which is one you can't afford.

If the reprint is only one or two pages, the probability that your target will read most or all of the article increases dramatically over that of a multipaged article. One sheet is also particularly useful to you because, along with your cover letter, the total package can be sent first class in a number-10 envelope at the minimum rate.

When abridging the original article, use as much of the first page as you can and write on the bottom of the page, "Abridged with permission of the publisher." When your camera-ready copy is complete, you have several options available: you can underline selling points by highlighting them or making marginal notes.

Your goal in using the article is to identify a central theme through the use of the hot button and then to support your position by highlighting paragraphs and sections containing evidence. If you choose to underscore any of the points made in the article, it is best to do this neatly with a light blue felt marker. Light green, light beige, and light orange are also acceptable, but blue is best because it has an authoritative hue.

What you have marked on the article reprint should be the focus of your cover letter. You may also use margin notes, arrows or stars to highlight particular passages, but they must be done very neatly. Post-It (tm) notes are not recommended because they can be pulled off and separated from the article reprint.

Avoid marking too many passages; usually you need only to highlight one to three sections to emphasize the point discussed in the cover letter. Remember, the purpose of the enclosure is to provide an authoritative spokesperson, to reinforce your point, to establish you as an insider, and to begin to alert the prospect about your capabilities in providing solution services.

The article you have chosen and the reprint you have prepared must attract the attention and emotions of the reader. As a general rule of thumb, the more prestigious the publication, the greater impact your initial mailing will make. However, pointed, on-target articles from less prominent publications have been used to great advantage.

Let's say, for example, you are a marketing consultant to the hospital industry. Figure 9.1 is the first page of an article that

*In a new competitive arena,
the challenge is
to maintain both
good care and a
sound financial base*

Strategies
for survival in
the hospital
industry

*Dean C. Coddington,
Lowell E. Palmquist, and
William V. Trollinger*

Hospitals, besieged by new competitors and pressured to cut costs, are entering a new and unfamiliar environment. As usage declines and the government's new prospective payment system makes itself felt, hospitals are feeling the pinch. Nonprofit hospitals face competition from newer, for-profit providers of health care. These authors discuss the factors that have led some hospitals to close and forced most others to consider how they can lower costs while maintaining high-quality care. Several strategies exist to help hospitals cope with their new problems. The authors point out the advantages and disadvantages of downsizing, diversification, and joint ventures, among other practical measures that hospitals can take.

Mr. Coddington is managing director of Browne, Bortz & Coddington, Inc., an applied economic research firm in Denver, and a trustee of Swedish Medical Center in Englewood, Colorado. Mr. Palmquist is president of Swedish Health Systems, Inc. in Englewood and immediate past chairman of the Association of Western Hospitals. Mr. Trollinger is a geologist, co-owner and vice president of exploration of Marsh Oil and Gas Company, an independent petroleum producer, and chairman of the board, Swedish Health Systems.

The health care industry has joined the list of major U.S. industries facing intensely competitive environments. Hospitals, in particular, are plagued by excess capacity, many new types of competitors, and pressures to cut costs drastically.

The United States has always been blessed with excellent health care facilities and services. Now, however, revolutionary changes are sweeping the industry, and it is unclear whether most of the nation's hospitals will be able to remain economically sound while maintaining high-quality care. In this article we discuss several possible strategies to help hospitals deal with these new challenges:

Downsizing, that is, finding ways to reduce the number of beds while remaining economically viable and providing an acceptable level of care.

Becoming a low-cost provider of medical care in order to compete on a price basis.

Increasing market share.

Becoming more specialized and developing centers of special competence.

Diversifying into related health care activities so as to become less dependent on inpatient revenues.

Editor's note All references are listed at the end of the article

FIGURE 9.1. Article Supporting Hot Button (Reprinted by Permission of the *Harvard Business Review.* Excerpt from "Strategies for Survival in the Hospital Industry" by Dean C. Coddington, Lowell E. Palmquist and William V. Trollinger (May/June 1985). Copyright © 1985 by the President and Fellows of Harvard College; all rights reserved.)

appeared in the *Harvard Business Review*. This article supports several hot buttons, including downsizing, specializing, and diversifying. An attractive reprint with the appropriate article section highlighted would strongly support your new-client development program.

Preparing the Cover Letter

A good letter gets right to the point and tells why a meeting with the sender will be beneficial to the receiver. Benefits deal with improving desired situations and correcting undesired situations. Use action verbs, such as *improve, protect, reduce,* and *enhance,* to convey benefits.

There are many advantages to using direct contact letters, including the following:

They are relatively inexpensive

They can offer a personal touch

They afford selectivity

They can be customized

They enhance a desired image

They can be controlled as to timing and content

They help present an organized message

They can be sent to many prospects at once

They help to boost your status, if you are already known by the prospect.

There are also some disadvantages that the following sections will help you overcome. Letters can easily be ignored, may hit the wrong target, or may not be delivered at all. Some prospects may see letters as a hard sell. The communication is somewhat impersonal and one-directional (although with your follow-up calls this attitude can be quickly circumvented). Finally, it may be difficult to differentiate your firm and its services from the scores of other businesses attempting to catch the attention of the target.

Base your letters on the AIDA structure:

Attention. In the opening paragraph or opening sentence mention a strong benefit to the reader. You only have about 20 to 30 seconds to grab the reader's attention. Here are three sample attention grabbers:

"When is the last time your accountant's management letter really talked to management?"

"Is it time to get back to basics?"

"There are two situations in which you will find my services to be an indispensable aid to your firm. First, when you are looking for new clients. Second, when you have got them."

As you can see, posing a question is an excellent way to gain immediate attention. A variation on this theme is to pose a question that is actually a dilemma to the client, such as "How can anyone expect you to manage your growing firm and provide training to your staff?" Here are other possible question leads:

"Is your inventory-control system doing everything that you want it to? For instance is it . . . . ?"

"Are your best clients getting the best of you?"

"How many of your top personnel really know how to . . . ?"

"When was the last time you really got something done about . . . ?"

Though we don't like to admit it, these thought-provoking

questions frequently capture our attention. Another powerful way to open is to describe a favorable circumstance. For example:

> *"When you need expert advice and assistance with XYZ, it is useful to know who you can call for prompt, responsive assistance."*

> *"When your key people say, 'We just have to do something about . . .' you just have to call us to take the first positive step."*

> *"You can provide your firm with its strongest defense against a sluggish economy—an effective marketing and sales training program."*

The attention-grabbing portion of the letter, which I also refer to as the "ho-hum crasher," is the most important feature. In today's competitive market, the typical executive each day receives at least a dozen well prepared appeals and pitches.

Interest. Your letter must stress how your need-driven service solution will enable the reader to better do what she is in business to do. Thus, one of your goals is to promise the prospect that she will be better off by agreeing to meet with you. Your service solution should give her a reason for investing some time and money, and for taking the risks involved in revealing her corporate needs.

Your service must be pitched in a nonthreatening manner. This is done by linking your enclosure to your interest and ability to solve the problem. Your goal is to tap the emotions and develop interest in the mind of the target so that she will agree to meet with you to discuss her concerns. The body of the letter stimulates interest and enhances the idea emphasized in the enclosure. First you make the target aware of a need; then you can emphasize your capability in handling it.

Desire. Next, tactfully remind the reader that she lacks the benefits you can provide, and these benefits can be discussed at a meeting with you. Offer compelling reasons why she should meet with you when you call for an appointment. This is where buying motives are triggered. Use a sentence such as, "Working with an experienced bank-consulting firm improves/reduces/protects. . . ." Notice how that links back to the types of need situations with which you are dealing.

Another motive sentence would be, "Experience shows that morale is the first factor to improve with a program such as ours."

Affirmation. This is the part that separates the men and women from the boys and girls. Make it easy for the contact to meet with you. "I will call you during the week of the 21st to determine if you're interested in meeting." Putting the date in the letter puts the onus on you to call, which is just how you want it to be. All of your work in researching the niche, finding a hot button, and supporting evidence gives you the confidence of knowing that your prospect wants to see you. This last section of your letter, which is literally the last sentence, paves the way for your call. Here are some examples of effective closings:

"I will contact you within five days for an appointment, so you can evaluate our ideas in terms of profit to your organization."

"I will call you in a few days to arrange a convenient meeting."

"I will call you next Thursday morning at 10:15 to arrange an appointment for the following week."

Once you have offered this kind of powerful statement, you are boxed in; you must make the call because you said you would. If you don't make it, you would negate everything else of value in the letter.

Before reviewing some good and bad examples of sample letters and discussing the mechanics of fine tuning your mailing program, here are some additional tips on preparing an effective letter:

Use lots of white space—nobody likes to read a long, involved letter.

Use a you-centered focus, as opposed to an I-centered focus. Remember the Platinum Rule.

Focus your attention on the central need and the benefit promise.

Point out tactfully that she is not alone, she is in good company.

How do you know when you have produced an attention-grabbing letter that paves the way for your forthcoming phone call? One clue is when the reader "marks up" the letter. Over the next few days, save some of the letters that you receive from others who are trying to get your business. Which letters invite your pencil to make margin notes? Those are the ones that are most effective.

Let's look at some sample letters (Figures 9.2 to 9.7). The notes at the bottom of each page have been added to indicate the positive and negative aspects of the letters. The names have been removed to protect the innocent.

FINE-TUNING YOUR INITIAL MAILING

Once you are happy with your letter and its supporting evidence, the next step is to carefully choose 10 contacts to whom you will send a test mailing. These contacts should be representative of the target niche, but shouldn't be among your 10 best prospects. You could also send one to a client, but let him or her know it is coming. In addition, you should include a note on top

First Name *Last Name*
Title
Address
City, *State* *Zip*

Dear Mr. *Last Name*

Ensuring profitability and long-term financial security just became a lot more certain, thanks to the GETTING NEW CLIENTS Workshop.

Where other workshops fail, this systematic approach to developing profitable new business succeeds. The reason is that it doesn't try to make salesmen out of professionals. Instead, it capitalizes on what they do best—solve important problems for clients.

The enclosed article points out the advantages of using "guerrilla" marketing techniques—dominating a niche, building leverage relationships with key players in the niche, earning an insider's reputation, and staying away from fee-sensitive selling situations, all the topics covered in the Workshop.

The GETTING NEW CLIENTS Workshop presents the strategies, tactics and techniques to take your firm profitably into the 90s. In only three days of intensive training your professional people will be out doing the things that produce results, at a fraction of the costs involved in traditional selling programs.

I will call you on Tuesday morning, March 16, to determine your specific situation, and answer any questions you might still have.

Very truly yours,

Richard A. Connor, Jr. CMC
The Client-centered (tm)
Marketing Mentor

FIGURE 9.2. Sample Letter by Dick Connor

February 11, 1987

Mr. Jeffrey P. Davidson, CMC
3709 S. George Mason Dr. #315E
Falls Church, VA 22041

Dear Jeff:

① Perhaps no word in the English language can strike fear—or even loathing—into the heart of a successful businessperson faster than the word . . .

"consultant."

Nobody enjoys paying to hear high-falutin' ideas from an outsider who doesn't know as much about your business as **you** know.

But **every** business, at one time or another, can benefit by sitting down with a "pro"—an interested, informed, experienced, <u>successful</u> person who can look at a problem (or <u>an opportunity</u>!) and cut through company habits, or industry traditions, to find a solution or a new road to profits.

Every "winner" I've ever met has told me, <u>point-blank</u>, that <u>he or she</u> ⑤ <u>learns more from competitors than from any other source.</u>

Now, **you** can talk with a competitor, too—without feeling guilty about it. Oh, maybe I haven't been your **direct** competition, but in 40 years as chief executive officer and chief operating officer of several multi-million-dollar companies, I've gone toe-to-toe with the giants AND the pygmies of American industry. And won. I'd be proud to talk with you.

The simple "brochure" I'm enclosing will take you about 7 minutes to ③ read. When you've read it, you may want to drop me a note, or talk with me on the phone. I'd be glad to hear from you! ⑥

Cordially,
Norman Rubin, President
N   R   G
The Norman Rubin Group
Consulting
771 Larchmont Road
Elmira, New York 14905
607–732–8810

POSITIVES	NEGATIVES
1. Good grabber	4. Longish
2. Vibrant style	5. Too many underlines
3. Timed reading	6. Passive finish

FIGURE 9.3. Letter from Norman Rubin. Reprinted with permission.

Dear

① At a time when every marketing dollar must be more productive in generating new sales, our work consistently provides that critical "plus" that builds effective results for our clients.

_____ is an established advertising and promotional design firm that focuses on successfully promoting its client's *products, services* and *identities* through in-depth marketing expertise, industry knowledge and award-winning design.

We can help maximize your image in the corporate/real estate and consumer community by emphasizing your firm's flexibility and creativity, characteristics that are essential in today's competitive real-estate world. This can be achieved through successful channels of corporate communications, promotional brochures, annual reports, trade and consumer advertising, and visual presentations.

At present, a variety of firms uses our services, including AIG Life ④ Insurance Company, GAB Insurance Corporation, International Commodity Services, Ogilvy & Mather, Cottage Technologies, Interior Design, Burlington Industries, and American Hospital Products, among others.

Based on our proven performance, I look forward to meeting with you to discuss your specific needs and make you aware of our corporate and promotional-design services. I believe we can prove to be a valuable resource for your present and future projects.

I will call you in a few days to arrange a convenient meeting. ⑤

Sincerely,

POSITIVES
1. Grabber opening
2. Original had attractive design
5. Good close but . . .

NEGATIVES
3. Wordy, unclear
4. Too much information
5. He never called!

FIGURE 9.4. Sample Letter

Dear

① Recognizing that your time is valuable, I will be brief and to the point.

② I would like to establish a working relationship with your firm by providing my expertise as a computer consultant to your clients. In this capacity, I would be pleased to involve and/or train your staff and share the work and fees with your firm.

③ This may be an added important resource for providing total service to your clients.

Thank you for your consideration. I will be available at your ④
convenience to discuss a specific client need or to provide additional ⑤
information.

A brief biographical summary is attached for your review. ⑥

Very truly yours, ⑦

POSITIVES
1. Brief
2. Good grabber

NEGATIVES
3. "I" centered
4. Indefinite
5. Passive
6. Too much like a job application
7. Overly affectionate
8. No call for action or mention of call

FIGURE 9.5. Sample Letter

Dear

Today's financial institutions are seeking new and innovative ways to (1)
market their services to corporate and individual clients. ABC has
emerged as a distinctive new option in the design, publication, and (2)
communication fields in the Washington metropolitan area.

ABC is committed to assisting your institution with the production of
superior quality print communications materials that today's intelligent
consumer has come to expect. Each of your creative promotional
programs, direct-marketing packages, and advertising campaigns
deserves the level of sophistication and style that ABC provides.

We offer a variety of services, including graphic design, production,
typesetting, copywriting, editing, and print and mail management,
which enables us to provide your institution with a host of print
communication packages, such as:

   ☐ Annual Reports   ☐ Publications
   ☐ Identity Programs   ☐ Signage
   ☐ Direct Mail Packages ☐ Advertising Promotions
       ☐ Audio-Visual Presentations

Quality control for each project is of paramount importance. Our
in-house capabilities allow us to monitor every phase of production
closely to ensure that the final product meets professional standards
and your institution's expectations.

(3) Timely service, personal attention, and a competitive pricing structure
are our assurances. The brochure, folder, and stationery enclosed are
examples of the high caliber of design produced by our award-winning
creative team.

(4) We look forward to showing you our portfolio.

Sincerely,

POSITIVES
Original had attractive print style on a good quality of
paper. The letter made a statement before it was read.

NEGATIVES
1. Laborious Reading
2. Not Client-Centered
3. Awkward Style
4. Indefinite

FIGURE 9.6. Sample Letter

①

Dear

② [Our company] is starting a syndicated survey of firms that we think you'll be interested in.

This new survey, [name], is designed to provide information that will help major accounting firms in the planning, implementation and evaluation of their marketing efforts.

The survey will be conducted nationally once a year among CFOs in large companies.

[Name] is designed to measure over time:

☐ Familiarity with major accounting firms
☐ Communications received from major accounting firms
☐ The images of major accounting firms
☐ Accounting firms used in the past year and would use if selecting a new firm

I've asked Jim Miller, a Vice President of [our company], to call you during the next few days to find out whether you would like to know   ③
more about [our system]. He's our "Accounting Firm Specialist" and
will be able to answer any questions you have about [our system].   ④

Sincerely,

POSITIVES	NEGATIVES
Good use of space	1. Original had name & title wrong
Simple wording	2. Starts with "We"
	3. Doesn't reflect insider's understanding
	4. Responsibility passed along
	5. He never called!

FIGURE 9.7. Sample Letter

of your grabber letter such as "Test Mailing No. 1." In other words, on this original mailing you are actively seeking input as to how to improve your presentation: You are not directly seeking an appointment or soliciting new business. However, if either occurs, you will certainly not turn it down.

When mailing, never send more than you can comfortably follow up within five to seven working days. I advocate mailing on Thursday and calling the following Wednesday or Thursday. Regardless of how well a letter is written, it is virtually useless unless followed up with a telephone call. And you must make a persuasive phone call if you want to progress with the right people.

Five days after your contacts receive your letter, it is time to call them. Your primary purpose in calling each contact is to determine the following:

Do they remember receiving the letter?

Is the need I have identified real and important to them? If not, will it be important in the future?

Were they the appropriate contacts within the organization? If not, who are the appropriate individuals?

During these calls, seek opportunities to gather additional insider information and to strengthen and expand your own comfort zone. If the conversation really gets rolling, then even on these test calls, make an appointment. If your test calls were representative of the target-contact universe, and your phone call suggested a fine tuning, the time to do so is now.

If the majority of contacts felt that your hot button was not of great concern to them, you will have to reexamine your niche data base and all the steps that led to your decision to choose that hot button. For some reason, it was not valid and something else needs to be selected. Perhaps the need was quickly solved in-house; or perhaps the author of the article overstated the case or relied on inaccurate figures. There are many reasons why you might have been off target. With very little time and effort, you will be able to make another selection that is on target. The hot button that you should be using may very well be handed to you while test calling.

What if you have identified an appropriate hot button, but your cover letter lacks punch? Reread the section on preparing your letter and graciously accept any criticisms that are made during the test calls. Remember, this is just a test; consequently, if anything requires modification, it is better to know now.

After you have restructured your letter or identified a new hot button to use, go to 10 new contacts.

For the test mailing and any other mailings, it is recommended that your contact package arrive during midweek. On Mondays, you are competing with too many other attention grabbers. On Fridays, you run the risk of reaching a contact whose receptiveness is less than desirable or who may cool off about your hot idea over the weekend. If you don't follow up with a call within five to seven business days, you have virtually lost them. Look at your own desk, and consider how much mail you get on a weekly basis. If it is under 30 or 40 pieces, I will be surprised. Any message that you send in today's junk-mail society simply has to be followed up by a human voice.

After mailing letters to your first 10 contacts, choose another 10 contacts representative of the target niche. These should not be your best possible prospects, but should represent firms and organizations that you would like to have as clients. Then repeat all of the steps outlined above. A third, fourth, and fifth test mailing is recommended until you have a winning package.

How do you know when your contact package is ready? When the recipients of the test mailing are very receptive, keep you on the phone for a long time, are interested in getting together, and start volunteering information that adds to your insider's understanding. When you have produced a contact package that is on target your confidence will shoot right up. Thereafter, getting appointments, and ultimately new clients, could actually become fun.

10

Getting Appointments with High-Potential Prospective Clients

In the previous chapter we examined the steps involved in developing and managing your initial mailing package, one of the two activities of developing and managing your initial-contact program.

Popular speaker and consultant, David Alan Yoho of the Professional Educators Group in Bethesda, Maryland says, "It is entirely possible for someone who dislikes using the telephone to employ it successfully in his or her work." If you ordinarily do things systematically, the phone can become one of your greatest marketing allies. This chapter presents a proven, step-by-step appointment-getting system that lets you "win at getting in."

IT'S EASIER THAN YOU THINK!

Many professional-service providers dread using the telephone for marketing purposes. Many regard making a follow-up telephone call on a par with making a cold call. A seasoned professional once confided, "Phoning for appointments is Maalox time at the old heartburn corral." Others worry it to death, and if they do make a few calls without getting an appointment, they quickly give it up as a bad idea.

I can relate to these feelings. Before I devised the approach I present in this chapter, I, too, experienced many of the same feelings. A throbbing headache and an occasional upset stomach were the payoffs for my investment. But that was before I developed the targeted-niche approach. Now I still don't *enjoy* making the calls, but they don't bother me as they once did.

Whether we like it or not, the winning professional-service marketers of the late 1980s and 1990s will be those who have mastered the use of the telephone.

A STEP BACK TO SEE AHEAD

Let's step back a moment and review why your targets *want* to hear from you. You have researched the niche, identified a hot button, gathered supporting evidence, developed a cover letter, test-marketed your package, refined the package, test-marketed it again if necessary, obtained feedback from test-market contacts, and, finally, produced a truly suspect-centered contact package. Now you are ready to step into the big arena and make the appointment-getting call. Contacts have received your package five business days earlier. In your package you told them you would be calling to discuss their needs.

PREPARING YOUR TELESCRIPT

I recommend using a telephone script, which is a road map to obtaining an appointment. Properly prepared, it can provide you with a proven track on which to run. Scripts enable you to adapt your rate of speech, timing and reflection, intention and vocal expression because you have the necessary data to handle the situations you encounter. Let's look at an effective telescript format that I use, which is based on the best ideas I gained during my 17 years of experience.

There are six steps to an effective telescript. I'll review each briefly and then discuss them later in greater depth.

1. *Introduction.* When the phone is answered, you introduce yourself and ask for the suspect by first name.

2. *Purpose in Calling.* You refer to the letter you mailed the previous week to see if the person remembers receiving it.

3. *Trigger the Buying Motive.* You review the grabber statement and the solution benefit mentioned in your cover letter.

4. *Trial Close.* Since your objective is not to sell the engagement, but to get the suspect to buy your recommendation of meeting with you, you determine if the contact is ready to meet with you. The trigger and trial close statements are made together.

5. *Contact Concerns and Objections.* You patiently and professionally answer your contact's questions and try again to set a date for the appointment.

6. *Confirm Next Step.* You confirm what will occur after you complete the telephone call. You'll send additional information, call again at a later date, strike the name from your mailing list, or set up the upcoming appointment.

For Telephobics Only

If you are still a bit uneasy about this topic, take heart—the number of negative incidents from making a telephone contact are very low. Let's examine the mindset of those who would rather do anything than get on the phone and ask for an appointment. What usually occurs is the feeling that the contact will loudly and roundly chastise you with one of the following responses:

> *"How dare you call me in the middle of a busy day to talk about your services."*

"Don't you ever call me again — you got that, I never want to hear from you again."

"I have no interest in you, your services, or anything you have to say.'

"Who the hell are you?"

"Where do you get the nerve to ask me for an appointment?'

"You G__ D___ SO_. You salespeople are all alike. Stop bothering me."

· *"Why don't you take a flying leap, buddy!"*

Read each possible response slowly and carefully. Now get them out of your system because you are never going to encounter them. And even if that remote possibility does occur and someone responds that way, it would be his problem, not yours.

The probability is medium to high that you will get a large number of rejections. However, using the client-centered approach developed in this book will effectively lower the probability of rejection because of your insider's understanding and reputation within the niche, your identification of a hot button, and your improving telephone skills. While the chance of getting an appointment is low, you must remember that every "No" brings you closer to a "Yes."

If you are concerned about tarnishing your image, forget it. You won't get a bad image because you use the telephone to secure appointments with target organizations. Recall that you are not trying to sell your services over the phone. You are simply trying to get the prospect to invest time meeting with you.

Many professionals still get anxious after having used the phone for 10, 20 years or more. The anxiety stems from feeling they are interrupting someone and trying to get them to buy something. A more useful and productive way to think is to remember how successfully served your Key and A clients were. Now, would you want to deny these types of benefits to others, just because they are not fully acquainted with you yet?

Unfortunately, the automatic response of mankind to any new suggestion, change, request, or idea is "No." The vast majority of rejections you receive have nothing to do with you, your firm, or the service need you have identified. Once you are able to depersonalize the rejection process, you free yourself to make more productive calls.

THE PROSPECT-CENTERED APPOINTMENT-GETTING SYSTEM

Now, it is time to put the structure of the telephone call into a larger perspective and discuss the specific steps involved in preparing for making effective telephone follow-up contacts.

1. Who am I calling and what is the best time to call? The chart on page 192, "Prospect Calling Times," shows the best hours for calling various prospects. Again, this is where the benefit of developing an insider's understanding comes in handy— you know the ebb and flow of the contact's industry and work environment.

2. Arrange for privacy. You don't want loud talking or ringing telephones to interrupt you. Nor do you want someone walking into your office and disturbing your concentration.

3. Clear your desk of everything not associated with making your appointment-getting calls.

4. Arrange your desk for action:

Put the list of names and telephone numbers you intend to make that day to your left if you are right-handed.

PROSPECT CALLING TIMES

Prospects	Best Time to Call
Chemists and engineers	Between 4 p.m. and 5 p.m.
Contractors and builders	Before 9 a.m. or after 5 p.m.
Dentists	Before 9:30 a.m.
Entrepreneurs	Before 8:30 a.m. or after 5 p.m.
Executives and business leaders	After 10:30 a.m.
Homemakers	Between 10 a.m. and 11 a.m.
Lawyers	Between 11 a.m. and 2 p.m.
Merchants, store heads, and department heads	After 10:30 a.m.
Physicians and surgeons	Between 9 a.m. and 11 a.m.; after 4 p.m.
Professors, instructors, teachers	At home, between 6 p.m. and 7 p.m.
Public accountants	Anytime during the day, but avoid January 2 through April 15
Publishers and printers	After 3 p.m.
Low-salaried people and government employees	Call at home
Stockbrokers and bankers	Before 10 a.m. or after 3 p.m.

Open your calendar to the week in which you are going to schedule appointments. Since my calender has a tendency to close by itself, I prop it open by putting my stapler on top of it; consequently, I don't have to fumble around trying to suggest times to meet.

```
┌─────────────────────────────────────────────────────────────┐
│                  SUSPECT INTERVIEW NOTES                      │
│                                                               │
│   Date:    / / ,  / / ,  / / ,  / / ,  / /                    │
│            1      2      3      4      5                       │
│                                                               │
│   Name of Organization: _____  │
│                                                               │
│   Name of Contact: _____  │
│                                                               │
│   Telephone Number: _____  │
│                                                               │
│   Results of Contact(s):                                      │
│                                                               │
│                                                               │
│                                                               │
│                                                               │
│   Next Step:                                                  │
│                                                               │
│                                                               │
│                                                               │
│                                                               │
└─────────────────────────────────────────────────────────────┘
```

FIGURE 10.1. Suspect Interview Notes

Place a pad entitled "Suspect Interview Notes" near the telephone to write notes. Figure 10.1 is a copy of such a form that has served me and my clients very well.

The form should be used to quickly capture essential information while talking with prospects over the phone. It has a twofold purpose, serving as a conversation guide and data sheet. Undoubtedly there will be many holes left open following most telephone conversations. These can be filled in as you gain more information about the prospect, hopefully after your on-site appointment. Consequences of not using this form are severe. You will be likely to make inconsistent margin notes on any paper from your prospect files. Or, you may end up not being able to retrieve and use complete information about the prospect that would support you in subsequent conversations. As new data are added, they should be dated. Later, this form can be used to update your niche data base.

Hereafter, keep track of all prospect calls that you make (Figure 10.2). There are several reasons for maintaining a tracking system of all prospect calls. First, you need to determine the number of calls required to get one appointment. As we saw back in Chapter 3, these kinds of statistics help you develop your hit ratio—the level of effort necessary to generate one new client.

If one appointment can be gained for every four calls you make, then obviously to get 10 appointments you will have to make 40 calls. If two new clients can be generated for every 10 appointments, and you have a goal of obtaining 12 new clients in the next three months, then you will have to make 240 calls. This sounds like a lot of work, but actually breaks down to only 10 calls each Wednesday and Thursday over a 12-week period. If you have more than one person responsible for making the calls, the effort is even less so.

If you have a telephone answering machine with a two-way recording device or otherwise have access to equipment that enables you to tape your telephone conversations, experts recommend that you do so. This is important for several reasons:

- ☐ You may miss many of the key points the prospect is making, no matter how fast you write.

- ☐ Upon second and third hearing, voice cues may reveal more information than you were able to gather upon first hearing.

- ☐ The tape will serve as an excellent instructional vehicle for helping improve your telephone performance.

- ☐ For conversations in which you are particularly pleased with your efforts, the tape can be used as an instructional tool for others in your firm.

```
┌─────────────────────────────────────────────────────────────┐
│                        CALLING LOG                            │
│                                                               │
│   Date:      / /                                              │
│                                                               │
│   Name: _____ │
│                            (or caller)                        │
│                                                               │
│   Name of Organization: _____ │
│                                                               │
│      Numbers Called            Results            Next Step   │
│                                                               │
│     1. _____        _____        _____   │
│                                                               │
│     2. _____        _____        _____   │
│                                                               │
│     3. _____        _____        _____   │
│                                                               │
│     4. _____        _____        _____   │
│                                                               │
│     5. _____        _____        _____   │
│                                                               │
│     6. _____        _____        _____   │
│                                                               │
│     7. _____        _____        _____   │
│                                                               │
│     8. _____        _____        _____   │
│                                                               │
│     9. _____        _____        _____   │
│                                                               │
│    10. _____        _____        _____   │
│                                                               │
└─────────────────────────────────────────────────────────────┘
```

FIGURE 10.2. Calling Log

☐ Taping is a sensitive subject with many. Obviously any taping you do must be done with equipment that is unobtrusive or you are liable to interfere with the communication process between you and the prospect.

☐ Set up your mirror so that you can catch yourself, and keep yourself smiling. I know this sounds silly, but the very best telemarketers use one at all times. Let's leverage off the experience of others whenever we can.

Over the years, I have found it valuable to produce a personal "confidence card" that I keep by the phone. Figure 10.3 shows

1. I have valuable services that many nonclients need and that will enable them to improve their operations.
2. People are somtimes hesitant to make appointments over the phone. This does not mean they are rejecting me or my idea.
3. I have succeeded before and I will succeed today!
4. I have a perfect right and responsibility to discuss my services with eligible prospects.

FIGURE 10.3. Confidence Card

what my card says. Have your confidence card propped up in front of you to derive support from this technique.

Next set your goals for today. I set a goal of reaching three contacts before I take a break. For every conversation I have with a target, my statistics show that four out of five attempts have been made. It's a fact of life that people are busy and have become increasingly resistant to accepting telephone calls from peddlers. Too many of the executives you will be attempting to see will have been burned by hustlers who use all sorts of lies and half-truths to try to get around the contact's "peddler protection shield," his secretary, or another third party—more on this subject a bit later.

Finally, place a copy of your telescript, Figure 10.4, and a reprint of your answers to their objections within reach. Now you are ready to get into high gear.

MAKING THE TELEPHONE CALL

This discussion of the telephone contact in-depth follows the advice of David Alan Yoho, a speaker and consultant from Bethesda, Maryland.

1. *Introduction.* Proper telephone use for prospecting begins with a natural-sounding conversation; do not sound as if you

---

TELESCRIPT: THE OPENING LINE

Mr/Ms/Miss _____ PLEASE

Mr/Ms/Miss _____ , I'M _____ WITH _____

_____

MY REASON FOR CALLING IS _____

_____

_____

Do you recall receiving my letter?

If no: "I'm glad I called you today. If it had reached you, you'd
know I'm calling to see if it makes sense for us to meet and

discuss ways in which you can improve _____."
                                                      (need situation)

If yes: "Good. As you recall, I mentioned that we work with

_____ in
                 (his type of organization)

_____ .
            (known/suspected need)

My reason for calling you today is to see if it makes sense for us to meet

and discuss ways in which you can improve _____ .
                                             (need situation)

If no

  Oh?

  "May I ask why?"

If yes

  Express appreciation

  Establish specifics

    Day and time
    Location
    Participants

FIGURE 10.4. Telescript

were reading from a script or following a prepared format. We have all encountered ineffective telemarketers who begin the conversation with "Good Morning Mr. X, how are you this morning?" The conversation is stilted, forced, canned, and uninspiring. It only takes a nanosecond to determine that this is a telephone pitch: our resistance starts immediately. While remaining polite, we wait for a break in the conversation to say, "Sorry, I am just not interested."

When the phone is answered, introduce yourself before asking for the suspect. For example, say "Good morning, this is Bill Jones calling for Ralph Winters." If someone else has answered and tells you that he is not available, determine if the contact person is his secretary. If this person says yes, say "Good! What is the best time for me to speak to him briefly?" Get the receptionist's name, offer thanks and call back at the given time. If you are transferred to Ralph Winters or you reach Ralph Winters directly, say "Mr. Winters, this is Bill Jones with Star Services Inc." The reason you repeat their name is to make them feel important and to reduce the psychological distance. At all times, remember to pause, keep smiling, and stay relaxed.

2. *Reason for Calling.* "I recently sent you a letter and article that you should have received by Tuesday. Did you receive it?" If the prospect has not received it, doesn't remember receiving it, or, for whatever reason, can't make reference to it, tell him or her that you will resubmit the letter and be back in touch. Then place that prospect in the next round of calls.

In those cases when the prospect says that he or she did not receive your package and you feel particularly confident, instead of offering to remail the package, you could launch right into "Well, I am glad I called you because in the letter I mentioned . . . ," then continue on to ask for the appointment.

If the prospect has received the package, the likely reply will be one of the following:

> *"Yes, I got it a couple of days ago, but I haven't had a chance to look at it."*

"Yes, I looked it over and then filed it somewhere."

"Yes, I know I have it here somewhere."

"I believe so. What did you want to say?"

3. *Trigger the Buying Motive.* At this point, you launch immediately into a brief review of what was in the contact package. "As we discussed in the letter and article, containing costs is a big factor in the plastics industry. Cost control is an area in which we have developed some effective methods that could be quite useful to your business. I would like to meet with you for no more than 30 minutes next Tuesday or Thursday. Does it make sense for us to get together?"

Here is another way to approach prospects: "Ms. X, a short time ago, I sent you a letter and an article that discussed the PQR situation facing organizations in your industry. As I mentioned in the letter, our firm works with companies like yours to [solve the problem mentioned in the article]. My reason for calling you today is to arrange a time for us to discuss your situation."

All the while, visualize a friendly person on the other end of the line who is seriously considering your message and the information you have sent. If you are cut off or rejected, consider that you're now one "no" closer to a "yes."

4. *Trial Close.* You'll note that the trigger and trial close are offered in the same paragraph, shown above. This is by design. You want to make the major buy decision for now, the appointment, the central focus.

5. *Handling any Objection.* No matter how prepared you are, and even if the prospect has the need you have identified, you are still likely to encounter objections. Why might a prospect object? The number of reasons is endless, but here are a few:

Fear that your services are costly.

So busy they can't find the time to meet.

Such bad shape that the need you have identified was fifth on the list!

Already retained someone to help them with this problem.

Are skeptical of you, your firm, its services (or anyone in your industry).

Afraid that in handling this problem you will encounter many other problems.

Don't see the consequences of not acting now.

Yoho classifies objections into four major areas:

1. *Money.* How much will it cost? Are your prices competitive? What is the payment schedule? What kind of return can I get on my investment?

2. *Indecision.* Who are you? How long have you been offering this service? Why should I buy from you? When do I need this?

3. *Weak Desire.* This doesn't fit our needs. We already have enough. It is being taken care of. It doesn't come up that often. I don't think it is that important.

4. *Time.* How long will this take? I don't have the time. How should I spend my time? How long will it take to provide this service?

Listed below are suggested answers to the most frequently encountered objections. Your task is to rewrite them to fit your personal and professional comfort zone.

"I'm not interested in buying anything!"

"Ms. Griffin, I appreciate what you're saying. It will only take 20 minutes for you to decide if my ideas are useful to you. I'll be brief and to the point. Would Monday or Wednesday be better for you?"

"I'm already served by ( )"

"Mr. Watkins, you don't want to waste your time meeting with me because you are satisfied with the service you are getting from your present accountant, right? I appreciate your concern. In today's environment, though, I find it unusual for anyone to have all the good ideas about STV. My purpose in calling you today is to see if it makes sense for us to share ideas; we'll both be better off for our meeting. Would Thursday or next Tuesday be better for you?"

"Tell me over the phone"

(Laughingly) "You like to get right to the point—that's great! You don't want to waste your time discussing something that isn't of value to you, right? Tell you what, let's meet for no more than 28 minutes to look at my plan for VWX. You'll be able to see how the ideas can work for you. Would Tuesday or Wednesday be better for you?"

"I don't have the time"

"Mr. McMahon, I appreciate that. We are all too busy to waste time on meeting people who can't contribute to our development. That's why I'm calling you. It's been my experience that we'd both benefit from meeting to discuss DEF. Would Tuesday or Wednesday be better for you?"

Notice that when answering an objection you close by asking for an appointment.

Veteran sales trainers regard objections merely as opportunities to gain more information about the prospect. They also serve as guideposts to make an appointment. Yoho says to use the objection to your advantage, such as, "I am glad we got this out in the open. I am going to enjoy meeting you."

If the prospect is still reluctant to give you an appointment, then thank him or her for talking with you and listening to your message. Send a follow-up thank-you note. Then file the information for future reference and use whatever information you learned to be more effective with the next prospect. If the prospect is a prominent member of the niche, you may be encountering him again. Your first contact, if it was professional and cordial, will pave the way for future discussions. Also, keep in mind that since you are developing an insider's reputation in the niche, those that won't meet with you will still be seeing your name and hearing about you from others. In essence, a good, qualified suspect remains one, even if you can't land an appointment now.

6. *Confirm the Next Step.* If the prospect agrees to meet you, you only have to establish the date and time, location, and the participants. Then, thank him and close by saying something like, "I look forward to meeting you."

Be sure to let the prospect hang up first. You don't want to convey that you are in a hurry, anxious, or happy to get this call over with.

Keeping the Momentum Going

One pitfall of using the phone is to stop after a few calls, whether or not you are getting results. When you obtain an appointment, feel free to celebrate. Stand up, stretch, get yourself some coffee. But, then get back to your *winning ways;* you have more calls to make. Don't consider the job done until you have made your quota of calls, including your callbacks. When you get an appointment, be sure to send out a confirmation letter that says nothing more than, "Looking forward to our meeting on Wednesday the 7th at 2:15 at your office."

If you are interrupted while making calls or have trouble getting started, rehearse mentally. Visualize yourself talking with a pleasant person who is willing to listen to your ideas for improving or protecting something of value to him or her. Each call you make is new. I don't care if you have encountered six "nos" in a row; the next call may result in an appointment that brings in a high paying, longstanding client.

Most professionals prefer to call in privacy. If you are among them, make sure you are not disturbed during this time. Continue to use the supporting materials you have assembled, such as your confidence card and telephone script.

Once you begin to become adept at calling for appointments, start establishing quotas for yourself. For example, if you have decided to make 10 calls on Wednesday morning between 9:45 and 11:45 a.m., how many appointments do you intend to get? Two? Three? Pick a number and go for it.

Dealing with Third Parties

Often, you will be encountering a receptionist or secretary who screens your target-contact calls. Obviously, the higher up the person is in the organization, and the larger the organization, the more well defined the screening process will be. Over the years, I found that the best strategy for handling a third party who stands between you and your target contact is to level with them.

"May I ask what this is in reference to?"

(Pleasantly) "I sent her a package last week and promised to call her at this time. Is she in?"

Even if the person is not in, the fact that you called when you said you would and properly left a message will score you some points. The probability of the target calling back increases when he is handed a message that says you called exactly when you said you would. Ask the intermediary if he or she could suggest the best time for you to call back. If given a time, thank the intermediary and convey the message to the target that you will be calling back at X o'clock. Then, of course, do so.

If the intermediary can't suggest a time to call back, then offer one. If you are calling in the morning, choose a time during the afternoon. If you are calling in the afternoon, choose a time the next morning.

If the intermediary is uncooperative, remain pleasant but professional. "He is very busy right now and won't be available for several days. Why don't you leave your number, and I will see that he gets it." If you are confronted with this type of response or one that is even less informative, you have several options. First you can use the technique of super seller Joe Gandolfo: State your business, using such words as "I have a message of importance." Then, issue a polite order, "Kindly put him through to me." Or you can inform the intermediary that you will be calling back on such and such a day at such and such a time. The day and time that you select should be one day after the "busy" period. Alternatively, inform the intermediary that you will send a follow-up letter. In essence, the letter will say, "When I called you last week, I learned it was a very busy period for you. I will give you a call next Wednesday at 11:30."

Whatever you do, don't make the intermediary wrong. They are paid to do what they do and may frequently be confronted by overly aggressive, rude, or otherwise unprofessional callers. Stand your ground, remain unflustered and professional, and convey your intentions. Your professional demeanor does get back to the target person and will pay off in the long run.

Joseph Sugarman in his insightful book *Success Forces* says that he can tell by the way the caller treats his receptionist or secretary whether or not he will want to get in touch with the caller. Those who behave as blowhards to the intermediary, and sugar and spice to the target, are revealing their true nature.

Sugarman tells of the time when the president of a major manufacturing firm was passing through town and called Sugarman, who was out of the office. The caller could have used considerable leverage with the intermediary to obtain information as to where and when Sugarman could be reached. Instead, he was among the politest and most cooperative callers Sugarman's company had encountered.

TELEPHONE DO'S AND DON'TS

DO'S	DON'TS
Come to the point	Ramble
Ask questions	Assume the answer
Accept the target's point of view	Argue
Compliment the competition	Knock the competition
Talk with them	Talk at them
Talk about the listener	Talk about yourself
Visualize the listener	Daydream
Sit erect (move around or even stand if it helps you)	Slouch in your seat
Control your emotions	React to their negativeness
Sell solutions	Sell hardware and techniques
Thank them	Hang up first

©1983 David Alan Yoho

FIGURE 10.5. Telephone DO'S and DON'TS

Above is a list of telephone do's and don'ts; some will increase your effectiveness, others will decrease it.

If you follow these tips, you will easily surpass 95 to 98 percent of all professional services marketers in effective use of the telephone.

11

Preparing for the Discussion

Conducting new-business discussions is very expensive in terms of time and energy invested: to make them cost-effective, they must be planned, managed, and leveraged. I am always surprised by the lack of preparation with which so many professionals enter a new-business discussion; too many veterans wing it instead of carefully preparing their discussion. "You never have a second chance to make a favorable first impression" is a truism that couldn't be more applicable than to marketing. Another such expression also has merit, "By failing to plan you plan to fail."

Why don't professionals prepare for new-business discussions? Because few have been taught how to do so. Even though the busy professional is told what to do, he or she is seldom told how to do it. The popular literature has not been very helpful, either. Consequently, effective planning is not undertaken.

This chapter will discuss the steps involved in planning new-business discussions, and the importance of getting to the prospect's office on time and in an alert, relaxed condition. In addition, it will also cover the issue of how long to wait for a prospect.

OBJECTIVES FOR NEW-BUSINESS DISCUSSIONS

There are seven basic objectives of a new-business discussion, two of which apply in all situations. These two objectives are creating a favorable awareness with the prospect even if he or she does not purchase your service at this time; and increasing your insider's understanding of the niche.

The remaining five objectives of new-business discussions are presented in Figure 11.1. Depending on the nature of the need situation, where the discussion leads, and the level of interest and enthusiasm on the part of the contact, one or more of them may be achieved. The five objectives are:

1. *Setting an Appointment for the Next Meeting.* When the contact is enthused, and you have more to talk about.

2. *Beginning a Proposal, a Survey, or Research.* If the need situation is complex and requires in-depth analysis in order to prepare your solution program, your objective would be to have the prospect agree to your recommendation that you conduct a survey or research project. If your solution program involves a large fee, or if it is likely that the prospective client will insist on a proposal being prepared, then this would be your primary objective. This occurs as a result of a need expressed by the prospect and is a prelude to possible new business.

3. *Obtain Referrals and Leads.* As a byproduct of sharing ideas regarding the target's situation, you can often obtain the names of others who may be interested in your service solutions.

4. *Place this Prospect in the Future File.* If there is currently little or no interest on the part of the contact, remember that needs can change quickly. Tell the prospect when you will call next.

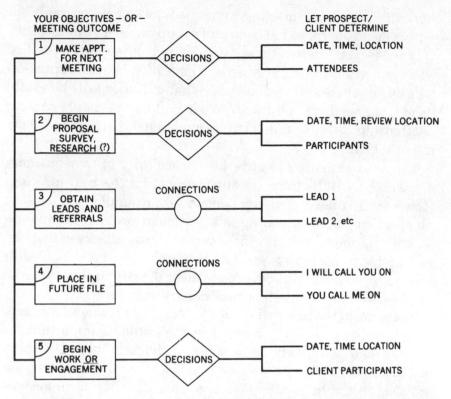

FIGURE 11.1. Objectives/Outcomes of a New-Business Discussion

5. *Begin Work.* As a result of your appointment, the prospect may actually become a client and work may begin shortly.

Usually, while making your appointment-getting telephone call, you have some clue as to which of these five objectives might be achieved as a result of your on-site visit. However, realistically you must be prepared for unpredictable situations. This is where you establish a fallback or contingency objective. For example, if the contact sounded enthusiastic over the phone and practically indicated that you could begin work immediately, your objective would be to close for the commitment to begin work. If during your meeting some roadblocks emerge, your objective then is to try to fall back and set up another appointment.

Now, as you review these five desired outcomes, visualize what you will be doing to make each a reality. What information will be acquired and exchanged? What attitudes will be established, changed, or solidified? What will be the nature of your relationship during this getting-acquainted period and how might it change?

The most realistic objective for the majority of new-business discussions will be to set an appointment for the next meeting. However, the unexpected often occurs. For example, you and the prospect may have agreed upon a particular problem area while on the telephone; on site, however, you may discover that the real problem lies elsewhere. Consequently, you must now shift your focus to the real problem and steer the discussion toward a needs assessment and other preliminary activities.

In any case, when meeting face to face, your fundamental task is to leverage your time invested in the available opportunities and proceed as quickly as possible to the next steps. In some instances, the next step may be nothing more than placing the prospect in the future file. When such a situation becomes apparent, the professional way to handle it is to conclude the discussion in as pleasant a manner as possible. Obtain any referrals or leads that you can, and then move on. This is far more beneficial than trying to sell an engagement to a prospect who is not ready or has very little interest.

I once met with the managing partner of a prominent management-consulting firm in the Midwest to discuss his new-business development needs. His firm was facing price-cutting competition that was eroding its profits. Although he agreed that the problem identified was certainly one that plagued his firm and many others in the industry, his main objection was the cost of my services. As I was about to leave, I said, "You know, Harry, you must know at least one other firm with this need that has a budget for training. How many names come to mind right now?" Like a light bulb suddenly switched on, he said, "Dave Jones, XYZ Company, Chicago." Harry set up an appointment for me using my telephone credit card number and it turned out to be one of the largest engagements that I handled that year.

PLANNING FOR THE DISCUSSION

Having contemplated the major objectives/outcomes of the new-business discussion, and your plans of action once on site, let's review what is necessary to plan for the first meeting. By planning for interviews, you will greatly enhance your relationship with the prospect, as well as your own image and confidence. When you know you are prepared to call on a prospect, you will do a much better job because planning enables you to anticipate the prospective client's concerns and expectations. Consequently, each prospect will regard you as a confident, well focused professional; and that is real leveraging of your time.

Here are the six stages of the interview-planning procedure:

1. *Get Totally Clear About the Need Situation You Wish to Discuss.* Although this point has been stressed in previous chapters, it is here that too many professionals begin to stray off course. There is a strong tendency, even among experienced professionals, to indicate their brilliance by discussing a variety of problem areas facing prospects in the niche and their ability to handle all of them. This tends to be counterproductive, however.

You need to focus on the hot-button need situation that got you the appointment. You must be prepared to answer for the prospective client, "Why are you bringing this need situation to me?" Your objective in answering this question is to have accumulated enough information to break through the "ho-hum" or "I-don't-need-any" barriers. You are the one who must develop a sense of importance and urgency regarding the need situation. After all, you are a highly accomplished professional with an insider's reputation and a thorough understanding of the niche.

It is your business to identify need situations and bring them to the attention of prospects within the niche, often before they themselves recognize the magnitude of the need.

2. *Identify the Solution Program for the Need Situation.* Here is where your understanding of the different types of need situations pays off. The nature of the need and the prospect's requirements and expectations dictate the solution program you must be able to provide. Solving a deficiency in the performance of a profit-affecting factor is quite different from assisting the prospect in making a decision. Different skills, information, techniques, and timing are required.

During this step you are doing the job in your mind. You start by identifying the end products of the engagement—what they are, how they will be used, and who will use them. You identify the tasks that will be required to produce the end products, and you identify the roles the client's people will play as they assist your people in preparing the products.

3. *Assemble Existing Information About This Prospect.* This is a two-step process. First you assemble all the information you have on hand for this prospect. Then you identify information that you must verify during the meeting. As a general rule, early in the meeting you verify any information about the prospect that you can't afford to be wrong about. This is information that will affect the nature and scope of your recommended solution program.

For example, I conduct workshops on getting new clients for professional-service firms. It is essential that I verify early on whether the prospects have provided traditional sales training programs. If they have, I know without a doubt that for every 10 people forced to attend a traditional sales skills program, at least four or five still have heartburn about the experience. My solution program must be different. It must include specially developed, comfort-building modules that will remove the lingering resentment brought into the training room by the reluctant and wary participants. Otherwise, they will tend to think to themselves, "Here we go again with another program that's going to discount my technical skills, make me wrong, and pressure me to develop a sales personality. No, thanks!"

4. *Identify Information You Must Obtain During the Meeting.* You must also identify your "information buckets" to be filled. Is there anything else you need to know to define the need situation and the desired solution program?

As a final check, put yourself in the prospect's shoes for a moment. What information should she expect me to have prior to the meeting? What information do I need that I can get only from this person or from someone else in her organization? If the information you need is not readily available from your contact person, you must be prepared to direct the contact in her search elsewhere in the organization.

Although all companies are somewhat different, you will get better and better at being able to get the needed information after conducting a few new-business discussions.

5. *Setting Objectives.* Now, you are ready to set the objective for this particular meeting. What is the primary objective/end result of the meeting you want to accomplish? Remember to set a fallback objective just in case the meeting bogs down.

6. *Developing Your Interview Plan.* Your interview plan should be in writing and contain the following elements:

1. Opening benefit statement—What you say after "Hello." You restate the solution goal you mentioned during the appointment-getting telephone call.

2. Information you feel you must verify.

3. Information buckets to fill during this meeting.

4. At least three compelling reasons why the prospect should buy now and from you.

It is essential that you present information to support your proposed solution and to justify why the prospect should authorize you to proceed with your recommended solution program.

INTERVIEW PLAN FOR _____

1. Opening Benefit Statement — ideas for using current engagements to sell additional work
2. Verify:
   Previous training?
   Currently busy with ongoing engagements?
   Leaving a lot of fees on the table?
3. Must get:
   Number of engagements
   Accomplished (or considered) regarding need
   Who is for and against program
   Desired/required specifications for the solution program
4. Reasons:
   Have red-card system that is automatic need generator
   Opportunity costs are staggering
   Cross selling is retention, too
   Firm X is 24% ahead since implementing red-card system

FIGURE 11.2. Sample Interview Guide

Figure 11.2 is an example of an interview plan I prepared for a meeting with a prospective client, an accounting firm located in the Southwest. Their positive need situation required instruction in identifying their clients' needs for additional services.

I frequently use Figure 11.3, "Structuring Your Sales Story," in developing my interview plan. It builds my confidence as I identify in advance at least three reasons why the prospect needs the type of service solution I will discuss and three reasons why my services are the best solution for the prospect. I also identify in advance why the prospect is justified in using my services now. Many times I have to provide the prospect with tangible reasons why he should hire me so he can convince his people.

STRUCTURING YOUR SALES STORY

STEP 1. Three reasons why this prospect needs the *type* of services I plan to discuss.

1. _____
Positive outcome if used

_____

2. _____
Positive outcome if used

_____

3. _____
Negative condition corrected/prevented

_____

STEP 2. Three reasons why *my* service is *the best* answer for the prospect.

1. _____

_____

2. _____

_____

3. _____

_____

STEP 3. Three reasons why this prospect should buy my service *now*.

1. _____

2. _____

3. _____

FIGURE 11.3. Interview Plan

215

I don't list the potential objections the prospect might raise because I have a mental template for handling them. If a short-hand note would be useful to you, by all means jot it down. It's your plan, and it demonstrates that you are organized for action.

I've asked prospects how they felt about the way I referred to my interview plan during the meeting. The most frequent response was, "I was glad you had a plan for the meeting. It built my confidence that I was dealing with a professional who was not here to wing it."

Once prepared, the interview plan should be reviewed with those colleagues who accompany you. I discuss below the idea of bringing others from your firm to the meeting. Type the plan and put it in the holding pocket on the left-hand side of the writing portfolio you use to take notes during your new-business meetings.

Planning for the interview and conducting the interview are not the same. Interruptions may occur, the prospect may not be attentive, the need you have identified may be the tip of the iceberg, and so on. Still, the more planning and preparation you undertake before making the on-site visit, the better.

BRINGING ALONG A COLLEAGUE

Another item to consider in planning for the interview is whether to take along a colleague. If so, coordinating schedules could be difficult; yet, having two people present at a meeting ensures compatibility and completion of coverage.

The fundamental reason why you would want to take along a colleague on new-business discussions is to minimize the time lapse from contact to contract. If you sense that including a colleague would improve your chances of success, you must take several steps internally. First, you must brief your colleague on the upcoming appointment. You will have to coordinate who leads and when; who takes notes and who follows up. If the colleague has only passing knowledge of the current situation, you may find it easier to provide three or four key questions you want him or her to ask in support of your presentation.

When should a joint contact be made? One answer is when a need solution requires a multidisciplined approach, or is outside your area of expertise. It is also advisable when the prospect represents a potential Key or A client. Finally, as a general rule of thumb it is best to bring a colleague when it will make it easier to communicate with the prospect.

Frequently, part of your interview plan involves asking the question, "Who is the person in my office who can most readily support this new-business quest?" Your answer will be the person you should take with you. In all cases be certain to let the prospect know in advance that you will be bringing a colleague along.

HOW TO PREPARE THE PERSONAL-CONTACT KIT

The personal-contact kit consists of those materials that will identify your ability to solve the client's needs, such as previous PARs (problem-approach-results reports), testimonial letters from other satisfied clients, and engagement deliverables such as monthly reports, PERT or Gantt charts, final reports, and so on. Other materials contained in your kit should include brochures or literature about your firm, the original article containing the hot button that you first mailed to the prospect, and any appropriate articles written by you or your staff. In determining what to include in your kit, you are really accumulating evidence and examples of "wins" in the need area. The items you include should be powerful. They should help answer the question, "Will the packet sell my services when I'm not around?" In preparing your contact kit, your goal is to be able to demonstrate via the materials that you are already an established force in handling the identified need.

If you are not an established force, and you don't have enough items to prepare a strong personal-contact kit, there are some alternative measures that can be taken. For example, you could develop a question-and-answer flyer that answers the most typical questions that prospective clients ask. Or you could develop a fact sheet, a one-page, typeset document that highlights the needs, current environmental conditions, and firm's capabilities.

In all instances, if you refer to clients, be sure to get their permission in advance; or don't use their names or any proprietary data that would identify them. This is particularly necessary when you are exhibiting a final report prepared for another client.

What Should Not Go into the Kit. If you are a national firm with branch offices, some prospects will be overwhelmed by a nationally focused brochure. Don't make the mistake of coming across as a national firm with no local roots. If your personal-contact kit contains too much overkill, the prospect may get the notion that you are too big for them. Limit the testimonials you present to five; presenting more than five can easily overwhelm your prospective clients.

The supporting materials in your personal-contact kit should show evidence of your ability to help others in the industry solve the kind of problem(s) you are there to discuss. The order in which you present these materials is up to you. What is important is that you effectively convey your firm's reputation, experience, and professionalism.

Your personal-contact kit should include such supporting items as a folder to hold a pad of 8-1/2 by 11-inch paper, a pen or pencil that indicates professionalism, and a professional-looking briefcase to hold everything.

PROSPECT CONTACT TIME

Once you have completed all of your preinterview planning and assembled the personal-contact kit, you are ready to start making appointments (see Chapter 10). Use your travel time wisely. Lay out your contacts by zip codes so that you are in the general vicinity of a large number of prospects. If your travel takes you out of town, contact in advance the local chambers of commerce, economic development offices, or tourism centers to obtain maps and other pertinent materials.

Keep stationery and stamps on hand so you can leverage your time on the road. I have a tape recorder that plugs into the cigarette lighter in my car, which allows me to debrief myself immediately following a new-business discussion. This information strengthens the proposal letters that I prepare because they are based on facts I have been able to verify and gather during the meeting. Finally, while traveling be alert to new suspects. Seasoned professionals called this "smokestacking."

Preparing Yourself for the Discussion

Always leave enough time to arrive at the prospect's office alert and relaxed. This is a very important step. Often, the busy professional will create inner stress by not getting to the prospect's location in time to relax. Because of poor planning, there is little time for sizing up the surroundings. For example, one professional had to fight bad traffic all across town to arrive at a meeting. I insisted that he call the contact and explain that he was running late because of traffic. Instead, he argued that being a few minutes late wouldn't create a problem. Is there a problem? When you arrive on time, or when you call and say you will be a few minutes late, you maintain control. You also convey respect for the time of the prospect. Few people enjoy meeting someone who is tense, has sweaty hands, and a rapidly beating heart.

It takes time and effort to arrive at the prospect's office fully prepared to talk about new business. The time to get your car washed is in advance of the call. If you are prone to sweaty palms, regardless of the situation, keep a towel or package of disposable premoistened towelettes in your car. How is your grooming? These may seem like basics, but everyday thousands of experienced professionals ignore them. If it is early in the day, or if you have just eaten a mild lunch, your breath will probably be okay. However, if it is later in the day and you have eaten a garlic-and-onions salad, or your stomach is empty, your breath will stop a clock. The prospect will know it. The obvious solution can be found in any drugstore.

There are numerous relaxation techniques if calling on a new prospect represents a tense situation for you. You can take long, slow, deep breaths for a few minutes. Or you can visualize having a pleasant experience, meeting someone who will be warm and friendly and take an immediate liking to you. Many professionals find it relaxing to review the goals for the meeting and to visualize their desired objective being accomplished.

If you are habitually late, it is time to examine the issue. You need to ask, "Why am I doing this to myself? What am I gaining by underallocating the time necessary to arrive alert and relaxed?" Some are quick to blame a traffic jam for making them late. Traffic jams don't happen exclusively to you. You put your car in traffic that occasionally can jam up.

Perhaps the greatest relaxation technique is to acknowledge the purpose of the meeting. "I am here to create an environment in which the prospect and I think together." Your goal is to define, uncover, and articulate what the prospect wants and expects as a result of engaging you. This can only be done by getting the prospect to talk.

On the Matter of Waiting

How long should you wait? A reasonable wait is often a function of how hungry you are for new business. In general, I allow 10 to 15 minutes slack time for all appointments. However, I will politely remind the receptionist of my appointment about seven minutes after the scheduled appointment if she hasn't indicated any other prevailing circumstances. After another 10 to 15 minutes have passed, I ask the receptionist to call the contact's secretary to see if the appointment is on the calendar and if the contact is going to be much longer. If it looks as though I will be late for my next appointment if I wait any longer, I take out my business card and write on the back:

Mr. X:

Waited until 10:15. Since you must be delayed, I will get back with you today to set up a more convenient time.

Letting the contact waste your time suggests that your time is highly negotiable. People treat you the way in which you educate them. If you indicate that your time is flexible or can be modified to meet a prospect's schedule, you are conveying the message that the prospect's time is more valuable than yours.

While waiting, use your time wisely. Make notes about the organization's atmosphere. Given your comfort zone, consider what is the realistic outcome of the first meeting. Stay poised and ready to greet the prospect with a nonoverwhelming burst of energy.

We have come a long way and our preparation has equipped us to conduct an effective new-business discussion. In the next four chapters we'll look at the specific phases involved, and the skills and techniques for winning.

Part 3
Conducting a Winning New-Business Discussion

You have arrived at the stage where your intensive planning and preparation pay off. It is time to have close encounters of the third kind with qualified prospects. In this part of the book, we will look at what is involved in opening a new-business discussion, defining the existing need situation, and scoping out the desired future situation. We will also examine what is involved in effectively presenting your proposed solution, handling concerns and information needs of the client, closing the discussion, and taking action.

Because you're prepared, you will find that you are more at ease on a prospect's turf than ever before. In fact, once you have made a couple of your new-business calls following the planning and preparation suggested earlier, you actually may begin to look forward to face-to-face discussions with new prospects. You may even find that it can be good fun.

Chapter 12, "Opening the Discussion," will get you off to a flying start.

12

Opening the Discussion

The purpose of the opening phase is to build a bridge from the appointment-getting telephone contact to the new-business discussion.

To effectively open a new-business discussion, you must handle several important tasks, including the introductions, and communicate in a manner that builds rapport. All the while, you should be alert to cues from the prospect regarding his or her knowledge of your firm, buying motives, initial attitudes, and communication style. It is during the new-business discussion that you must also establish your credentials. Your ultimate task is to find out how to proceed to the next step: defining the existing need situation. Let's examine further the tasks involved in opening the new-business discussion effectively.

MANAGING THE INTRODUCTIONS

The contact is walking over to you. You stand up, exhibit an open posture—hands at your side, good eye contact. You are directly facing him. You have a smile on your face. You offer your dry, warm hand and present a firm but not overpowering handshake. In all ways, and on all levels, you offer positive vibes.

You know that in the business world, the time during which you first shake the prospect's hand is probably the most intimate you will ever have. You must manage this time effectively. In dealing with women, if they do not extend their hand, extend yours. Be careful: Many people believe the stronger the handshake, the lower the self-esteem or sensitivity to others. When you have managed this portion of the greeting properly, the contact knows who you are and has had interaction without being intimidated, bruised, or made to feel inferior. The contact feels that there just might be something in it for him.

You say, "Good Morning! I'm Elizabeth Goodwin." You have already established some of the ground rules, including how you would like to be addressed and the level of formality. During the discussion, you maintain eye contact with the prospect. You know well that you will never have a second chance to make a favorable first impression. You know that you should not hand out your card at this point. If you are going to present your business card, you do it shortly after you sit down or at the end of the discussion. If you bring a colleague, presenting your business cards in the order in which you are seated is both helpful and courteous.

Your briefcase is in your left hand. Your voice sounds natural and relaxed because you took the time to take a few deep breaths while you were waiting for the contact to appear. As you enter the contact's office, you scan the office to get some clues about the person: How is the office arranged? Is it messy or neat? What pictures are on the desk and walls? Are there any plaques, awards, or mottoes posted?

You take your cue regarding seating from the contact. Many times the contact will head directly to his desk. If so, don't read "power game" into this act too soon. The contact may just feel more comfortable doing this. Or, he may direct you to an area used for more intimate discussions.

This point in the new-business discussion process is critical. You need to be prepared to take the lead if the contact suddenly throws the ball to you. One of the easiest ways to begin the discussion is to comment on some aspect of the contact's environment. If you have been hearing some good things about the organization you should mention it.

As an alternative opening, you may say, "How is business? Based on what we are seeing with clients in your industry, it looks like [state your observation]." This gets you down to business quickly and establishes your knowledge as an insider, provided you have done your homework.

All the while, your goal is to establish effective human interaction. In addition to what you are saying, you also want to communicate that you are easy to talk with and that you are interested in what the contact has to say. All this should be done before proceeding to the next phase. Each of you has your own agenda. You each have had your own experiences in meeting and dealing with strangers, which are affected by your respective comfort zones and personal levels of self-esteem.

What you are really doing during the introduction is building a bridge from the initial phone contact to the face-to-face new-business discussion. In building such a bridge, you restate the central theme you used in the letter and in your phone call. Meanwhile, the client-centered marketing approach must be maintained. You must talk in terms of the contact's interests. Remember, the relationship you develop may well outlast a single engagement. You want to make the contact feel unique and special. Everything about you must communicate that the contact is the focus and beneficiary of your time and intention.

If you are not met by the contact on time, follow the instructions, presented in Chapter 11, on how long to wait. Meanwhile, also make good use of this time: Review your notes; check your calendar; make some phone calls, if possible. While seated in the reception area, you can also assess the tempo of the organization, review available literature, or talk with other vendors who may be waiting. If you have to use the restroom, that is fine. It is far better to begin a new-business discussion with an empty bladder than a full one.

Do not make the mistake of reviewing a lot of internal notes or having to stand up quickly when the contact arrives and end up quickly gathering or spilling papers. This builds your anxiety and says to the prospect that you are not prepared or confident. The notes that you review or the paperwork that you undertake while waiting must be in a small contained area, which you can quickly and readily close up and take with you should the contact suddenly arrive.

REDUCING TENSION

The way that you communicate goes a long way toward reducing tension and building rapport. Your easy dialogue and open posture communicate that you are not a threat. The prospect has made a good decision in agreeing to meet you. It is important to try not to judge the other person, which is fairly easy to do if he does not meet your expectations. Communication specialist Janet Elsea, Ph.D., says that "You *cannot* not communicate."

In all new encounters, the first several minutes are critical. You might get lucky and encounter a prospect who is as good at reducing tensions and creating a safe arena as you are, but don't count on it. This remains your responsibility. The better you are at reducing initial, normal tension, the faster you can build trust and rapport. The importance of arriving on time, relaxed, and alert pays off at this stage. I like to follow the three L's for reducing any residual tensions:

Lighten up
Listen
Lay back

If the conversational ball remains in your court, be sure to emphasize that you were looking forward to meeting the prospect. During this time, the contact is making a lot of snap decisions about you, such as you are okay, you are not okay; you are safe to be with, you are not safe; and so on. Most importantly, he is determining whether it will be easy to do business with you. Most professionals, including myself, are a bit tense during this time, especially when discussing a need that the contact person may see as a problem or threat. Remember, to reduce tension, keep it light!

BUILDING TRUST AND RAPPORT

Rapport has been defined as *being in harmony or agreement with another*. By establishing rapport early, you begin to build a relationship that is profitable to your contact. The rapport-building process continues throughout the discussion; it is facilitated by listening, accepting his or her ideas, sharing information and experiences, and virtually vibrating at the same frequency.

You build rapport by listening and showing interest in what the contact has to say, which requires no less than 100 percent of your attention. Few have mastered this feat; Jacqueline Kennedy Onassis is one who has. One of her greatest strengths is that she makes the person she is listening to feel that she is interested in no other person in the world.

Besides listening, you must also indicate that you understand what the contact is saying. This can be done by offering small supporting statements such as "I see," "Hmmm," and most importantly, rephrasing what the other person has said. Another component of rapport building is respect—you must show that you accept the views of another no matter how vastly they differ from yours.

Be careful not to assume too much. For example, if there is a picture of children on a bookcase, say, "Is that your family?"

instead of saying, "You have a nice-looking family." If the answer is yes, you can then say, "I have daughters, too—are you still smart in their eyes or have you suddenly contracted a case of the 'dumbs?'" Any small story that touches areas of mutual interests or concern helps build rapport. The stronger the connection you can establish, the more the prospect will feel that you are alike. Then you may have access to the contact's mind and emotions and pave the way past such questions as, "How long has this person been with the company," or "What jobs did he have on the way up?"

What diminishes your ability to build rapport? Some barriers are physical, such as a poor setting in which to discuss business—noise, interruptions, and so on. If you have made a poor first impression or let preconceived notions interfere with your discussion, your ability to build rapport will be hindered. If you haven't done your homework, you will be anxious, which will be picked up by the contact. Finally, if your manner or presentation is overwhelming or threatening to the contact, your chances for building trust and rapport on a long-term basis start off behind the eight ball.

IDENTIFYING BUYING MOTIVE(S)

Buying motives are the factors that drive the contact. While I will focus on this in more detail in Chapter 13, you should be alert to what may be driving your contact's behavior.

In Chapter 9, I introduced the idea of determining the buying motives to be triggered by the initial-contact mailing program. Figure 12.1 depicts prospect buying motives. Two factors have been added—quality and price. Hopefully, most of your prospects will be interested in quality, but many prospects are driven by price.

There are three other factors that can be used to gain further insights into the contact's buying motives.

PROSPECT BUYING MOTIVES

Need Situation	Fear of Failure	Unknown	Meeting Requirements of Job	Feeling Good—Self-Approval	Looking Good—Approval by Others	Quality	Price
1. Negatives							
a. Fear	X						
b. Threat		X					
c. Decision		X					
2. Positive							
a. Wanted factor is lacking			X	X	X		
b. Wanted factor is in short supply			X		X		
3. Task			X		X		

FIGURE 12.1. Prospect Buying Motives

Short-term gain versus long-term gain

Personal objectives versus company objectives

Defensive posture in market versus offensive posture in market

SIZING UP THE CONTACT

Whether or not you want to, you will immediately begin sizing up the contact; it's simply human nature. However, your goal is to do it so that it enhances your chances of obtaining the engagement. First, determine how best to pitch him. You don't want to tell him what he already knows, and you don't want to talk over his head. You need all the clues you can get to size up the contact; that way, once you are ready to bridge to the body of the discussion, you can fine tune your approach to the prospective client's needs and communication style. An important aspect of sizing up the contact is to gauge his initial attitude toward your firm and its services.

The contact's initial attitude can be classified into one of three categories.

1. *Accepting or Interested in You and Your Firm/Service.* This is entirely likely as a result of a client-centered marketing approach to a new-business discussion.

2. *Indifferent to You and/or Your Firm/Service.* The question that immediately comes up is, "Why might this attitude be present?" One answer is that the prospect cooled to the idea of handling the need. He might have been told by his boss to curb all expenditures, and he felt embarrassed in calling you to cancel. Another reason may be that he is preoccupied with something.

3. *Hostile to You and/or Your Firm/Service.* Why is this attitude present? Since you were successful in obtaining the appointment, it is unlikely that you will encounter this attitude. I once accompanied a client on new-business calls and ran into this situation. My client was an executive search consultant who

Perceptive	Myopic
Risk Taker	Risk Avoider
Leader	Led
Big Picture	Nitty Gritty
Open Communications	Closed Communications
Trusting	Suspicious
Conservative	Liberal
Macho	Wimp
Suave	Earthy
Loud	Quiet

FIGURE 12.2. Sizing Up the Contact

had obtained an appointment with a newly hired vice president. We were ushered into the prospect's office and greeted with verbal abuse. We even had our legitimacy questioned. The reason soon became obvious. The contact had been outplaced from his previous organization and felt a great deal of anger toward consultants. The only close made that day was the door, which was slammed as we left his office.

Figure 12.2 offers 10 additional factors for sizing up the contact.

The reason one attempts to size up another is not to manipulate this person. Rather this is done so the professional can better relate to the person as an individual. Fortunately, certain patterns of behavior and communication tend to repeat themselves and the alert professional can learn from them.

ESTABLISHING YOUR CREDENTIALS

Your task here will be to briefly establish your credentials by qualifying yourself and your firm as a team worth knowing. This will also ensure that the contact is receptive to additional discussion. To establish your credentials, you must synopsize your industry experience and relate the experience to your captive audience. Offer a small bit of information on yourself and others in the firm. Briefly mention your referral sources if appropriate.

BRIDGE TO BODY OF DISCUSSION

So far you have managed the introduction, helped reduce tension, and built up some trust and rapport. During this time, you have been sizing up the contact, looking for tip-offs to the buying motives. The next step after opening the new-business discussion is to move to the body of the discussion that is to take place. This is done in two simple steps. First, you obtain agreement to proceed. Then, you reiterate the opening benefit statement. For example, you wait for a pause and then say, "Mr. Prospect, if it's okay with you, (agreement) I'd like to share some ideas about improving your cash flow." (opening benefit statement)

You may be thinking that we're overusing the benefit statement. Not a chance—that's why he's investing his time in seeing you.

The opening benefit statement represents the moment of truth. If you are a professional in the new-business development game, you have thought about your opening statement and practiced its delivery. This statement significantly affects the balance of your discussion. It is precisely now that your preliminary need and solution analysis pays off.

Always, always, *always* put the prospect first by structuring the initial statement in his or her terms. For example, begin by mentioning a need, problem, or interest to the client in the form of a general statement:

"Many professionals are interested in improving their client-development capabilities to meet increasingly stiff competition."

"Mr. Scott, since talking to you by phone last Wednesday, I have been thinking about the way in which we have been assisting our clients in winning at the new-client game."

Immediately after presenting your statement, observe and listen to the contact's response and classify his attitude toward your statement. This is a repeat of the initial attitude check I mentioned earlier. Be alert for any signs that the positive attitude has slipped.

Now you're into the body of the new-business discussion. Your immediate objective is to define the scope, costs, and consequences of the existing need situation. This will be covered in the next chapter.

13
Defining the Existing Need Situation

You have successfully opened the new-business discussion and bridged to the body of the meeting. Now it is time to prepare a very carefully developed description of the prospect's need situation. This is done by putting a picture frame around the situation so you can deliver a verbal snapshot of the situation at a given time. That way, you can compare the way things presently are with what is desired or required in the next step. Your suggested service solution will fill the gap between what is and what is desired.

Defining the existing need situation is a 6-step process. First you verify the *nature* of the need situation to be certain that you and the prospect are singing out of the same hymnal. Next you define the *scope* of the need situation: the who, where, when, and how. Then you estimate the *costs* to date associated with the need situation. Next you get the prospect to look at the probable *adverse consequences* to her and her organization if the situation is not resolved. Because you have covered a lot of ground in your definition phase, you stop for a moment to *verify mutual understanding*, to be certain you and the contact are in sync.

Finally, you *restate* the opening benefit statement in terms of *the central solution goal*. This goal statement serves as a bridge into the next phase where your task is to define the desired future situation. Each of the six steps will be discussed separately, with examples to illustrate the ideas as needed.

UPSETTING THE EQUILIBRIUM

If you are doing your job correctly, you are going to disturb the equilibrium in the minds and emotions of the buying team. To do this, you will discuss and probe the need situation so that the contact person becomes the one who identifies the magnitude of the problem. This eliminates the burden of having you deliver the bad news; instead, your role as the professional advocate will be enhanced and preserved.

As I will discuss later, it is crucial in the new-business discussion that the prospect be the one who mentions that the current situation is not up to the desired or required level of performance. Moreover, the contact must tell you that the expectations of the management team or the organization's publics are dissatisfied in some way. This strategy also involves having her tell you the costs to date, and the consequences of not proceeding with direct action. You must then skillfully bring a level of anxiety into play and allow the prospect to marinate in her misery. The questions or directive probes that you use will generate yes/no answers that highlight unwanted conditions or insufficient resources. Let's step back now and examine how we steer the new-business discussion toward this desired outcome.

Verifying/Determining the Nature of the Need Situation

By the time you have sent your letter and made a telephone call, presumably the need situation you are going to discuss and define has already been nailed down. Yet you must first verify that the need situation is indeed similar to that discussed in the initial-contact package.

It is possible that the need situation will have changed by the time you arrive. This has happened to me several times. The task is to determine the *exact nature* of the need situation.

Defining the Scope of the Need Situation

There is always a history to a need situation. There are always players with different stakes. Some will champion your efforts; others don't want you to succeed. You must understand the prevailing environment to be successful. This involves determining where the need exists within the organization, and what impact it has on operations.

Next you must determine when the need started. Who became aware of the need, and how? Then try to determine what has already been done to address the situation. Who has taken the lead? What kind of effort has been expended? What are the results?

Determine the Cost to Date—Extrinsic and Intrinsic

Your goal here is to get the contact to determine the out-of-pocket, as well as the emotional and opportunity, dollar costs to date. When you have caused a contact to attach a dollar figure to the need, you are then in a position to empathize with her about her difficult situation. Then suggest that the contact sum the dollar amount of the total costs to date. This can be done with a leading statement, such as, "My experience is that it costs the average consulting firm about $25,000 to $35,000 to replace a three-year supervisor. Does that square with your experience?" If she says yes, the fee mentioned later by you as the budget for your solution program will be only a fraction of the costs mentioned earlier.

There are several important reasons for determining the costs as early as possible in a new-business discussion. First, you gain a sense of the magnitude and difficulty the prospect has had with the particular need situation. You also convey the message that, "Hey, this is getting more costly all the time." You have thus paved your way to introduce your cost-effective service solution. Moreover, the contact is less likely to be shell-shocked by your fees.

Getting the contact to talk about costs is a critical step in the definition of the existing need situation. Without a ballpark figure of the dollar amount of the costs being incurred, you are really lacking the ammunition you will need to disturb the equilibrium and emotions of the buying team, and influence decision-makers that this is a need that must be addressed now. By attaching an air of urgency to the situation, you have helped the contact realize that it will be far more costly not to take action immediately.

Determine the Consequences of Not Proceeding

At this point, you must get the contact to recognize the dire consequences of not proceeding. In other words, saying no to your solution to the problem will be saying yes to additional costs and courting disastrous consequences. This is a powerful strategy and one that must be approached delicately. You must expose gently the consequences of not taking action, by saying, for example, "Ms. Henderson, given the widespread dissatisfaction surrounding the forced merger of the two departments, what is the probability that this situation will work itself out, without some focused and specialized attention?" Let's suppose her reply was:

> "I don't see much hope of it correcting itself. God knows I've tried my best. It won't let go."

Now you get to be the good guy and use a supporting, reinforcement statement such as:

"You're absolutely right, Ms. Henderson, this is an important and difficult situation that is not healing itself. As you say, unless something is done you run the risk of (you mention the likely adverse consequences)."

Let's take a moment to look at the structure and power of the supporting-reinforcement statement given above. The statement was preceded by your probing question. . . .

Dialogue	Analysis
You probe. . . "Ms. Henderson, given the widespread dissatisfaction surrounding the forced merger of the two departments, what is the probability that this situation will work itself out, without some focused and specialized attention?"	The probe was done in a gentle, conversational manner that led to the prospect's admission that self-correction was not probable. Because you did not mention that her own attempts have been costly, futile, or ill-advised, she did not have to defend her actions. In fact, you have been saying all along that the situation is difficult to handle because it requires special expertise.
Her reply. . . "I don't see much hope of it correcting itself. God knows I've tried my best. It won't let go."	
Your reply. . . "You're absolutely right, Ms. Henderson, this *is* an important and difficult situation that is not healing itself. As	You support her remark made in response to your probe, then reinforce her position and make her "right" in being there. You

you say, unless something is done you run the risk of. . . [you mention the likely adverse consequences]."

are not the bad guy trying to push her into something you are trying to sell. Instead, you are thinking along with her in sharing ideas in a compassionate manner.

Triggering the Buying Motive

During this step, you will be repeating the probe, support-reinforcement, and consequences loop until you have the situation defined. When you have the picture frame and verbal snapshot of the existing situation completed, you bridge to the next phase in the new-business discussion by restating the solution goal. Of course, you won't use the same words every time.

Verify Mutual Understanding

You have verified or determined the nature of the need situation, defined the scope of the need situation, and determined the cost to date. You have also helped the prospect determine the consequences of not proceeding. Hopefully, you have triggered one or more buying motives. Now, before proceeding to the next phase, you must be certain that you are again singing from the same hymnal. If there is disagreement regarding the nature and scope of the need situation or of the costs and consequences, then your suggested solution will not tie up all the loose ends in the prospect's mind. The solution program will not fit the prospect's specifications of the existing and desired future situation.

At this juncture, slow down and say, "Let's see if we are both tracking this thing the same way. What I hear you telling me is GHI. Am I on target?" If not, use nondirective probes to round out or clarify the situation, such as "How is that?" "Why?" or "In what ways does . . . ?" Should you discover that you two are not singing in harmony, you must slow down and ask, "Where have I gone astray?" You must take responsibility for the variance.

The prospect will often raise a question about a topic that you thought you had covered in sufficient detail. Patiently discuss the same topic using other words. Try making a sketch to illustrate a point if possible.

Verifying your mutual understanding of the need situation is a critical point in the new-business discussion. If you are able to achieve mutual understanding, your next task is to use a mutual solution goal to bridge to the next phase. (See next section.) If you don't achieve a mutual understanding, you will have to make a decision. Does it make sense to try to get in harmony at this time? Should I suggest that the prospect invest another minute to state her concerns/questions/considerations so I can go back to the office to think through her responses? The last option is a poor third choice because it lets the prospect off the hook. But it may be the best one in the situation.

Restate the Solution Goal

This step is as simple as saying, "Ms. Henderson, I feel comfortable that I understand the background and circumstances surrounding the fall-off of morale in the newly formed departments. Your analysis and candor really have been valuable. Together, let's think about the way your department is going to perform when we get the people working fully as a team."

This is a simple statement with a lot of power embedded in it. Let's analyze this statement to identify the power element in it. . . .

> Ms. Henderson, (1) I feel comfortable that I understand (2) the background and circumstances surrounding the fall-off of morale (3) in the newly formed departments. (4)

In the first phrase, I was again respectful in using her name. Had she asked me to call her Elizabeth, I would have done so immediately. Phrase 2 is a personal statement of the way I work—I probe until I'm comfortable and confident that I understand. I don't wing it and run the risk of misunderstanding the situation. Phrase 3 is a more positive description of the mess she has been living with. I didn't mind her marinating in her misery during the definition step. But, at this point I'm beginning to promise her that better days are coming. Phrase 4 refers to the newly formed departments as not being her direct responsibility.

"Your analysis and candor really have been valuable (5). Together, let's think (6) about the way your department is going to perform (7) when we (8) get the people working fully as a team." (9)

Phrase 5 rewards her for her communication style and openness. Praised behavior is likely to be repeated, so you are shaping her communications with you. Phrases 6 and 8 create the partnership that is going to enable her to win. She admitted earlier that her approach did not work. Phrase 7 is the solution goal stated a bit differently. This solution goal is again used to trigger the buying motive(s) that you think are driving the prospect's buying behavior.

To test your mastery of buying motives, jot down what motives are driving her behavior on the line below:

If I were conducting the interview, I would work on the assumption that fear of failure and need for approval from others are driving this woman's buying behavior.

Phrase 9 holds the end result of your solution program, which you have not yet introduced. When you get to the point of discussing your approach, she will be primed to listen and think along with you.

A very skilled accountant who had attended my Getting New Clients workshop engaged me to accompany her on a number of new-client business discussions. During one meeting, the discussion focused on the accounts-receivable problem experienced by the prospect. After defining the need situation, the accountant made the solution goal statement, "Let's see what is involved in improving your cash flow, so you can get your organization out of the bank's pockets."

The effect on the prospect was dramatic. The accountant's statement had hit the prospect's emotional target. She activated the buying motivators of fear of failure and need for approval, both of which added up to a powerful combination.

After you have examined and agreed upon the nature and extent of the situation and made a bridge using a mutual solution goal, it is time to move to the next step. We will pick this up in Chapter 14, Defining the Desired/Required Future Situation.

The following chart, Guide for the New-Business Discussion, should be copied and taken with you on calls. Questions 1 through 3 relate to the points made in this chapter, questions 4 and 5 relate to material presented in Chapter 14.

GUIDE FOR THE NEW-BUSINESS DISCUSSION

1. What is the REAL NEED this prospect wants to discuss?
2. What is the SCOPE of the need situation?

Where is the need?

☐ Located organizationally?

☐ Felt or observed?

☐ Impacting on operations?

When did the need start?

☐ Become evident?

☐ To whom?

☐ How?

What has been done/tried/thought of?

☐ By whom?

☐ When?

☐ With what results?

How URGENT is the need?

3. What are the COSTS and CONSEQUENCES?

What COSTS have been incurred to date?

What are the probable CONSEQUENCES of not proceeding?

4. What is the SOLUTION goal?

What is the desired/required SOLUTIONS PROGRAM?

☐ Objectives

☐ Solution alternatives

☐ Work team—who and why?

☐ Deliverables

   ☐ What, in what form?

   ☐ When needed?

5. Who are the players?

What authority does each have?

What is their stake in the engagement?

☐ Who will make the PURCHASE decision?

☐ Who will serve as POINT OF CONTACT?

☐ Who will EVALUATE the RESULTS?

14

Defining the Desired/Required Future Situation

In Chapter 13, we wanted to sit on the same side of the desk as the prospect to understand what he is facing. Our task was to develop the ability to see as the prospect sees and describe the need situation in his terms.

In this chapter we will acquire new clients by helping the prospect define the desired or required future situation. If a prospect views a situation as *required*, it will be easier to trigger and reinforce buying motives.

Up to this point, we have worked with the prospect only in defining the existing need situation. We developed a carefully defined word picture of the situation today.

Now, our task is to develop a word picture of what the prospect feels is desired/required. We also need to determine when he would like the desired/required situation to become a reality. This can be shown as the following equation:

DESIRED/REQUIRED		(Future Situation)
−	IS	(Existing Situation)
OPPORTUNITY GAP		

DEFINE THE SCOPE

The best professional-service marketers always have the prospect tell them in advance what they expect before they suggest a service solution. Conversely, a novice attempts to find out the need and then quickly jumps in with a solution. Yet it is a simple procedure to have the prospect define the specifications for the solution; he must be coached to describe what that improved situation will look like. What will be eliminated after the need has been addressed? What doesn't exist now that will?

At this point, it is essential that you think *with* the prospect rather than *for* him. You want to have the prospect visualize the positive future situation, which both of you will create together. Rather than keep him marinating in misery, you focus on future potential. You ask him to identify the positives that will be added and the negatives that will be deleted when you have completed the engagement.

You have yet to describe your service solution. The reason is that you want as much of the prospect's input as possible to ensure that your proposed solution will be desirable, achievable, and understood.

Let's look at an example. Prospect A has a very restricted cash flow that is hampering operations. You walk through the desired future situation by asking him what would change if he had an adequate cash flow. First the negatives are eliminated (in discussion): The contact no longer has to be embarrassed sending out letters explaining the delay in payments; he doesn't miss opportunities to gain new business because of a lack of funds.

What are the positive developments that the contact envisions? Foremost is a checkbook with a positive balance. Another important benefit is the ability to plan effectively in the short run, at least. And what about being able to focus on other issues confronting the firm?

As the prospect is visualizing the positive conditions, the buying motives are again being triggered without your trying to sell him anything.

What about a situation the prospect describes that you know is not feasible? Actually, this is a favorable situation. Both you and the prospect want to know as soon as possible if the desired outcome is feasible.

The worst time you could learn of the prospect's future scenario is when your closing statement has gone down in flames or when the prospect says, "My God, that doesn't fit what I had in mind." At that point, you get a sinking feeling in your stomach and realize that you and the prospect miscommunicated. However, there is no use blaming the prospect. The responsibility for conducting successful new-business discussions is all yours.

How can this situation be avoided? You create an environment in which you and the prospect think together. Your goal is to define, uncover, and articulate what the prospect wants and expects as a result of engaging you, or someone who provides your type of services. This can only be done by getting the prospect to talk.

Determine Solution Criteria

Now the contact is talking and feeling a little more confident, and may even be excited. So this is the time to ask the prospect, "Mr. X, probably the easiest way to get at this is, how will you and I both know when I am doing a good job?" That is the money question. Then he might say, "You'll be meeting with me to keep me informed, staying on budget, hopefully saving me money. But most importantly, you'll be building me a system that is doable with my people—no bells or whistles for me!" Whatever he says with which you agree becomes the solution specifications. His response becomes the yardstick to measure your service.

Be certain to write down his exact words so you can refer to them later in the discussion. If you get the engagement, his words will be used at the conclusion of the engagement. During

a client "satisfaction" meeting you will review his solution specifications, assure satisfaction, and seek to obtain a referral.

I remember a tough situation with a seasoned and wily managing partner of a prestigious management-consulting firm.
This firm positioned itself as *the* premier firm offering its type of
services. The situation was a positive one. The need was to fill a
lack of required performance factors. The firm had a cadre of
rainmaker partners who regularly brought in high-potential new
clients. But the partners-in-training were noticeably deficient in
the number of contacts made to actively seek new clients.

His reply to my question, "How will you and I both know
when I am doing the job for you?" was instructive: "When this
year's crop of potential partners is landing more work than we
can handle, and you're just a memory." This did not give me a
lot to work with, so I returned to my notes regarding his existing
situation and began reprobing the elements of the situation. I
asked, "When you visualize the associates coming out of training, whom do you see emerging as the early leaders and why?"

This opened the floodgates and his real solution criteria began to emerge. What he really wanted was to have his preferred
candidates for partner be the stars. I hastened to add that I could
not guarantee this result, but would be willing to devote extra
attention both during and after the training to ensure the very
best results possible for the high-potential PITs.

Very often, the prospect's response to the question, "How will
you and I know when I am doing the right job?" involves some
outcome that may take place a year or two down the road, beyond the time and scope of your solution program.

If the prospect says, "When I have a million in sales per year,"
and his best year so far has only been $350,000, you must assert
yourself. Novices buy into the prospect's banter. The pros know
how to say, "Well, that is certainly a good long-term goal. For
now, let's focus on what we can achieve in the foreseeable future." Again, the strategy is to return to the notes regarding the
scope, costs, and potential adverse consequences of the existing
situation, and then to focus on the "must" and "can-do" factors

in the solution program. You might say, "Specifically, let's determine what can be achieved by the time we have completed our work with you." Then you might say, "I will be able to produce the new organizational plan. Will you want me to stay on to assist in its implementation? Or will you handle that?" In this manner, you are literally mapping out with the prospect (who is soon to be a client) the immediate future and your respective roles. At the same time, you are conveying the message that these steps do contribute to the prospect's long-term goals; yet it is still best to walk before you run.

The prospect now begins to acknowledge that you are a professional who offers practical results to needs. The chances are high that the prospect has been given a pitch by others who fell prey to his "million dollars in sales revenue" goal, when the prospect really didn't believe it himself.

When you redefine the scope of work, and make a stand for integrity as in the above illustration, you are able to stand above the other professionals the prospect may have encountered recently.

DETERMINE THE TIMING

Continue to scope the future situation by probing. Steer the prospect toward a realistic time frame on which both of you can agree and in which you know you will be able to deliver. At any point in the process, you have the option of selling your services in phases or rethinking the situation, if the situation will require a significant and continuing effort on your part.

I frequently have to sell in phases. The majority of clients face one of two situations: A large number are in trouble—they've lost or are on the verge of losing important clients, a rainmaker has left or is burned out, or competition is moving in for the kill. Another sizable number has provided traditional sales training and earned the resentment and resistance of their senior and high-potential people, which has manifested itself in missed targets, or with the complaint of "I'm already too busy serving the clients I have. How can you expect me to bring in more? Aren't you concerned with *quality* anymore?"

In these complex and highly emotional situations, the first phase of my work usually consists of a combination of fact finding and ego soothing. I look for opportunities to catch them doing something right. I stress the fact that until recently, the technology just wasn't available for a professional, new-client-getting sales program. What has been done to date can be modified and can serve as a launching pad for even better performance—*if* the same mistakes are not repeated. This implies that *I'm* the new factor that will now ensure success and begin to heal the wounds, and so on.

Subsequent phases involve providing working on site with them in mentoring assignments, developing an in-house marketing director, and the like. This requires patience from the client who wants to get the problem solved yesterday, and a lot of counseling and hand holding by the professional.

As you'd expect, I lose my share, too. One of the satisfactions and frustrations serving these professionals is in their personality and talent mix. They tend to be very bright, have sound analytical skills, and a desire to have things handled yesterday.

Just recently, a managing partner of a firm whose growth had suddenly taken a nosedive was talking with me about my Getting New Clients workshop. He told me his expectation was that I could and would condense the 3-day workshop into a Friday-evening-and-all-day-Saturday program, and still achieve the results of the 3-day program. His rationale was that he could not afford to have 18 participants miss 24 hours of potentially billable time, especially in light of the recent fall-off of billable hours. To sweeten the deal he told me, "I'm willing to pay you the full amount for the workshop because you'd have to push harder, and besides, you're giving up another weekend for me."

I pointed out that the three days I allocated for the workshop was not a capricious decision on my part. I had developed a program that worked. He agreed that my data were sound, but he insisted that his needs still superseded mine. Then I tried to reduce the scope of the program to fit his time frame, but to no avail. We wound up at loggerheads. I declined to serve him at the time.

Many professionals I have trained are concerned that the prospect may paint too rosy a picture for his future scenario. They are concerned that the prospect may ask for results that exceed their abilities. Yet this has not happened in my experience. For those prospects who do have a grand, long-term scenario, you can be a part of the process.

I was more successful with one client who agreed to my conducting an introductory 1-day client-centered marketing program, to be followed later with a 2-day niche-marketing program. This fit into his longer range goal of developing a marketing consciousness among all the professionals in his firm prior to investing in the niche-development process.

If not handled skillfully, on occasion it may look like you are turning business down. Or you may be setting up a situation in which the next professional-service provider actually gets the job. Continually bring the prospect back to reality. Yes, there are other professionals who promise to meet all the client's long-term expectations, regardless of how reachable they are.

Your professionalism and integrity must prevail. Let the prospect feel that you are in charge and are trying to figure out the very best way to get the job done. What you are advocating is a realistic progression toward long-term goals by dividing the tasks into bite-size portions. In dealing with a prospect's unrealistic expectations, I have often used this thought-provoking statement, "I would rather turn you down up front than let you down at the end of the engagement." I have found that prospects appreciate and respect this type of candor.

What about a situation where you know that the prospect needs a variety of services but is only asking for services in one area? If the prospect will be better off with your solution in this area, then strive to sell your solution. Perform the work profitably. However, make sure that the prospect maintains realistic expectations.

SURFACE EXPECTATIONS

The reason professionals don't get the second, third, and fourth engagement is that the new client is disappointed. The disappointment stems from not determining with the prospective client what the desirable future scenario will be and how you will know when you have done the job correctly. Often, the final product has not been thought through or negotiated. The prospect had some expectations about what was going to be delivered. The professional-service provider had some thoughts on what was being delivered; and, unfortunately, the two did not mesh. This is a situation that need not occur. And if you follow the approach presented in this chapter, it won't.

By now you are chomping at the bit to tell the prospect about your service solution and the benefit he can obtain from working with you. In the next chapter you'll have the opportunity to tell your story in a client-centered way.

15

Presenting Your Proposed Solution

You have opened the new-business discussion and defined the existing need situation in the prospect's terms. You have thought through with the prospect the desired or required future situation. You are now about to present your proposed solution. Figure 15.1 below summarizes the steps that lead up to your discussion of the proposed solution.

The need situation on the left side of Figure 15.1 includes both favorable components of the present situation, A, and unfavorable components of the present situation, B. The need situation conveys the client's uncertainty in achieving the desired situation.

How you define the problem, the approach you use, and the results you offer bring you to the desired situation, labeled C. Roughly speaking, A – B = C. In other words, when we drop off the negative components of the present situation, what we have created is a desired situation, C. PAR in this chart represents the word *par* just as in golf. The B section of the need situation is literally below par.

Continuing with the chart, the elapsed time is the time frame

PRESENT
"P"

FUTURE
"F"

FAVORABILITY →

PROBLEM — APPROACH — RESULTS

DESIRED SITUATION →

NEED SITUATION

(A)

(C)

(B)

P A R

TIME →

[A − B = C]

ELAPSED TIME

(C) = ENGAGEMENT DETAILS

FIGURE 15.1. Assessing A Need Situation

you have in which to achieve the desired situation. This sets a
tone of urgency and limits the scope and depth of your solution
program. After thinking through the situation, you are ready to
move from point P, the present situation, to point F, the future
situation. You can now offer a verbal proposal to the prospect.
Your goal is to have him think through the situation and say,
"Your ideas make sense." It is here that analysis ends and judgment prevails. For example, to get the prospect to think about his
goals and strategies to achieve them, should you present a variety of options or one main solution? When the prospect is shop-
ping around or can't articulate his wants, you must use your
judgment, that is, offer a range of solutions, determine the best
single solution, and so on.

WEAVING BETWEEN THE FINE LINES

Your proposed solution program is the vehicle for delivering the desired/required future situation. In effect, we are going to transform the existing situation into the future situation by means of the proposed solution program.

This conversion process puts you on the solution track. All the while you are including the prospect as an active participant in the process. Instead of saying, "Let's see how we (your firm) will develop your improved accounts-receivable system," you are saying, "Let's see how we can work together to improve your cash flow to accomplish XYZ." Although the first statement is accurate in defining what you will do, your terminology is not client-centered; consequently, you use the second statement, which is more representative of the prospect's interests. The end of your conversation should be upbeat; it should focus on the positives so the prospect can visualize obtaining the desired or required situation that will result from working with you.

If you feel comfortable, you may offer a more detailed statement to move the action forward. For example, you could say, "Let's see how we can work together to speed up your cash flow (a desired, favorable, future situation—the central theme of your solutions program) so you can stay out of the bank (an undesired condition) and reduce the killing interest charges you have been carrying (the cost and consequences of the present situation)." It is a mouthful, but if said slowly and in a conversational manner, it is music to the prospect's ears. All along, that is what he had been hoping to hear. Your detailed statement also tells him that what he says is important to you.

DISCUSSING SOLUTION ALTERNATIVES

If you choose to discuss a range of solutions, there is a prescribed way to do so. But first let's briefly review the potential negatives involved in discussing a range of alternatives. The potential for confusing the prospect is greater when she has to deal with multiple options. Mentioning alternative solutions may also provide a resistant prospect with more opportunities to argue and disagree. Now back to the way to discuss solution alternatives.

Introduce service solutions with confidence. After all, you have handled the situation before. I said earlier that the proposed solution program is the vehicle for delivering the future situation. Now you want to determine how the prospect wants to travel to the required or desired future situation. The following vehicles offer different options:

Rolls Royce. No skimping on quality. Produce a solid, fully functioning product that will yield dividends for years to come.

Oldsmobile. Pay top dollar, but not through the roof, for a dependable, modest prestige vehicle (service solution) that borders on the luxurious, but is rooted in the practical.

Volkswagen. Get the job done as economically and efficiently as possible; never mind the frills. If it works, that is fine; we can always dress it up in the future.

Here is how to work with the three alternatives. First you start by mentioning the Rolls Royce solution program and watch closely for signs of prospect flinch or resistance, such as facial changes, including a tightening of the lips or a squinting of the eyes.

For example, I might say in discussing a solution program for a firm that has never had any marketing training, "For firms that are just now considering installing a marketing function, I have structured my work to include the entire professional staff in some form of marketing and business development."

If the prospect remains silent, or says, "No, I'm not interested in training all the troops. I can't afford it. They wind up leaving after a while, and it's too costly," then I continue with the Olds-mobile solution: "We could limit the program to your long-term, high-potential troops and the existing partners." Again, I observe and listen to assess the situation. If this alternative fails, I wind up a bit more forcefully by saying, "Given the nature of your situation, *you* should get your marketing program underway by training your existing partners who voluntarily agree to the training."

If the prospect doesn't respond, or if the response is unfavorable, it's a clear tip-off that you do not have all the facts. Refer back to your notes and verify their accuracy. My experience is that the apparent trappings of the person's office and the organization's reputation or standing in the industry are poor predictors of the amount of money the prospect will invest. My working principle is to never assume that a prospect will buy or set a budget limit until given the opportunity to do so.

OUTLINING THE PROPOSED WORK APPROACH

Once you have determined the appropriate service solution, restate the solution goal to confirm that you are communicating effectively. Your goal here is to make the service solution tangible. Keep in mind that you are still communicating on a verbal level; you have put nothing in writing, other than notes. By remaining in the discussion mode, you gain more information on how to prepare a winning written proposal, if one is required, and ensure that the actual engagement will proceed smoothly.

When outlining the proposed work approach, you must first discuss the methodology with the prospect. Don't overwhelm the prospect with too many details. He wants assurance that you know what you're doing. Focus on the broad tasks and the results you will achieve for the prospect. You must be very specific in stating the nature and level of assistance that you expect from the prospect and upon which the budget will be predicated. Then spell out with the prospect what he will do, how he will do it, and what he will provide.

Next spell out what you *won't* be doing—what is not part of the engagement. This discussion will reduce misunderstandings further down the road. (Note: Try not to discuss fees in specific terms until you are convinced you have an interested and qualified prospect. More on this in Chapter 16.)

In a similar manner, spell out exactly what deliverables will be supplied and in what level of detail as a result of this engagement. This includes interim reports, monthly reports or progress reports, and the final product. If the prospect will be receiving any additional benefits, spell these out.

This kind of precision may seem tedious, and appear to create more work than is necessary. However, it is precisely this type of effort that separates the novices from the pros in getting new clients. It is not advantageous to have vague or nebulous notions of how the engagement will turn out. Such unforeseen developments occur, but in most instances, the number of surprises will be minimized if you've first thought through the situation.

Next discuss who will be leading, participating in, and supporting the engagement team. Likewise, find out who will be the engagement coordinator. It is to your advantage to have the *prospect's best person* serve as the engagement coordinator. This person must be a credible source, well trained, and able to serve as a continuing point of contact.

Ask, "Does it make sense to proceed?" The phrase has been carefully designed. It quietly and powerfully communicates to the prospect that from this point forward it will be a mutual decision to proceed. The manner in which you communicate during the new-business discussion educates the prospect and shapes his response to you. If you communicate that you are hungry for business, that you are at his beck and call, many will attempt to take advantage of the situation.

During a new-business meeting with one of my clients, I was astounded to hear him tell a prospect, "I'm at the disposal of my clients; call me anytime you need to. I'll always be available to talk to you. I'd like to have you for a client." After a long discussion about the inadvertent implications of such statements, he vowed to be more careful with his promises.

Viewed in the proper perspective, the new-business discussion is really a miniconsulting engagement in which the classic problem definition, fact gathering, analysis, and recommendations are employed.

Making a verbal proposal is desirable at this time because it enables you to quickly move in for the close. If what you have verbally presented is of interest to the prospect, you have effectively shortened your selling task and can proceed more quickly with the initiation of the engagement. And even if what you have presented is not exactly on target with what the prospect has in mind, you can still quickly regroup, redefine the scope of work, and make a second verbal proposal that may hit the jackpot.

Your verbal proposal should build excitement and confidence in the mind and emotions of the contact. She must feel that she is making a good purchase because you have convinced her that you are the best one to provide a service solution to her need.

Following the verbal proposal you must test for "fit" or agreement. This can be done by posing questions such as the following:

"Does this make sense?"

"Have we covered the essentials?"

And the power statement, "How will you and I know when I have done a good job for you?"

By this time, the response of the contact should be, "That sounds about right." Or, "Yes, plus X." Or, "When can we start?" If you followed the steps outlined in this book, it would be a surprise if your verbal proposal weren't right on the mark, or at least very close.

SELLING THE SOLUTION AND ITS BENEFITS

To sell the solution and close the sale, you must outline the approved future picture frame of the prospect situation. Then, through your verbal proposal, you put the contact in the picture. How? You use her actual words and expressions from your interview notes. (Note: These would also appear in a written proposal.)

You stress your understanding of the many supporting elements within the prospect's organization. By using these elements as anchor points in the service solution, you enable the contact to maintain her own concept. It also positions you as an advocate for improving her situation, without making her wrong about retaining your services.

You conclude by stressing that the contact's positive attitude and the strength of her organization and staff, coupled with your experience and staff, will create the desired or required future situation on time and within budget. The benefits of this approach are that you and the prospect will be working from the same side of the fence, supplying resources to arrive at the cost-effective service solution.

16

Handling Concerns and Information Needs

Objections and concerns traditionally have been the bane of the salesperson's existence. You put in a substantial amount of time and effort to ensure that your services are needed by your prospect.

Yet no matter how compelling the need, no matter how precise the definitions of the desired and required future situation you develop, prospects are naturally going to have objections, concerns, and requests for additional information. Don't take it personally. It is a normal response to the introduction of new ideas.

Objections and client concerns should be welcomed. They give you the potential energy to close the discussion and move to action (Chapter 17). In this chapter we will look at ways to handle objections, including the "big three" facing us all:

Skepticism

Misunderstanding

Stalling, indecision

Your manner in handling these objections and concerns is to appear as a knowledgable, interested insider whose only mission is to help the contact achieve his objectives and his desired or required goals.

ANATOMY OF AN OBJECTION

To surface a prospect's objections and resolve any doubts and concerns, let's examine an objection. An objection is a reason for not buying that generally arises from a prospect's lack of understanding. Objections have a structure that enables you to analyze them and determine their cause. Happily, their structure also enables you to minimize their occurrences, and cope with their effects should they arise.

You must respond to objections with a positive attitude. Respect the prospect's doubts and view them as legitimate concerns.

Just as you have done in defining the existing need situation and the desired or required future situation, you must work with the prospect to understand the nature and scope of his objections. The information or facts you provide should be relevant to the prospect's way of thinking so he can gain better insights into how the service will benefit him. In short, the client-centered approach works well in handling objections.

As used here, the term *objections* refers to any barrier that is voiced by the prospect and that prevents you from moving on to the next step in the new-business discussion. The key word here is *voiced*. In the second half of this chapter, we will discuss client concerns that have not been voiced. The proper strategy to handle objections is to:

1. Welcome them
2. Build on them
3. Communicate openly and fully

It has been said that reasonable people will often disagree after searching for the right facts, data, and reasoning needed to achieve a meeting of the minds. You must take the lead in resolving disagreements. The most successful commissioned sales representatives know that the way they view objections determines the commissions earned. For example, the sales representative who welcomes objections is communicating to the prospect that the prospect's information needs are important and addressable.

A good approach would be, "I appreciate what you are saying. Many of our existing clients said the same thing before retaining us." You can then build on objections by offering the following, "Here is how we worked with them in overcoming the problem," or "If we can deliver it according to your schedule, would that still be a concern?" Or "I am glad you brought that up because it gives me an opportunity to highlight a superior aspect of our service solution."

When conducting a new-business discussion, being candid always pays. Yes, there are many who will fudge a little here and there and tell the prospect what he wants to hear, instead of the full truth. In the long term, maintaining 100 percent integrity works best. The few clients you lose will be offset by the many you gain because of your outstanding reputation for integrity.

Today's consumers are far better educated and far more sophisticated than ever before. They have the ability to check out facts, to make comparisons, and to determine whether you are telling it like it is. Realistically, you will not be able to adequately defuse every objection you encounter. But if you listen to the prospect and acknowledge her points as being valid for her, you have offered additional proof and justification for buying into the proposed approach.

Here are five steps that address prospect objections:

1. *Expect* and allow them to occur.
2. *Welcome* them when they do arise because they indicate

the prospect's interest. See them for what they are—a request for more information or a clarification of information already provided.

3. *Acknowledge* the prospect by restating the objection as a question to be verified. ". . .then you are concerned about XYZ?"

4. *Present* your evidence, give examples, offer testimonials, and so on.

5. *Support* the prospect's observation only if he has identified a real drawback. Then present an offsetting benefit. Say, "While your concern about DEF is justified, wouldn't you also agree that GHI more than compensates for it?"

I have found that after the prospect has brought up an objection, it is best to wait about 10 seconds before responding. Often the prospect continues talking and may offer even more clues as to how you should respond. If this happens, pause for an additional 10 seconds. This allows you to fully contemplate what you have just been told. The pause also signals that you are preparing a reply to the question.

Objections are really nothing more than a prospect's request for more information. Before the closing discussion can take place, this information must be provided. If you approach objections as requests for information, all of your new-business discussions will proceed more smoothly. Each time an objection is handled effectively, you have moved the prospect one step closer to a buying decision.

Not all objections are real; some objections are simply delaying tactics. A real objection is specific and represents signi'icant concern about your proposed solution on the part of the prospect. Some real objections are based on finite resources, limitations, or other constraints, such as, "It has to be finished by August 2 or we will lose several major contracts." Most real objections, however, center around a lack of information.

We all use false objections to fend off others. What you are proposing may be needed, but the prospect may not want to deal with it, or may not want to deal with it now. Those who offer false objections often don't really know why they are objecting. They may have some underlying fear about acknowledging the validity of your message. If you are not aware of these concerns, you will have a hard time responding appropriately.

Skepticism as an Objection

When the prospect is skeptical about you, your presentation, or your proposed solution, it often stems from one of the following factors:

1. *"Heard you Screwed Up Previously."* The prospect may have information about a previous engagement where you encountered some difficulties. Your task is to admit to any problems that were encountered and why (without placing blame) and to emphasize positive benefits the client gained as a result of your efforts.

2. *Qualitative Benefits.* Your explanation to the prospect may be fuzzy. He or she doesn't get it. Have you highlighted the benefits in the prospect's terms?

3. *Differing Favorable Futures.* What you have portrayed may not match what the prospect wants to achieve. Your task here would be to reexamine the desired or required future situation to achieve a better meeting of the minds.

4. *Insufficient Industry/Company Experience.* The prospect questions your ability to handle his or her situation because you haven't presented your capabilities adequately. You must offer compelling evidence that your experience is valid and up to the demands of this prospect.

5. *Disease vs. Symptoms.* The prospect doesn't think you have done the proper analysis; you have been focusing on the symptoms instead of the disease. For example, the prospect's initial concern is finding good replacements for key executives who have been leaving. If you neglected finding out why they

are leaving in favor of discussing your executive search procedures, the fun part of the job, this objection could and probably will arise.

6. *Low Confidence.* Based on your appearance or presentation, you have been unable to inspire confidence in the prospect. This requires asking the prospect to tell you exactly what it is she needs to agree to move the action forward. This may necessitate gathering additional information and attempting to reschedule an appointment so that you can invite a colleague or other expert to assist you.

7. *Contact's Inexperience.* The contact person or prospect may be inexperienced. Perhaps they have never worked with someone in your profession. In this case, testimonial letters and endorsements from others in similar positions will be helpful.

The factors outlined above triggered the objection and can be reviewed in advance and *prevented* from occurring. By presenting information and evidence designed to deactivate the trigger, the skepticism/objection rate should drop dramatically as you improve your ability to communicate in a client-centered manner. In addition to the above skepticism triggers, there may also be factors that *maintain* or *sustain* skepticism on the part of prospects.

1. *Failure to Gain Rapport.* The biggest culprit here is not listening and responding effectively. If the prospect thinks you are offering lip service or just nodding blank approval, skepticism may set in quickly. Active listening takes work. In *Marketing Your Consulting and Professional Services* we offer several checklists you can use to evaluate your listening effectiveness.

2. *Not Asking the Right Questions.* The ability to ask good questions is fundamental to getting new clients. In her recent book *Smart Questions*, Dorothy Leeds says that asking good questions can be just as important, if not more so, than having the right answers. Your insider's understanding of the niche and your preparation for the new-business discussion should arm you with the capability to ask the right questions. Also, by tier-

ing your new-business contacts, you can call upon low-priority suspects first to gain the insider's knowledge that will enable you to interact powerfully with your higher priority leads.

3. *Not Answering Questions.* Whatever the prospect brings up, no matter how trivial, should be regarded as a contribution to the new-business discussion. If you duck a dumb-sounding question, the prospect may wonder what you are trying to hide. This advice runs counter to that of other authors who believe you bypass trivial questions. As an advocate for the prospect, you can't afford to duck any questions.

4. *Defensiveness.* If you're at all defensive in handling a prospect's queries and concerns, you are likely to turn the prospect off. Remember, your reaction to objections is optional. As Wayne Dyer, Ph.D. says in *Your Erroneous Zones,* "You can choose your emotions," so choose to be responsive.

5. *Not a Client-centered Approach.* This occurs when you speak in global terms or offer evidence that really doesn't relate to the prospect. For example, "We are the biggest in the world," or, "Our partners get 40 hours of CPE training every year." Such statements offered at the appropriate moment can be beneficial in your marketing effort. However, extrinsic techniques that are not client-centered nor germane to the discussion should be avoided.

6. *Lack of Time Commitment on Your Part.* If you seem rushed or you haven't given enough consideration to the prospect's points, you will end up making the prospect feel uneasy. While it is not recommended that you linger endlessly within a prospect's office, you must be willing to listen patiently and handle the client's objections within reason.

7. *Presumption.* By promising too much too soon or minimizing the unique factors of the client's situation, you are likely to contribute to the prospect's skepticism.

The maintaining and sustaining factors should be reviewed before the interview so you can plan a coping strategy. Skepticism occurs when your communication is not in sync with the prospect's. I encountered more than my share of skepticism early in my consulting career because I was too quick to respond and my answers were too pat. A partner in one of my target firms told me, "I know you're good, but don't be too quick to show and tell. You're an outsider talking to people who hate the whole notion of marketing, so go slow and don't solve in five minutes what we've been struggling with for years."

Objections Due to Misunderstanding

Objections due to misunderstanding between you and the prospect fall into three basic categories.

1. *Inadequate Definition of the Need Situation.* In this instance, you must return to an analysis of the existing situation and verify, verify, verify. Remember, defining and solving problems is your stock in trade. You earn your keep by immersing yourself in the misery of others and showing them how, by working with you, the misery can be eliminated. The prospect earns his keep by avoiding or getting beyond problems that affect his operations. It is your responsibility to get the facts and engineer understanding.

2. *Inadequate Definition of Desired State.* This is handled in the same manner as that of inadequate definition of need situation in number 1 above.

3. *Inadequate Definition of Benefits and Features.* Your task is to provide specific examples of how this prospect will benefit from your proposed solution program. It is also helpful to rely on a colleague, should one be present, to provide clarification and additional information.

Stalling

Figure 16.1 summarizes how to handle situations in which the prospect does not wish to proceed due to six different and common factors.

STALLING TECHNIQUES AND THEIR RESOLUTION

Factor	Resolution
1. He is not decision-maker	Ask to meet with decision maker
Find out who makes decisions	Who do you think?
2. Not sold (uncertain/afraid of price)	Probe
Explain benefits	Explain
Probe beforehand	
3. Wants other proposals	Have client talk to others first
Ask if job is competitive	You set selection criteria
Be last to propose	Why other proposals?
	What info do you need?
4. Lack of understanding	Probe
Explain beforehand	Explain
Probe in previous conversation	
5. Too busy right now	When should we start?
Ask about schedule	Can he delegate?
Be prepared	Our project will ease burden
Plan	Increase scope
6. Project Not Budgeted	Cost/Benefit
Illustrate benefits	Adjust scope
Be prepared	

FIGURE 16.1. Stalling Techniques and their Resolution

HANDLING UNSPOKEN CONCERNS

For the balance of the chapter, we will focus on unspoken concerns of the prospect. You might ask, "How can I possibly deal with objections that have not been presented to me?" The answer is to anticipate concerns not voiced by the client based on your insider's understanding of the niche and information you have gained during other new-business discussions. Through planning, you can develop strategies that will deal with the unspoken client concerns. Thus you will be able to head them off at the pass.

The key to handling unspoken client concerns is to flush them out, or to initiate a discussion about them when you sense the concern is present. Allow me to clarify. Near the close of a new-business discussion, if the prospect appears to be reluctant to proceed or is otherwise holding back in some way, you say, "Are there other points that we haven't discussed that you would like to bring up now?"

Your mission is to uncover what the prospect feels uncomfortable talking about. Many professional-service marketers would prefer not to do this. They feel that if they skirt the issue all will turn out well. But this is usually not the case. Keep probing until the underlying concern is voiced. Until the human race learns how to master extrasensory perception, you are going to have to get the missing information straight from the prospect's mouth.

Here are five specific examples of unspoken client concerns and suggested responses.

1. *The Professional Will Not Understand my Business or Industry Because my Business or Industry is Different.* Stress your extensive experience in industry, maintain objectivity, discuss the commonality of the prospect's problems and how you have addressed them before.

2. *Engaging an Outside Professional is an Admission of Incompetence, an Indication of Trouble.* You must stress that bringing you in is a positive indication that the situation is important. The mark of a professional manager is taking positive action to preclude negative occurrences.

3. *We Have Worked With Other Outside Professionals in the Past and Their Recommendations Did Not Work.* This situation calls for allowing the prospect to describe the problem in detail. Then you point out your experience and ability to tailor and presell solutions to ensure results.

4. *Consultants (or Lawyers, Accountants, etc.) Have Only One Concern: Maximizing Their Fees.* This requires a cost-benefit analysis and discussion of how you strive to offer service solutions that are needed and produce results that far exceed the fees involved. You can handle this using a story: "You know, the fee involved in tackling tough situations can look huge if taken out of context. But when you look at the payoffs to clients who engage good consultants, the fees are right in line."

5. *Firms in your Industry have a High Turnover in Personnel and Cannot Provide the Continuity We Will Need.* Be candid about staffing and turnover, and if this is a high-potential prospect, try to guarantee that top-level staff will be assigned this job.

As a rule of thumb, any time it appears to you that the prospect is concerned about something she is not talking about, you must probe for information. "It seems to me that you look doubtful about something I have said. Am I correct in my feeling?" Successful relationships are enjoyable, enriching, open, and perceived as everyone-wins situations by both parties. This cannot be achieved if you allow unvoiced concerns to go unaddressed. Your explanation is, "I am here to try to be of assistance, but can't be without an adequate understanding of the situation." This may shake the prospect loose and get her to open up in a way that she hasn't previously; or it may confirm your suspicions that this would be too tough a sale to give it much more time.

QUESTIONS ABOUT FEES

Problems related to fees generally start in the mind of the service provider, not the prospect. Let the prospect bring up the matter of fees. If it does come up too early in the discussion, I respond by saying, "I appreciate your wanting to know what your budget for the engagement will be. In order to give you a sound answer, I need to get a little more information."

Put in perspective, fees are just a normal part of business. When the topic does come up, you want to control but not dominate the discussion.

I've made it a rule not to discuss fees until I'm prepared to justify what is required to produce the results the prospect and I agreed to. I never use the words *costs* or *fees* in connection with my services. The term *budget* is preferable.

To summarize, here are a couple of general principles in dealing with fees:

1. Don't make the prospect wrong for introducing fees, but
2. Handle the discussion of fees on your terms—when you are ready to discuss them and in the context of expected performance.
3. Build your case based on the benefits the prospect will receive.

Getting new clients involves encountering lots of objections. Relax. Everybody faces them, but few will handle them as well as you.

17

Closing the Discussion and Moving to Action

The closing process gets blown out of proportion by many authors and professionals. The prospect is either portrayed as a tethered goat who is mauled into submission or a giant who must be overcome by brute force. By following the steps outlined throughout the chapters of Part III, Conducting A Winning New-Business Discussion, you will find that the close isn't a big deal. Rather, it is the logical end result of a successful new-business interview, an agreement to proceed to the next mutually beneficial step.

Since you are calling on prospects in a targeted industry niche, and discussing hot-button needs, your close becomes much easier. In fact, the client-centered marketing approach and identification of specific needs is a powerful combination that takes a lot of the effort out of closing. Thus, if you are having closing problems, you probably need to improve the way you handled earlier steps in the new-business discussion.

It is both unnecessary and unproductive to put on your closing manner. Your personality doesn't have to change; there is no need to become anxious. Properly handled, closing is a mutually satisfying and normal wrapup to your discussion. In many cases, the prospects will set up a closing for you by asking, "When could you get started?"

PURPOSES OF THE CLOSING PHASE

Your purpose in closing the new-business discussion is to obtain an agreement to proceed to the next mutually beneficial step. This has been your primary goal all along. If things are not going according to plan, you fall back to your secondary or contingency plan (see Chapter 11).

A second major purpose of the closing phase is to assist the prospect in overcoming inertia and resistance to change. This is done by suggesting ways to produce a more favorable future and by continuously speaking in terms of client benefits.

Three Steps to Closing

When it comes to marketing professional services, there are three basic steps to the closing process: recognizing the time to close, debriefing the prospect using a client-centered scenario, and making the closing statement. Let's examine each of these in detail.

1. *Recognize When it is Time to Close.* Selling your service solution is the sum total of the steps you have taken from the time you first contacted the prospect until the time she is satisfied with her purchase. Everything you do during the new-business discussion is preparation for the act of closing. For example, you observe closing signals on the part of the prospect. These occur when the prospect leans forward, offers more open posture, starts taking notes, asks another person to listen to the discussion, and communicates her agreement with your ideas. You might take a moment to recall the signals you have observed.

It is also time to close when the prospect *asks signal questions*, such as who will do the work, what technology would you use, and when would you be available. Think back to the times when you closed business recently. What questions did the contact person bring up? Also, what was there about the situation that made you know that the close was imminent?

Another tip-off that it is time to close is when the prospect *indicates requirements*. If he says, "If we are going to proceed, the start day would have to be the second Tuesday." Or, "My vacation will not be over until the 18th." Or, "Of course Mr. Walston would have to be involved in any decisions such as this . . . ." Such statements strongly indicate that it is time to close.

Finally, when the needs have been confirmed, the benefits have been established by you and accepted by the prospect, and the objections have been resolved, it is time to move to the second step in the closing process.

2. *Debrief the Prospect Using a Client-centered Scenario.* Using reinforcing statements, it is time to briefly restate the benefits the prospect can expect as a result of the service solution you will introduce into the organization. Create a positive word picture of the client's desired or required future situation, calling attention to the positive purchase motivation trigger mentioned earlier.

Debriefing is truly a leverage operation! Here, you summarize your understanding of the prospect's central interest or concern. By restating benefits, you are activating their buying motives with substantial leverage and encouraging them to retain your services.

Debriefing begins with a statement such as, "Let's take a moment to see what we have covered so far." You communicate slowly while you leaf through your interview notes. Then you say, "If I am on target, you are interested in XYZ." Or, "You are concerned about ABC." You knew this when you determined the need situation. You then say, "Specifically, you need. . .," and restate the solution specifications that you identified when you were scoping the desired or required future situation. You also include any concessions you made in response to earlier objections or negotiation points.

> "As I mentioned, we will. . ."

Then restate the actions you will take to produce the results promised and restate what the prospect must do.

> "Which means that you will. . ."

Again mention the solution goal that you used throughout the entire contact process. You have now completed a loop: You need, we provide, you get, your need is met.

You need ——————————————————→ We provide

↑   ↓

Your need is met ◄——————————— Solution

Making a Closing Statement

With the client-centered scenario established, you are ready to make the closing statement. This step moves the prospect to the final A in the AIDA process.

As you close, you make the major decision for the prospect and give him the final word on the subject by offering him options. This is also known as the "assumptive" close and is most appropriate for professional services:

"Mr. Levitt, to produce the accounts-receivable system we have been discussing, I need to come back and get some information about the current setup." You then look at your calendar and say, "Monday afternoon or Thursday about 10:30 is open right now. Which time would be best for you?"

You have made the major decision to meet again. Yet you've

allowed the prospect to have the final word by allowing him to choose the date and time to meet.

If the discussion has not gone according to your plan, then make a secondary close. "Mr. Levitt, I understand your desire to be on hand if we are to proceed. Since your vacation will be over in two weeks, I will call you midweek when you return. This will allow you to go through your mail and backlog. Would Thursday, morning or afternoon be best for you?" You ask this with a smile and wait for a response.

At this time, the prospect will suggest a meeting time or will raise some objections. In the latter case, you should employ the coping strategies presented in Chapter 16.

Suppose you have been having a good discussion, but you are still uncertain whether the prospect has made up her mind. You say, "Ms. Johnson, may I use your phone for a minute? Getting your marketing audit under way will require the use of our analyst Bob Richardson. I would like to make sure he will be available."

Another approach in dealing with a prospect's uncertainty is to ask him a question that leads down one of two closing paths, such as, "We need a great deal of information to start a project like this. Our people could gather it directly or we could outline the data requirements for your people. Which approach makes the most sense to you?" The prospect is bound to select one of the choices. This gives you a new vantage point from which to proceed.

Some Closing Do's and Don'ts

As indicated in Chapter 3, a win in the process of getting new clients consists of getting a prospect to meet with you. At the conclusion of your new-business discussion, a win consists of getting the prospect to meet with you a second time, so you can move to action. If you are lucky, you might be asked outright to prepare a bid proposal or to start next Tuesday. Figure 17.1 gives tips to remember when going for the close.

SOME DO'S AND DON'TS

DO'S	DON'TS
Stay in normal discussion mode	Change hats and telegraph that you are going to close
Include all necessary information the prospect agreed was relevant or important	Add benefits not brought up or agreed to by prospect
Remember you are not asking for the order	Pressure for a sale—continue the relationship by moving to a next step
Expect your close to "fail" due to information needs not raised and handled	Resent the failure—look on it as an opportunity to get more information
Use nondirective probes when close fails and be positive	Show resentment at stalls

FIGURE 17.1. Some DO'S and DON'TS When Closing

Exiting the Prospect's Office

After making your closing statement, you will encounter one of three responses:

1. An outright rejection of your closing options
2. An "I'm not ready to proceed yet" type of reply, or
3. An "Okay, let's get this show on the road" type of reply

Let's examine each one in turn.

Because you are promoting solutions to important needs, the number of outright rejections should drop dramatically. Don't panic should a rejection occur. Just stop talking for a moment and then ask, "May I ask why you're saying that?" Don't sound cross or appear pushy. Ask the question in a conversational manner and listen to the prospect's answer while observing his body language. The usual cause of an outright rejection is anger; the prospect's feelings got hurt or you inadvertently pushed his anger button. Who knows, he may be steamed at himself for overlooking something you said you would do in solving the problem.

If you think you can still salvage the situation after you have listened to him, say, "If it makes sense, let's take a few more minutes to discuss our solution goals for producing the results you want." Try to keep the "we" feeling.

If you feel it is futile to continue in the selling mode, then say, "Ms. Henderson, I wish that we could have worked something out. I'm glad I had the opportunity to meet you." Then shift the tone and focus of the meeting by discussing a current industry concern as you pack up and leave her office.

The "I'm not ready" reply can be handled with a simple response, such as "Oh?" or "Not ready?" After your reply, be quiet. Since you were the last person to talk and the pressure of silence is building, the prospect will often blurt out the reason for his unwillingness to proceed. If this happens say, "Thank you for telling me why you were not ready to proceed." Note the shift in tense from *are not* to *were not*. If the prospect lets this slide by, I begin to handle each concern in order. This is a critical point in the discussion. Your goal is not to shoot down his reasons, but to close by converting the energy behind the reasons for not proceeding into justifications for moving to action.

The way you do this is as follows. If, for example, he is reluctant to proceed because he is uncertain that a reorganization can really be effective when managed by outsiders, you deal with his concern by saying, "Mr. Henry, your concern about using outsiders is well founded. When you are dealing with a sensitive issue such as reorganization, you have to have outsiders who know how the industry works and what it takes to organize and harness the talents and temperaments of a large number of people. Frankly, it requires talent and experience such as ours, which has been developed and tested in dozens of reorganizations."

Examine the anatomy of my responses. They always include an acknowledgment of the prospect—he's okay, he's no dummy. Then, I indicate that I've listened to his response or I pose a question by using some of his words in my response. I conclude by introducing the benefits of working with my firm and the dangers of not using the best available talent.

It would be valuable for you right now to list the "not now's" you encounter and to apply the model described above. Train yourself to reply in systematic fashion without getting into an argument or sounding too glib or rehearsed.

The favored reply, *"Okay, let's go"* will be encountered much more frequently as you build your skills and confidence using the methods discussed in this book. Attempt to schedule a start date without having to prepare a proposal. Get agreement that a confirmation letter will suffice.

Many readers of this book are fortunate in that they are not required to prepare proposals. They simply outline their work approach, quote budget or billing arrangements, and schedule a start date. Others are not as fortunate. The next chapter will address the techniques involved in preparing winning proposals.

18

Preparing a Winning Proposal

As a result of your new-business discussion, you may find yourself preparing a proposal. From your standpoint, however, the best proposal is one you don't have to write. Your time, energy, and expenses can be kept to a minimum when a confirmation letter containing the specifics of your service solution will suffice. With today's stiff competition in the service sector, however, proposals are required more often.

Entire books and training programs have been written on the subject of proposal writing. The purpose of this chapter is to present the anatomy of a winning proposal. Ernie Kosty, president of Kosty and Associates in Chicago, is a very effective proposal writer. Kosty, who is also president of the Midwest Society of Professional Consultants, has perfected the proposal process over the last 25 years. This chapter incorporates parts of his method with our own 18 years of experience in this area.

TO BID OR NOT TO BID

When you agree to write a proposal, one thing is certain: You *will* incur costs. So you must first determine whether you should bid. The following questions will help you decide whether to bid.

Do you have a chance of getting new business?

Does the prospect have the money and desire to proceed?

Do you have the necessary resources to be successful?

Will this work be profitable and move your firm in the direction you want it to go?

Are you willing to do everything necessary to produce a winning proposal?

Proposals don't sell the job, but they can unsell it. This occurs when you give a doubtful prospect "hard copy" justification for not proceeding.

Many professionals make the mistake of preparing proposals even when they don't believe they will get the job. Obviously, most of the proposals you write will not be winners. However, a proposal should only be undertaken when there is an identifiable chance to gain new business, or the proposal will be of use with other prospects, or you need to propose to get your name on an authorized bidders list used by government agencies.

Preparing the Draft Proposal

A proposal has three basic purposes. First, it educates the prospective client about the nature and dynamics of his need situation. Second, it convinces the prospect that you are willing and able to deliver results. Third, it justifies the prospect's investment in terms that are useful and understandable to members of the decision-making unit.

In producing a proposal, I recommend first writing a draft. This allows for prospect input. Let's discuss the steps to preparing an effective draft proposal.

1. *State the General Theme of the Proposal.* For example, "To describe how (your service) will enable the client to counteract the negative effects of previous indebtedness and maintain a positive cash flow."

2. *Develop a Written Outline.* Determine the major elements/ sections to be included. Most proposals contain the sections presented in the chart below:

PROPOSAL SECTIONS

1. Introductory paragraphs
   Indicate broad nature of job
   Cite meeting that occasioned proposal
   Indicate how proposal is organized
   May have some kind words about client

2. The present situation, or our understanding of the problem
   Expanded definition of problem
   Details of problem (includes "you are concerned. . .")
   Confirms our understanding of the situation
   Includes our thinking through the implications of what the prospect told us
   Puts the problem in context

3. The objectives and scope of the work
   Objectives to be met
   What we will do and not do

4. Our approach to solving the problem
   A prediction of what the assignment will involve stated in such detail that prospect appreciates and understands our approach, without committing us to an inflexible course of action

5. How we would work with you
   Work closely with key people
   Draw upon the creative thinking of client people
   Hold frequent progress meetings

6. Anticipated benefits/end results
   Stated from top-management viewpoint
   Implicitly justifies why client should hire us
   May be stated as final product or proposed outcome of
   project
7. Estimate of time and charges
   Time charges stated either in range (e.g. $15,000 to
   $17,000) or an appropriate dollar figure per month
   Reimbursable charges stated separately
8. Starting date
   Typically gives two-to-three-week period for assignment
   planning
   Frequently close with, "We await your approval to pro-
   ceed"
9. Closing paragraph
   Statement of interest in doing work for prospective client
   May include generalized statement on benefits
10. Qualifications statement
    Not in all proposals
    State why we are qualified to do job
    Background of principals
    Corporate history
    Facilities
11. References when appropriate
    Normally provided only on request
    Often submitted by separate letter or attached to proposal
    letter

3. *Organize and Distill Your Interview Notes.* Include other
related client data for each section.

4. *Review Each Section from the Prospect's Viewpoint.* Identify omissions, points that require proof, and nonessential re-
dundancies. Winning proposals have deliberate redundancy in
regard to benefits, experience, and the consequences of not proceeding.

5. *Write the Initial Draft.* Let it sit for a while before reviewing it.

6. *Type the Proposal in Semifinal Draft Style.* Leave lots of white space for notes by either you or the prospect.

7. *Stamp the Words "Working Draft" on the Cover.* Schedule an appointment with the "champion" in the prospect's company to review the proposal.

What Makes a Winner

Even if you have followed to the letter the items listed in the chart entitled Proposal Sections, there are some elements that will make your proposal stand out.

1. *Introductory Paragraphs.* You want to provide introductory comments that are warm, are tailored to the audience, and exude confidence that a mutual understanding will be achieved. Don't be overly solicitous, using such statements as, "We are grateful for the opportunity to propose. . . ." The prospect is not doing you a favor by asking you to prepare a proposal. Indeed, if you do the job correctly, he is going to derive value from it. Some prospects obtain proposals so they can do the jobs themselves. We will talk about avoiding that trap momentarily.

2. *The Present Situation or Understanding of the Problem.* Winning proposals provide a balanced description of the situation. This section is written to avoid embarrassing the reader and to avoid undue criticism from significant others. The 1987 *Tower Report* on the Iran arms affair, for example, could have blasted President Reagan's loose management approach. Instead, it used terminology that did not embarrass him or cause him to criticize the way the report was written. You must take great pains to positively present the need situation and prior actions. Then you convey your prospect's concerns and interests and how they relate to the present situation.

3. *The Objectives and Scope of the Work.* The solution objective, the benefit that will accrue to the prospect, and supporting

goals are spelled out in this section. You must also spell out precisely who will do what and what will be included in the solution program.

4. *Our Approach to Solving the Problem.* This section discusses what the solution engagement will involve. Winning proposals generally follow this structure: (1) The tasks required to produce the future situation are listed; (2) The products of each task, including the deliverable and intangible factors such as morale, confidence, and so on, are identified; (3) The benefits statements are fully defined for each task. Your task is to offer just enough detail to make the prospect appreciate and understand the approach, without committing your firm to an inflexible course of action.

For example, I've figured out the process involved in formulating a strategy and positioning a firm in its niche. Instead of giving away the store, I write,

I will personally work with you and your key people in determining the current and preferred strategic posture for your firm. The posture will contain a definition of the current strategic direction, an analysis of the scope and service mix, and recommendations for using this analysis to position your firm as a leader in the niche.

5. *How We Would Work With You.* Surprises are the enemy of good relationships. Your proposal should pinpoint the submission of early and frequent progress reviews. This is especially necessary if the engagement is complex or of long duration. You want to avoid the adverse consequences of being wrong. Your goal at all times is to avoid the nagging question "I wonder what the professional is up to now?"

Give the client credit for having a competent staff, with which you can work and communicate well. Offer such statements as "We will draw upon the experience and creative thinking of your people to . . . ." Build a relationship between your firm and the organization's employees. Keep the prospect's confidence level high.

6. *Anticipated Benefits/End Results.* In an eye-catching manner, state in specific terms what you will strive to produce given the resources and time constraints. For example, as a result of the reorganization of department XYZ, management can expect a substantial improvement in morale and personal performance. Also implicitly justify why the client should hire you, using statements such as, "Using our unique approach. . ." or, "We will rely on our 15 years' experience to produce a . . . ."

7. *Estimate of Time and Charges.* You should state the amount that you will charge in a range. Remember, this is a draft proposal and chances are you will modify what you have written. If the norms of your profession dictate an alternative way of presenting estimated charges, then use it. Any reimbursable charges (i.e., out-of-pocket expenses) should be stated separately.

8. *Starting Date.* Your availability to start is an important selling point, a fulcrum on which the action proceeds. You need to strike a balance here. If you are available on too short notice, the prospect may wonder why you're not busy: "No good?" On the other hand, having to wait six to eight weeks can cool off a hot prospect. Even if you are working flat-out, you can still find a half day to get the engagement started.

9. *Closing Paragraph.* Your closing paragraph should reemphasize your interest in doing work for this prospective client. "Working with you and your staff to (solution goal) will pay dividends to (name of prospect). We await your approval to proceed."

10. *Qualifications Statement.* Depending on how familiar the prospect is with your firm, it may not be necessary to include this section in your proposal. The qualification statement outlines the general capabilities of your firm and why you in particular are qualified to do the job. The key point here is to ensure that you are a known quantity to all members of the decision-making unit.

11. *References (When Appropriate).* Don't underestimate the power of a previous client's positive comment on a job well done. The support and endorsement offered by someone outside your firm can be the deciding factor in your ability to gain a new client.

Proposal Preparation Hints

Use graphics when needed, but don't overdo the dramatic. Consider making the proposal look more like a report by using sidebars and headlines. Your goal is to have it read. If it looks inviting, it will be. Start each section on a separate page because it allows you to make changes easily, and facilitates easier reading.

Review the language you have used and make sure your proposal contains a majority of active verbs. If you have included a qualification section with biographical sketches, make sure they appeal to the prospect. Your proposal is literally a sample of your professional skills. Moreover, it is the most tangible product you will offer the prospect until the promised results are delivered.

A winning proposal blends technical and managerial competence to deliver a cost-effective result. It must demonstrate your firm's professionalism loudly and clearly. The checklist in Figure 18.1 can be used to examine your proposals.

PROPOSING WITHOUT GIVING THE JOB AWAY

I wish this section were not necessary, but some prospects ask for proposals just so they can learn how to do the job themselves. To avoid this problem, follow the principle of going long on benefits to accrue, and short on how you are going to produce the benefits. For example, instead of telling how you assemble a market-focus study group, describe what you will do. You could say, "After forming a focus group designed to capture the full range of buying dynamics for your type of product, our inter-

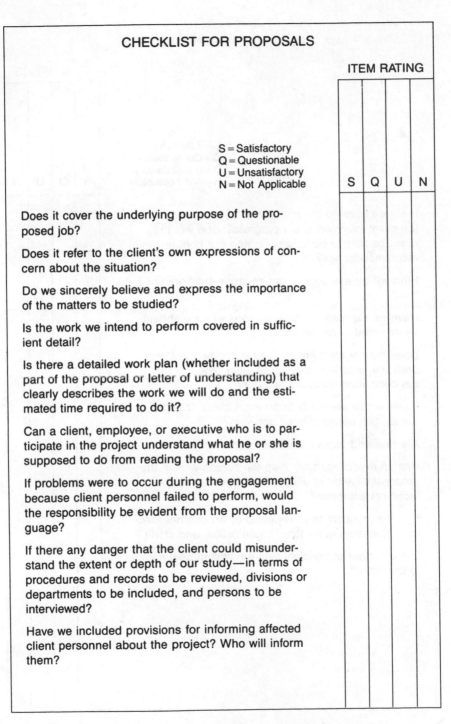

CHECKLIST FOR PROPOSALS

ITEM RATING

S = Satisfactory
Q = Questionable
U = Unsatisfactory
N = Not Applicable

	S	Q	U	N
Does it cover the underlying purpose of the proposed job?				
Does it refer to the client's own expressions of concern about the situation?				
Do we sincerely believe and express the importance of the matters to be studied?				
Is the work we intend to perform covered in sufficient detail?				
Is there a detailed work plan (whether included as a part of the proposal or letter of understanding) that clearly describes the work we will do and the estimated time required to do it?				
Can a client, employee, or executive who is to participate in the project understand what he or she is supposed to do from reading the proposal?				
If problems were to occur during the engagement because client personnel failed to perform, would the responsibility be evident from the proposal language?				
If there any danger that the client could misunderstand the extent or depth of our study—in terms of procedures and records to be reviewed, divisions or departments to be included, and persons to be interviewed?				
Have we included provisions for informing affected client personnel about the project? Who will inform them?				

FIGURE 18.1. Checklist for Proposals

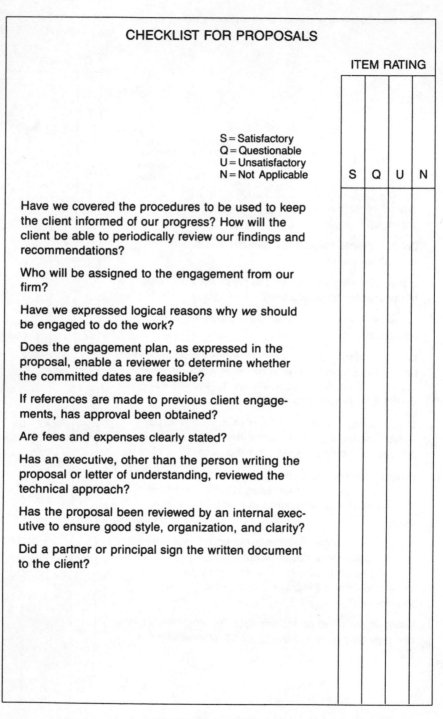

	ITEM RATING			

CHECKLIST FOR PROPOSALS

S = Satisfactory
Q = Questionable
U = Unsatisfactory
N = Not Applicable

	S	Q	U	N
Have we covered the procedures to be used to keep the client informed of our progress? How will the client be able to periodically review our findings and recommendations?				
Who will be assigned to the engagement from our firm?				
Have we expressed logical reasons why *we* should be engaged to do the work?				
Does the engagement plan, as expressed in the proposal, enable a reviewer to determine whether the committed dates are feasible?				
If references are made to previous client engagements, has approval been obtained?				
Are fees and expenses clearly stated?				
Has an executive, other than the person writing the proposal or letter of understanding, reviewed the technical approach?				
Has the proposal been reviewed by an internal executive to ensure good style, organization, and clarity?				
Did a partner or principal sign the written document to the client?				

FIGURE 18.1. Continued

viewing team will ask six to eight questions, which, based on our extensive experience, will yield the information you need to make the go/no-go decision regarding product X."

PROPOSAL DELIVERY

I believe you never should allow the prospect to present the proposal to the ultimate decision-maker(s) for you. Your goal is to be present during the review with the decision-making unit. If this can't be done, seek to meet with at least two or three members of the decision-making unit prior to the decision. Otherwise, it may be best not to propose because you are telling the prospect he is in charge of the project. I realize this may sound harsh and not be your standard practice, but I urge you to reconsider your position.

The advantage of presenting your proposal to the decision-making unit is that nothing is lost in the translation. You are able to answer questions and provide immediate feedback to the contact persons. The disadvantages of being present are few, if any. Perhaps your being there may inhibit full and open discussion, but this can be overcome, especially if you have developed an in-house champion who will work and sell on your behalf.

PREPARING THE FINAL PROPOSAL

If the draft is accepted, ask your new client to write the words, "Accepted as noted," and the date on the bottom of the draft. You can sign it and send a copy to the client. This becomes your engagement-detail-confirmation letter.

Larger organizations typically insist on a finished, final draft that is letter perfect. To paraphrase Confucius; When you have to prepare a final proposal, do the best possible job because it is visible evidence of your ability to deliver a useful and informative product on a timely basis.

If the draft proposal is not accepted, you have to determine why it died. Otherwise, you run the risk of repeating the same mistake throughout the niche.

A continuing question asked by professionals is, "How do I follow up on an outstanding proposal without being perceived as pushy and hungry?" I don't have the answer; I don't think there is one answer. But I send a note to the contact person thanking him for his efforts on my behalf. If I haven't heard from him in a week, I call him and find out what is happening. Does he need any additional information? If he says he does not, I ask him when the organization will be making a decision. Should I call him shortly after that time?

Remain focused on the prospect you have been tracking. If you don't hear from them in a few weeks, send them a letter telling them you're still interested in working with them, but you will not be able to guarantee a quick start-up time because you're getting into your busy season. Much like spending too much time waiting in the reception area, you must consistently demonstrate that your time is valuable.

19

Reinforcing Your Client's Choice

MAKING THE "GO" DECISION A REALITY

When it comes to actually making the "go" decision a reality, many professionals get heartburn. They eagerly wait to hear that the client is going to proceed, but then hesitate to follow up to garner a decision to proceed. The rule on following up is simple: Do it early and do it often. There are a variety of engagement killers that can creep up at any moment:

The prospect might be going out for additional proposals now that you have brought your solution approach to his attention.

The prospect may be getting into hot water internally, facing budgetary concerns, office politics, and so on.

The key to effective follow-up is always to offer something to share or have something to check up on every time you make contact. For example, say you called to get some information you need to develop computer software. Listen for clues that the opportunity may be hanging by a thread:

> "It is going to be a while before we can get started because. . ."
>
> "Are you really certain that you will be able to. . .?"
>
> "We need to discuss this further. I was talking with. . .and he raised the issue of. . ."

Any of the above responses demands your immediate attention. Review the techniques for handling objections and client concerns. If you sense that face-to-face discussion is necessary, arrange another appointment and be sure that essential members of the decision-making unit will attend.

HANDLING POSTPURCHASE CONCERNS

You know how it feels. Tonight you are going to pick up a new gizmo that you just bought. You mention your purchase to a good friend who says, "Gosh, I wish you would have let me know before you did that. I could have saved you a ton of money and gotten you a better deal."

You are feeling lousy now: It is called postpurchase concern. It is manifested in a lot of ways, but mainly by worry: Did I really make the right decision? Have I been taken? Will I look like a fool?

No matter what the purchase, the bigger the price tag and the more closely it affects your personal and professional life, the greater the level and intensity of postpurchase concern. Experienced professionals are aware of this phenomenon and take a number of steps to manage and minimize its consequences:

1. They call the new client with a bit of good news. "I was just reviewing the work plan, and thought you would be inter-

ested in knowing that Bob Henry is going to have more time to work on JKL. This means that you will have our best manager handling your project."

Joe Gandolfo, who is listed in the *Guinness Book of World Records* as the world's most successful insurance salesperson, says, "You would be surprised how much a brand-new customer appreciates a phone call saying how much you appreciate having the opportunity to do business with him." Gandolfo always makes it a point to send a handwritten note, such as:

Dear Mark,

Tonight does not seem too soon to congratulate you on this afternoon's decision about _____ . This is certainly a major step in establishing _____ . I hope that our meeting was the beginning of a long and enduring relationship.

> Sincerely,
> Joe Gandolfo

2. They send something that relates to the upcoming engagement. This could include a relevant article, a previous PAR summary, or some other item that solidifies the initiation of the engagement.

3. They schedule a lunch appointment with the new client and with another client for whom the same type of services were performed.

4. As soon as possible they send someone from the professional-service firm to visit the client firm and be seen in action. Your visibility on site will calm the client.

The purpose of these actions is simply to reassure the purchaser that he made a good decision to proceed. The subtle message that you are conveying is, "You chose the right firm to do the work. Consequently, the results will be forthcoming, and your organization will get the benefits they need and are paying for. You will be safe and well regarded."

You will have a lot more opportunities to make the "go" decision a reality by using the niche-marketing approach presented in this book. You made a good choice when you bought it. Jeff and I have enjoyed presenting it to you.

Glossary

Affinity Factor the behavioral characteristics and communication style of your best existing clients that enable you to feel comfortable in relating to them.

AIDA Process creating a favorable *awareness* (A), sharing *information* (I) to develop an interest in seeing you, conducting need-driven *discussions* (D), and building a desire to proceed to *action* (A).

Alert, Yellow-Red the zone of unacceptable performance of a factor deemed to be important in the operation of a prospect's business.

Benefit the satisfaction your client receives from your service solution.

Buying Motive the internal force that activates and directs the behavior of members of the decision-making unit to accept your recommended solution program.

Champion a member of the decision-making unit who wants the company to purchase the solution you are proposing.

Client-Centered Marketing the continuing process of developing and enhancing relationships with clients and other receptive people who are or can be useful to you in using, retaining, and referring you and your services.

Client Referral an existing client that has provided you with leads, introductions, and/or has vouched for you.

Clones nonclient suspects in your niche that have many, if not all, of the positive characteristics of your best existing clients.

Close the self-initiated step designed to obtain commitment to move to a mutually beneficial next step in the new-business development process.

Comfort Zone the range of effective, self-initiated behavior in an activity area; the area of professional behavior where one is productive, confident, and forthright in communications and actions.

Confidence Card a list of positive statements used to keep the professional on track and motivated while making follow-up telephone contacts.

Critical Success Factors—CFS's the five to seven areas of performance in a prospect's business where things must go right for survival and profitable growth.

Data Base the accumulated information about the niche that can be entered and accessed in a variety of ways.

Decision-Making Unit the members of the prospect's organization that are involved in the purchase and use of your solution program.

D&B the things you do and provide to prospects that are perceived by them as being *different* from and *better* than others who attempt to serve them.

Industry all clients, prospective clients, and suspects in your practice area having the same 4-digit SIC number.

Infrastructure the clients, prospects, suspects, nonclient influentials, competitors, and others who serve and affect the niche in some way.

Initial-Contact Mailing Package the cover letter and enclosure that are prepared and mailed to suspect organizations in your niche.

Initial-Contact Program the mailing and telephone follow-up contacts made in relation to a need-specific mailing program.

Insider's Reputation the favorable awareness of you and your firm by members of the infrastructure.

Insider's Understanding your in-depth knowledge of how the niche works, what it takes to make a profit and compete successfully.

Integrity an unfailing consistency between what you promised and what you actually delivered.

Leveraging concentrating on the smallest number of clients, prospects, niches, and targets that will produce the largest amount of profitable revenue; a multiplier type of activity that produces a cascade effect of results.

Market the postal ZIP codes that comprise your practice area for a specific SIC; a defined geographical area.

Menu of Needs the list of hot-button, recurring, and emerging needs identified as a result of developing your insider's understanding of the niche.

Motive—see Buying Motive

NCIs Nonclient influentials, people in the infrastructure who can assist you in meeting your marketing objectives and goals.

Need a generic term referring to an existing unwanted situation, a desired situation wanted and in short supply or lacking, and a task to be completed.

New-Business Discussions the face-to-face meetings with prospective clients to define the existing and desired situations, and the solution program for delivering the required results.

Niche an abbreviated term for industry-market niche.

Objectives, Closing the primary decision you make and seek to obtain from the prospect to move to a mutually beneficial next step in the new-business development process.

PAR Report a report that summarizes the *problem* statement, *approach* used by your firm, and the *results* achieved for a given engagement.

Players—see Infrastructure

Potential Clients—see Suspects

Preferred Prospective Client Profile the list of desired characteristics, and the factors that "knock out" a suspect from being considered for attention in your niche.

Preliminary-Need Scenario a worksheet prepared to get in sync with targeted suspects for your need-specific mailing.

Probes purposeful questions with a specific structure and desired outcome.

Promotion the process of informing, persuading, or reminding targets of opportunity and influence about your firm's ability to meet selected needs in the niche.

Proposal a document designed to describe the firm's ability to perform a specific task(s). Indicates that the firm has the facilities, human resources, management experience, and track record to assure successful project performance and completion.

Prospect a former suspect who has agreed to meet with you to discuss a need situation and has not yet purchased your proposed solution program.

Prospecting the activities involved in obtaining appointments with qualified suspects.

Referrals clients and nonclients who mention your name to others and provide you with introductions and leads to new-business opportunities.

Scenario a word picture describing the outcomes of your application of resources.

Scope the range in which something occurs.

Services Delivery Program the activities and work steps involved in delivering and installing your recommended solution program.

Services Promotion Program the activities and worksteps involved in bringing a need and proposed service solution program to the attention of suspects in your niche.

Solution Goal a statement describing a favorable outcome.

Suspects desirable nonclient organizations possessing suspected opportunity who have not yet agreed to move with you.

Standard Industrial Classification (SIC) a 4-digit number assigned by the U.S. Department of Commerce to identify commercial entities.

Target Niche—see Niche

Targets of Influence nonclients such as attorneys and bankers with whom you do not yet have a referral relationship.

Targets of Opportunity existing clients with needs and budget, prospective clients, and suspects in your niche.

Telemarketing using the telephone for marketing purposes, especially to obtain appointments with prospective clients to discuss potential new-business situations.

Telescript the written guide used by professionals in preparation for and making follow-up telephone contacts.

Value-Added Service Solution service deliverables/products and activities that fully create the desired/required future situation within the agreed-upon time and dollar budget and exceed expectations.

Visualization a technique for doing a job in your mind to identify the outcomes etc.

Index